THE HOLY SPIRIT IN
THE THEOLOGY OF
MARTIN BUCER

To My Mother

THE HOLY SPIRIT IN
THE THEOLOGY OF
MARTIN BUCER

BY

W. P. STEPHENS

CAMBRIDGE

AT THE UNIVERSITY PRESS

1970

Published by the Syndics of the Cambridge University Press
1970 Bentley House, 200 Euston Road, London N.W.I
American Branch: 32 East 57th Street, New York, N.Y.10022

© Cambridge University Press 1970

Library of Congress Catalogue Card Number: 79–96100

Standard Book Number: 521 07661 7

Printed in Great Britain
at the University Printing House, Cambridge
(Brooke Crutchley, University Printer)

CONTENTS

PREFACE

For almost four centuries Martin Bucer has been the neglected reformer. Leaving behind him no followers who bore his name, he became little more than a footnote in the history of the reformation.[1] While generations of Christians looked to Luther or Zwingli, Cranmer or Calvin, as their fathers in the faith, none looked to Bucer. Though he belonged in some measure to three great reformation traditions, Lutheran, Reformed, and Anglican, none of them honoured his memory or recalled his work.

With few critical studies of his life and thought, with no complete edition of his works, with no disciples tenacious of his memory, Bucer's theology was ignored or misunderstood. Even the studies of Johann Wilhelm Baum, August Lang, and Gustav Anrich did not at once lead to a renaissance of Bucer studies. Not until the thirties of this century did the renaissance begin. Since then French and German scholars have produced a series of historical and theological monographs on the Strasbourg reformer, their research culminating at last in the first volumes of a complete, critical edition of his works.

The neglect Bucer has suffered in the last four centuries does not reflect the way his contemporaries judged him. Whatever the opposition or criticism he evoked, he was in his own day honoured and esteemed as a reformer and theologian. Sir John Cheke wrote of him with enthusiasm as a man of learning and godliness:

And although I doubt not but the king's majesty will provide some grave learned man to maintain God's true learning in his university, yet I think not of all learned men, in all points, ye shall receive Mr. Bucer's like; whether we consider his deepness of knowledge, his earnestness in religion, his fatherlikeness in life, his authority in knowledge.[2]

---

[1] This is true of such a considerable work as Joseph Lortz, *The Reformation in Germany*.

[2] Sir John Cheke's letter to Matthew Parker in John Strype, *Memorials of Archbishop Cranmer*, vol. 2, p. 657.

Preface

At his death Peter Martyr wrote a moving testimony to his friend in a letter to Conrad Hubert:

I am so broken and dismayed by his death, as to seem mutilated of more than half of myself, and that the better half; so that I am almost worn out by anxieties and tears, and seem scarcely to retain my senses by reason of the bitterness of my grief.

...Hitherto I have had a faithful companion in that road in which we were both of us so unitedly walking. I am now torn assunder from a man of the same mind with myself, and who was truly after my own heart, by this most bitter death which has taken him off.[1]

Bucer was a man of many parts—biblical scholar, reformer, statesman, apostle of unity. Any appraisal of his work and thought needs both to see him whole and to see him for himself. To see him in one period of his life or one aspect of his work to the neglect of others, or to view him in the shadow of Luther, Zwingli, or Calvin, is to miss the man and misunderstand his work.

This present study endeavours to see Bucer in his own light and to see his theology as a whole. It grew out of research in Strasbourg and Münster and was in its original form presented as a dissertation for the doctorat ès sciences religieuses in the University of Strasbourg. In this work I owe a debt to many, but in particular to three. At Cambridge it was Professor Gordon Rupp who first opened my eyes to the reformers and stimulated my study of them by his learning, interest, and encouragement. Then in Strasbourg Professor Rodolphe Peter pointed me to the Holy Spirit in Bucer's theology and helped me with his books and his ideas, while Professor François Wendel guided me in my research and offered me a critique of it which was broad, searching, and deep. To all three I would express my thanks.

Bucer's works are not easily available. Hardly any have been translated—and still only a few have appeared in modern editions.[2]

---

[1] Written on 8 March 1551. Hastings Robinson, *Original Letters Relative to the Reformation 1537–1558*, vol. 2, pp. 490–1.

[2] Five volumes of the modern critical edition have now been published. The last, vol. 3 of *Martin Bucers Deutsche Schriften*, appeared in time for references to be included in the footnotes.

Preface

For this reason several passages have been quoted at some length and the argument of many others has been summarised in the text.[1] Passages that have been translated generally keep close to the original, even though this has meant reproducing some of the complexities and uncertainties of Bucer's involved style.

The time has come for Bucer to appear as he appeared to his contemporaries: not the pale shadow of other men, but a man in his own right. When this happens we shall understand how Peter Alexander could write to Bucer on 24 March 1549: 'That good old man Master Latimer, formerly Bishop, but now the principal preacher before the King, salutes you; he earnestly desires to embrace you, and the like of you, as Simeon did Christ.'[2]

PETER STEPHENS

Shirley, Croydon
January 1969

[1] An explanation of the way references are given is found on pp. 275–6.
[2] G. C. Gorham, *Gleanings of a few scattered ears, during the period of the Reformation in England and of the times immediately succeeding: 1533–1588* (London, 1857), p. 76.

INTRODUCTION

The centrality of the Holy Spirit in the theology of Martin Bucer was noted by August Lang in 1900. In his magisterial study, *Der Evangelienkommentar Martin Butzers*, he argued that one could speak of Bucer's theology as a 'theology of the Spirit'.[1] Yet surprisingly, no examination of Bucer's theology has appeared that seeks to present the role of the Holy Spirit within it, or to understand his thought in terms of this pivotal doctrine.

There have been many references to the Holy Spirit in works that have treated other aspects of Bucer's thought. They have, however, concentrated on isolated elements in the doctrine of the Spirit, and have usually failed to see its relation to Bucer's theology as a whole. My concern here, by contrast, is to see the role of the Holy Spirit, not in this or that period of Bucer's thought, nor in this or that aspect of his theology, but in the total context of his theology, from his earliest writings in 1523 to his final ones in 1551. It is this that has determined both the method used in this presentation of Bucer's theology and the form it has taken.

THE METHOD

In considering the role of the Holy Spirit in the theology of the other reformers various methods have been followed, some more systematic, some more historical. In this it is rightly the reformer himself and his theology that determine the method of presentation, and not the author. For this reason a treatment of Bucer's theology differs inevitably from one of Luther's, Zwingli's, or Calvin's.[2]

[1] August Lang, *Der Evangelienkommentar Martin Butzers und die Grundzüge seiner Theologie*, p. 120.
[2] Regin Prenter, *Spiritus Creator: Studien zu Luthers Theologie*, A. E. Burckhardt, *Das Geistproblem bei Huldrych Zwingli*, Werner Krusche, *Das Wirken des Heiligen Geistes nach Calvin*, and Makoto Morii, 'La notion du Saint-Esprit chez Calvin dans son développement historique'.

Unlike Calvin, for example, Bucer left no systematic writing that affords an outline suitable for an exposition of his theology.[1] There are, however, in his works some dominant concerns that can be grouped together under 'The Holy Spirit and Salvation' and 'The Holy Spirit and the Word'. They cover the whole action of God in the salvation of man. Under 'The Holy Spirit and Salvation' we consider God's action in predestination, vocation, justification, sanctification, and glorification. Under 'The Holy Spirit and the Word' we consider the means whereby God once accomplished and now mediates salvation. Thus 'the word' embraces not only Christ the incarnate Word and the written word that bears witness to him, but also the people of the word, the servants (that is, magistrates) and ministers of the word, as well as the audible and visible words of preaching and sacraments. It is within this total context that the role of the Holy Spirit is presented.

A satisfying treatment of Bucer's theology, however, requires that the manner, as well as the form, of presenting his thought be true to him. Some studies of Bucer have sought to view him in terms of Luther (or some other reformer), so that he has been assessed according to his success in faithfully reproducing what Luther taught. By this criterion his standing as a reformer and his theology itself have been judged. This method, it is true, takes account of some of the influences at work in shaping Bucer's thought, but fails ultimately to do justice to him and to his theology.

Here, by contrast, an endeavour is made to let Bucer speak for himself. This is not done by abstracting his thought from its historical context, as though it appeared straight from heaven written on tablets of stone, uninfluenced by the tradition which he inherited and the situation in which he lived and worked. Some account is taken of these historical influences, but they are not

---

[1] Of all Bucer's works the *Articles*, despite its brevity, would be the most suitable for an exposition of his theology.

allowed so to dominate the scene, that Bucer is seen simply as a particular combination, whether good or bad, of the diverse people and movements of his time. In a form shaped by his own theological concerns and not by those of his contemporaries, and in quotations drawn from his voluminous writings, his theology is allowed to stand in its own right and to speak in its own accents.

The very size of Bucer's works raises a further question of method, that is, the question of selection. Many of the unbalanced and often contradictory studies of Bucer that have appeared, derive in some measure from the unrepresentative selection of works that their authors used. Too great a use of the commentaries presents either a static view of Bucer's thought or a view in which the changes from one commentary to another are not adequately accounted for.[1] Again the ignoring of a significant group of controversial writings[2] or the passing over of a whole period of Bucer's work (whether from 1530 to 1536 or from 1538 to 1548) presents an unbalanced and often one-sided picture of the whole.

The use made of selections from Bucer is equally important. A gay passage through the works, gathering quotations at random, will make Bucer's thought seem utterly consistent from beginning to end, or totally contradictory, according to the whim of the author. It ignores the many-sidedness of Bucer's thought and the importance of the context if his thought is to be genuinely understood. The context may be the historical context in which he wrote, which may account for a difference of accent between

[1] Lang's fine study (*op. cit.*) suffers in this way. He is too dependent on *Gospels* and *Romans*, and does not pay sufficient attention to Bucer's earliest works or to those written in the thirties. He thereby misses something of the controversial context of the writings, as well as the subtle nuances and changes in Bucer's thought, not least between 1530 and 1536.

[2] Wendel, pointing out that the *Articles* was written in an anabaptist context, as *Tetrapolitana* had been written in a catholic context, comments 'Aucun de ces deux documents ne pouvait donc prétendre donner une synthèse complète de la doctrine strasbourgeoise que leur juxtaposition ne réalisait pas davantage d'ailleurs'. François Wendel, *L'Eglise de Strasbourg: sa constitution et son organisation 1532–1535*, p. 127.

I-2

works directed against the radicals and those directed against Lutherans or catholics. It may, however, be the biblical context, as, for example, in the commentaries, where the historical context is sometimes less important. Thus Bucer's apparently spiritualist view of prayer is misunderstood where attention is not paid to the context of the passage in St Matthew which Bucer is expounding.[1] Moreover, a change in one edition of the *Gospels*[2] should not be seen in isolation from the fact that sometimes a great deal that is similar is not changed.[3]

The selection of material in this study has been made as representative as possible. Besides the commentaries, which are fundamental for the understanding of one who sought above all to hold a biblical theology, the treatises and the diverse controversial, catechetical, pastoral, and ecclesiastical writings have been drawn on. To a much lesser extent the letters have been used, though for most aspects of Bucer's theology they have no new light to shed. The selection is drawn from most types of Bucer's writings and from every period.

There has, moreover, been a deliberately differentiated use of the material. In the chapters on 'The Holy Spirit and Salvation' the presentation has been more systematic, as there is less development from one period to another. Change is noted where it occurs, but there is no need to unfold Bucer's thought from year to year. In this section, moreover, the commentaries have been used more extensively than elsewhere, as it is in them that these issues are most fully treated.

In the section on 'The Holy Spirit and the Word', however,

---

[1] Köhler, as Lang (*op. cit.* pp. 127–9), misinterprets Bucer for this reason. See Walther Köhler, *Dogmengeschichte als Geschichte des christlichen Selbstbewusstseins. II: Das Zeitalter der Reformation*, pp. 434–5.

[2] The immense length of many of the titles of Bucer's works makes it impracticable to give them in full. They are given in the bibliography where reference is given to the bibliography of Stupperich, in which a fuller version of the titles can be found.

[3] The fact that Bucer did not change large sections cannot be dismissed by saying that he did not have time to change them, for he had time to change a large number of matters of no theological importance. See Lang, *op. cit.* pp. 49–73.

several chapters (notably Preaching and Holy Communion) have required a more detailed historical presentation, unfolding Bucer's thought from year to year, so that the nuances of each period can be thrown into sharper relief. For this the varied treatises, together with the controversial, catechetical, and ecclesiastical writings have been essential. They alone enable us both to see how his thought developed in contact with his opponents (as well as in wrestling with the biblical text) and to follow that development in some detail. Nevertheless, a more systematic presentation is offered within or at the end of these chapters.

In both sections some care has been taken to treat the works in their historical order. Though this method lacks a certain elegance, it is an indispensable testimony to whatever change or development there may be in Bucer's theology. By this test alone theories of change within and of influences upon his thought can be judged. Where there are no references to writings from a given period, it may be assumed that there are no changes in the writings from that period.

THE CONTEXT

This is not the place for a sketch of Bucer's life and work. A number of biographical studies exist which can complement what is said here.[1] What is offered instead is a bare outline of the events that illuminate those works of Bucer which form the basis of this presentation of his theology.

Bucer's years of study at the famous school and then at the Dominican monastery in Sélestat led him in 1517 to Heidelberg, and in the following year to the decisive encounter of his life. In April 1518 he heard Luther at the Heidelberg disputation and later met him and talked with him. It was this event that shaped the rest of his life. However great had been the influence of Erasmus on him up to this point (and however much it was to remain after-

---

[1] See especially Johann Wilhelm Baum, *Capito und Butzer: Strassburgs Reformatoren*, Gustav Anrich, *Martin Bucer*, Hastings Eells, *Martin Bucer*, and François Wendel, *Martin Bucer*.

wards), it was never so profound nor so overwhelming as this experience.[1]

The next significant moment came four years later when Bucer stopped at Wissembourg and spent the winter there preaching and reforming the church. This was his first really independent work as a reformer and served as a dramatic prelude to his life's work which was to begin the following year in Strasbourg.[2] The winter at Wissembourg and the first years at Strasbourg were primarily years of conflict with the catholic opponents of the reformation. It is against them that his earliest works were directed.[3]

Already, however, at the end of 1524 the beginnings of differences with Luther emerged. Whether influenced by Carlstadt or Zwingli or some other tradition[4] Bucer diverged from him in his understanding of holy communion. This issue divided them for more than ten years until the Wittenberg Concord of 1536, although from 1529 Bucer had an increasing appreciation of what Luther was trying to say in his doctrine of the word and sacraments as a means of grace, and the polemic of the early years was accordingly modified. The mid-twenties are, nevertheless, the years in which Bucer stood more closely with Zwingli, though this does not mean that their positions were identical.

The mid-twenties mark the beginning of another conflict, that with the anabaptists and the spiritualists. This conflict was not just a theological one, to be resolved by private conversation and public

[1] See the judgment of Wendel: 'On peut prétendre, sans exagération romantique, que l'évolution religieuse de Bucer, commencée sous le signe d'Erasme, prit sa véritable signification à partir de ce moment (Avril 1518).' *Martin Bucer*, p. 7.

[2] His leaving the Dominican order, his marriage, and his excommunication were all significant events, the importance of which should not be underestimated when considering the depth of Bucer's commitment to the reformation at this stage.

[3] Among the works from this period of catholic controversy are *Das ym selbs*, *Summary*, *Against Treger*, and *Grund und Ursach*.

[4] The whole climate of opinion is much more equivocal than is sometimes supposed. G. H. Williams offers a picture of the various movements of thought that abounded at the end of the fifteenth century and the beginning of the sixteenth, together with an account of the visits to Strasbourg of Carlstadt and others. G. H. Williams, *The Radical Reformation*, especially chs. 1 and 2.

debate. It was a struggle for the establishing of the church in Strasbourg. The liberal policy of the council had made Strasbourg a haven for those chased from other cities for their non-conformity.[1] Many of them were welcomed by Bucer and the other reformers, but soon the reformers saw that fundamental differences over the church, the ministry, the word, and the sacraments were causing division in their midst and the alienation of large sections of the population from the reformation for which they had fought. The struggle which seemed no more than a theological debate in *Getrewe Warnung* and the commentaries became a matter of the life or death of the church in the early thirties. The reformers eventually persuaded the council of the seriousness of the situation and in 1533 a synod was held to bring order into the life of the church. It is against this background (the need to safeguard the life of the church, the necessity of outward forms to secure this, of the co-operation of the magistrates to effect it, and of theological debate to justify it, together with the catastrophe at Münster) that the writings of this period are to be understood. They include the *Articles*, the *Handlung*, *Quid de baptismate*, the *Bericht*, the *Catechism*, and the *Dialogi*.

The mid-twenties, which saw the beginning of a conflict on many sides, were also a period in which Bucer was grappling anew with the Bible. At first this found expression in his lectures, but then increasingly in his commentaries. In less than three years he published *St Matthew*, *Ephesians*, *St John*, *Zephaniah*, and *Psalms*. Too much significance must not be read into the choice of books on which Bucer commented; for, although it is the publishing of

---

[1] A picture of the Strasbourg scene is given in G. H. Williams, *Radical Reformation*, pp. 234–98 and Eells, *Martin Bucer*, pp. 54–64 and 127–59. Besides the refugees from other cities there was also a radical movement native to Strasbourg itself, boasting its own vivid characters, like Clement Ziegler. For Ziegler see the article by Rodolphe Peter, 'Le Maraîcher Clément Ziegler, l'homme et son oeuvre', *Revue d'Histoire et de Philosophie Religieuses*, 34 (1954).

Magnificent documentation of the radicals and their encounters with Bucer and the Strasbourg reformers is given in Manfred Krebs and Hans Georg Rott, *Quellen zur Geschichte der Täufer. VII—Elsass: I. Stadt Strassburg 1522–1532, VIII—Elsass: II. Stadt Strassburg 1533–1535.*

the commentaries on the gospels that dominates this period, he had already lectured on the epistles of Paul. Nevertheless, it may be expected that a theologian who concentrates on the exposition of the gospels in a given period will produce a theology that bears the stamp of the gospels. It is also clear that a theology that is drawn from commentaries on the gospels is likely to have different stresses from one drawn from commentaries on the epistles.

One thing is certain: the context of the book that is being expounded is no less important than the historical context in which the commentary is written. To some extent what is said in a commentary depends upon what is there to be commented on. The differences between the theology of *Romans* and the theology of *St Matthew* and *St John* (and indeed of the 1536 edition of the *Gospels*) are in some measure differences between the theology of the gospels and that of the epistles. This is not to deny that the precise selection of books that a theologian chooses to expound may reveal his theological predilections.

Already in the twenties Bucer's wider concerns were apparent. He helped to introduce the reformation in other places and at the same time sought to hold the reformation together, in particular its leaders, Luther and Zwingli. His whole life bears these two marks: a pastoral and missionary concern on the one hand and an ecumenical concern on the other. It is the second that is most open to misunderstanding, especially when isolated from the first. It easily suggests the time-server or the man of compromise. Those who judge Bucer in this way fail to grasp one of his distinctive insights into the Christian faith. For him the unity of the sons of God is to be found not in doctrine alone, but in a common life of faith and love. One could say that for him unity in holy communion is to be found not in abstaining from it (as with Schwenckfeld) or in insisting on doctrinal agreement on all its aspects (as with Luther), but in celebrating it together. Given that there was a fundamental unity in the gospel, Bucer's aim was to manifest this unity and to safeguard it. To achieve this one could leave secondary matters on one side or one could find a formula that affirmed what was important and left liberty in what was unimportant.

In the pursuit of unity for theological and (in a positive sense of the word) political reasons, Bucer attended and organised colloquies, visited both friend and foe, wrote letters, composed statements of faith, indeed used every method that an ingenious mind and a growing experience taught him. In his endeavours he made mistakes. His readiness to listen and to learn, his eagerness to find a formula that could hold two parties together, his willingness to interpret the formula in the way most agreeable to his hearers, all this laid him open to the charge of compromise, deceit, or surrender. But it was precisely these qualities that enabled him to bring some unity to a divided protestantism, and strengthened him in some measure in his missionary endeavour. It is against such a background that *Tetrapolitana* and the *Apology* in 1530, the Wittenberg Concord in 1536, and the *Acta colloquii* in 1541 can best be understood.

The thirties brought some peace to the church in Strasbourg, and marked the endeavours of Bucer to establish an independence of the church from the council and to introduce a pastoral discipline into its life. His understanding of church discipline and the relation of the church with the magistrate in this period owed something to Oecolampadius and, it may be, to the anabaptists. It found expression in *Von der waren Seelsorge*, and a wider expression in his work in Hesse, seen in the *Ziegenhainer Zuchtordnung* and the *Kasseler Kirchenordnung*. The growing importance of the forms of church life for securing a true and lasting reformation led him to new thinking about ordination, confirmation, church discipline, and groups for Christian fellowship (*Gemeinschaften*).

The forties which began with colloquies ended with exile. The vision of a wider unity for which he worked gave way to banishment from Strasbourg, but at the same time to a new and scarcely less important work in England. In between came the reform in Cologne with its renewed debate with the catholics, of which the *Bestendige Verantwortung* offers a superb testimony, the commentary on Judges,[1] and *Ein Summarischer vergriff*. This last gives a summary of Bucer's faith over the previous twenty years.

The English period presented a new situation and a new conflict with catholic opponents of the reformation. This conflict is apparent in Bucer's lectures on Ephesians which deal explicitly with questions like the scholastic understanding of merit. But the establishing of a true reformation occupied more of his time. His comments on the prayer book, his discussion of ordination and the sacraments (in *De vi et usu* and *De ordinatione*), his opinion on vestments, all form part of his concern with the shape of the reformed church in England.[2] A fitting and characteristic climax to his life and work is his *De Regno Christi*. It shows both the breadth of his vision of the rule of Christ on earth and the detailed and practical means he envisaged for its realisation. This work is a witness both to the source of Bucer's inspiration in the Bible and to the way in which he sought to let the biblical word take body both in the life of men and in the structure of society.[3]

THE INFLUENCES

The simplest outline of Bucer's work in its historical context lays bare the variety of influences that played upon his thought and personality. It is most convenient to consider some of them in a little more detail here. It would, however, be wrong to do this without a word of warning. The search for the antecedents to a man's theology often fails to do justice to his originality and individuality. Other men subjected to the same influences will respond differently, for no man is merely the sum of the influences that affect him. Above all, with the reformers the fresh impact of the Bible on each of them must be taken seriously.

[1] In this the date suggested by Pierre Lutz (that is, 1544) is accepted. Pierre Lutz, 'Le Commentaire de Martin Bucer sur le livre des Juges', p. 145. Koch suggests 1539–40. Karl Koch, *Studium Pietatis*, p. 258.
[2] See Constantin Hopf, *Martin Bucer and the English Reformation*.
[3] A discussion of his intentions is to be found in François Wendel, *Martini Buceri Opera Latina. XV: De Regno Christi*, pp. ix–liv.

Introduction

The difficulty in discerning the real influences at work is illustrated by the contradictory judgment of scholars when they assess the factors that influenced a particular treatise. Heitz notes that in the *Summary* Baum found reminiscences of the medieval mystics, Seeberg a résumé of the insights of Luther, and Courvoisier evidence of spiritualism.[1] To this it may be added that Rudloff in his edition of the text points to the influence of Erasmus.[2] Only a detailed study of Bucer and each of the people or movements alleged to have influenced him can offer solid results. There is no pretension to such a study here, simply a recognition of some of the factors that Bucer's life and work reveal.

Erasmus and Humanism

If Lang gave insufficient attention to the influence on Bucer of humanism, and of Erasmus in particular, more recent studies fall into the opposite danger.[3] Yet there can be no doubt of the importance of humanism in his life. Born and educated in Sélestat he came into direct or indirect contact with the humanism of Wimpfeling, Gebwiller, Rhenanus, and Erasmus. The scholarly methods and concerns that humanism taught him remained his throughout his life; so probably did some of its religious influence. Still in 1542 in *De vera ecclesiarum* he could regard Erasmus as the initiator of the reformation with his opposition to man's finding his salvation in ceremonies rather than in faith in Christ. The reference to Erasmus is quickly followed by one to Luther, but it shows that Bucer valued Erasmus, despite all that had happened in the twenty-five years since he had left Sélestat for Heidelberg.[4] Erasmus had opened his eyes to the inwardness of religion

[1] Jean-Jacques Heitz, 'Etude sur la formation de la pensée ecclésiologique de Bucer', p. 35. Heitz offers a sober review of some of the influences on pp. 31-5, mentioning particularly Luther, humanism, spiritualism, and Zwingli.

[2] Ortwin Rudloff in *Martin Bucers Deutsche Schriften* Band 1, p. 77.

[3] One of the main weaknesses in Koch, *Studium Pietatis*, is his over-emphasis on Bucer's humanism. A more just appreciation of the relation with humanism and Luther can be found in Henri Strohl, *Bucer, humaniste chrétien* and 'Bucer interprète de Luther'.

[4] DV 161.4–17.

(leaving aside all the other influences that may well have been at work in his youth), fired him with a strongly moral and practical understanding of the Christian faith (again leaving aside the whole tradition of Alsatian piety and the movement of modern devotion), and kindled in him a love of the language, literature, and thought of antiquity. After his encounter with Luther he could still call himself an Erasmian, and two years after the break between Luther and Erasmus he could praise the paraphrases of Erasmus and, indeed, continued to use them with eagerness and profit. It remains to be proved, however, that the emphasis on genuine piety in Bucer's theology is Erasmian rather than biblical, and that his opposition of inward and outward and in particular his understanding of the Spirit owes more to Erasmus and through him to antiquity than to scripture.[1] In this study Bucer's theology is seen as fundamentally scriptural, and is presented as such.

On the other side the points of difference between Bucer and Erasmus need to be seen clearly. The evidence that his booklist in April 1518 offers[2] should not be exaggerated. Apart from the fact that it describes Bucer's development only up to his encounter with Luther, it is no evidence for his theological convictions, only for his theological (and other) reading. In the letter of November 1524 he could speak of Erasmus' having harmed the gospel more than he had previously helped it, both perverting people by his disputation on free will, and preferring his own opinion to scripture. 'May the grace of the Latin language perish, may the miracle of erudition perish, by which the glory of Christ is obscured. By his word we are saved, by that of others rather we are lost.'[3] For all his debt to Erasmus, Bucer was capable of discerning where Erasmus does not measure up to the test of scripture. It need not be assumed that he was capable of doing this in one point, but not in others.

There are also some marked contrasts between Bucer's thought

[1] Köhler, *op. cit.* p. 418.   [2] BW 1.281–284.
[3] W.A.Br. 3.386.207–387.224.

and that of Erasmus. Some of these are apparent in such a work as the *Enchiridion* with its strong insistence on inward reality as opposed to mere outward forms. The opposition of letter and spirit,[1] the presence of a certain legalism,[2] the absence of any vibrant doctrine of the Holy Spirit with the sense that the Holy Spirit leads to faith and then produces the fruit of the Spirit, and the use of spirit primarily in opposition to what is outward[3] all suggest an orientation and an understanding of the Christian faith different from Bucer's.

Moreover, in the understanding of holy communion, where many see an influence of Erasmus, there is a clear distinction between Bucer's view even in 1524–8 and that of Erasmus. Erasmus' view, which tended 'to free the faithful from the physical consumption at the Mass and to replace it with a spiritual communion',[4] could lead him to go for a long period without receiving holy communion;[5] Bucer's did not. This in itself is some testimony that Bucer did not see an opposition between the Spirit and what is outward, but only a distinction.

It would be too much a half-truth to say that if the mind of

---

[1] Matthew Spinka, *Advocates of Reform* (Library of Christian Classics: vol. XIV), p. 304–7. Ernst-Wilhelm Kohls, *Die Theologie des Erasmus*, p. 103, and Lewis W. Spitz, *The Religious Renaissance of the German Humanists*, p. 222.

[2] See, for example, the words at the end of the fifth rule of the *Enchiridion*: 'Thus to him who comes nigh unto the Lord, He in turn will come nigh unto him, and if you will make a strong effort to surmount your blindness and the clamor of your senses, he will come forth fitly from his inaccessible light, and that unthinkable silence in which all tumult of the senses disappears and even the images of all intelligible things keep silence.' (Translation by Matthew Spinka of the *Enchiridion* in *Advocates of Reform*, p. 349.)

There are other similar expressions (for example, on page 377), but at the same time there are sentences like 'Let him love the pious in Christ, the impious for Christ's sake, who already so loved us as yet enemies that he gave himself wholly for our ransom' at the beginning of the section 'Opinions Worthy of a Christian' (p. 358). Compare also the end of the eleventh rule: 'In conflict, distrustful of your strength, flee unto Christ your Head: and place all hope of victory in his benevolence alone' (p. 364). Kohls (*op. cit.*) is inclined to overemphasise the evangelical, as opposed to the legalistic, note in the *Enchiridion*.

[3] Spinka, *op. cit.* pp. 335–42 and 346–9.

[4] G. H. Williams, *Radical Reformation*, p. 34.

[5] Spitz, *op. cit.* p. 227.

Bucer remained that of a humanist, his heart became that of a reformer. Nevertheless, an exactness in scholarship, an ongoing appreciation of the thought and writing of antiquity, a willingness to learn from whatever source, whether Christian or pagan, a universal breadth of vision, these are some of the signs of the humanist. But in the overwhelming sense of the sovereign and free grace of God in Christ and of the liberating power of the Spirit, together with an unassailable conviction of the supreme authority of scripture, one hears the heartbeat of the reformer.[1]

The Reformers

The influence of Luther on Bucer was profound, but it is not possible here to pursue it in detail. Quite apart from the encounter in 1518, which was the decisive turning point in Bucer's life, there is the fact that Bucer read an immense amount of what Luther wrote, traces of which are to be found throughout his writing. It is to Luther that he owed his fundamental insights into the Christian faith.

Yet there are a number of significant differences of accent or understanding, that indicate that Bucer was no pale copy of Luther. A peculiar stress on election and sanctification, a stronger sense of the church and of the pastoral ministry, a different conception of the magistracy and of the relationship of the Spirit to word and sacraments, these are some of the most obvious points which mark off Bucer's from Luther's understanding of the gospel and the church.

Zwingli's relation with Bucer differed from that of Luther. It was marked with fewer ups and downs and with less suspicion and misunderstanding. The nearness of Strasbourg to Zürich and their

---

[1] Koch argues in some detail for the dominant influence of humanism in Bucer. See *Studium Pietatis*, pp. 13–49, 77, and 99–100.

A comparison with a humanist like Mutian (with his universalism, his use of Jupiter for Christ, his lack of a sense of sin, his trust in his own piety and his ability to lead a good life, and his emphasis on Christ as the new and highest revealer of true ethical principles) reveals the diversity of humanism and the profound difference between some of its forms and the faith of the reformers. See Spitz, *op. cit.* pp. 141–51.

links with the other cities of Switzerland and Southern Germany made mutual understanding easier and more necessary. It is probably in the understanding of the sacraments that Zwingli's influence is most clearly to be seen. 'The Spirit makes alive, the flesh profits nothing' was a text common to both, even if Bucer learnt it from Erasmus or the spiritualists rather than from Zwingli. Though their views of holy communion were not identical, they sensed themselves as standing together over against Luther on the crucial issue of the word and sacraments as the means by which the Spirit is given. On many other points their views were similar, though in most cases it would be hard to argue Bucer's dependence on Zwingli. However, in his understanding of infant baptism, more especially in his defence of it against the anabaptists, he almost certainly drew on what Zwingli had already written.

If the influence of Luther, Zwingli, and other reformers, like Oecolampadius, is allowed, it should not be at the expense of ignoring the reformers who shared with Bucer in the work in Strasbourg, among whom for a period was Calvin.[1] Daily contact with Capito, Zell, and a host of others, both reformers and radicals, is not likely to have been without its impact on Bucer's thought and his attempts to link thought and action. To these last, the radicals, we must now turn.

Anabaptists and Spiritualists

There are certain clear distinctions in principle that can be made between anabaptists and spiritualists,[2] but they are less easy to sustain in practice. Not only were there different types of anabaptist and spiritualist, but there were those who passed from the

---

[1] Bucer's contacts with Calvin during his stay in Strasbourg are not likely to have been without influence on him. Bucer was a person ready to learn from others, and Calvin, moreover, was someone for whom he had a high regard. A careful examination of Bucer's writings during Calvin's Strasbourg period might offer tangible evidence of Calvin's influence.

[2] See, for example, Köhler, *op. cit.* p. 87, G. H. Williams, *Radical Reformation*, pp. 181–5, and G. H. Williams and A. M. Mergal, *Spiritual and Anabaptist Writers* (Library of Christian Classics: vol. xxv), p. 23.

one to the other, or indeed held something of the convictions of both at the same time. A study of Bucer's theology does not give evidence for any clear and direct dependence of Bucer on either, but it indicates some of the points of conflict and some of the parallel convictions.

The areas of conflict with the anabaptists are clear—baptism, free will, a certain literalism in interpreting the Bible, an insistence on a pure church safeguarded by discipline and upholding a high standard of personal morality (leading in the judgment of some to Pharisaism), a separation of the power of the magistrate from the life of the church, and a sense of the distinctiveness of, even the opposition between, Old and New Testament. Bucer's response to these situations differed from one to another. He argued for infant baptism, influenced by his doctrine of election and his understanding of the church. He attacked free will as taking away from the saving power of Christ's death and the sovereignty of God. He asserted the essential role of the magistrate in establishing the gospel and the life of the church. In all this his view of the Bible, in which he gave equal weight to Old and New Testament and at the same time avoided a literalism of interpretation, played a decisive part.

In some of the points of conflict, however, Bucer's reaction was much more positive. The importance of sanctification in his theology enabled him to be more open than Luther could be to the anabaptists with their desire for discipline in the church and their concern that faith should not overthrow works. His success in winning them to the life of the reformed church in Hesse is a token of this. What he deplored there, as in Strasbourg, was their separateness and the lack of love that so often marked their dealings with others.[1]

The point of conflict with those whose convictions were more spiritualist than anabaptist lay in their opposition to outward means, in particular such outward forms as church and ministry,

[1] These points are discussed and illustrated in the course of the following chapters.

Introduction

word and sacraments. They saw no need of the church,[1] regarded outward means as unnecessary to those with the Spirit,[2] and could view possession by the Spirit as setting them free from the Bible.[3] In this the inward inspiration of the Spirit, as they judged it to be, was not tested by the word of the Spirit in the Bible. For Bucer it was otherwise. The Bible was for him the place where the Holy Spirit speaks with clarity; by it, therefore, everything is to be tested. Moreover, it commends to us the outward means of church and ministry, word and sacraments. Bucer's opposition to spiritualism is different from Luther's, but no less resolute. It was strengthened in the thirties, but was already present in the mid-twenties.

Other Influences

One continuing influence was that of the fathers, and in particular Augustine. From his earliest works Bucer referred to them and listened to their judgment. From the end of the twenties his study of them seems to have intensified. This is especially evident in *Romans*, as well as in works directed against the catholics. His anthology of the fathers is an indication of the importance he attached to their views.

Other influences have been adduced, and require critical examination. This is not the place for it. South German Augustinian

---

[1] For Schwenckfeld's attitude in this, see G. H. Williams, *Radical Reformation*, p. 257.

[2] In Franck's translation of the *Türkenchronik* there is reference to a spiritualist sect, distinct from Lutherans, Zwinglians, and anabaptists,'which will eliminate all audible prayer, preaching, all ceremonies, sacraments, and ordinances such as excommunication, and also the ministry '. G. H. Williams, *Radical Reformation*, p. 265.

[3] G. H. Williams comments in *Spiritual and Anabaptist Writers*: 'For all of them spirit was central in their life and thought, as the driving spirit, as the enlightening spirit, or as the rational spirit. These Spiritualists, like Christians generally, knew that the spirits had to be tested, but they were always confident that the source of their particular authority was none other than the Holy Spirit. Moreover, they felt that the Holy Spirit as the inspiration of Holy Scripture, of the prophets of old, and of the present day, and also as the cohesive power of the Christian fellowship, was superior to any historic record of the work of the Holy Spirit, be it the Bible (or any part thereof, like the New Testament) or the church (or any institution thereof, like the clergy).' (Pp. 31–2.)

Introduction

spiritualism,[1] mysticism,[2] and Thomism[3] are factors in Bucer's development and background. A study of them would illuminate Bucer's theology at many points. In some cases, however, the parallels are only verbal. Bucer uses their language, but not their thoughts, or he may use their thoughts, but they are placed in a different context and have a different role.

The Bible

Decisive for Bucer is the Bible. He studied it as a reformer, though without neglecting the understanding he had gained as a humanist. This was the profound influence on his theology. Before it Luther, Erasmus, the fathers, and the tradition of the church had to give way. It was to the word of God that he strove to be true.

As he wrestled with one theological issue after another, his primary concern was to discover what the Spirit taught through

[1] See, for example, Martin Brecht, *Die frühe Theologie des Johannes Brenz*. He refers to the influence of Augustine, adding 'Brenz steht hier unter demselben Einfluss wie seine Freunde Bucer und Oekolampad...Mit dem augustinischen Spiritualismus, von dem er herkommt, unterscheidet sich Brenz von Luther, der sehr bald die Kirche eindeutig auf das Wort gegründet hat.' (P. 31.)

In this context it is interesting to note the similarity between Bucer's and Oecolampadius' understanding of the outward and inward word. See Gordon Rupp, 'Word and Spirit in the First Years of the Reformation', in *Archiv für Reformationsgeschichte* 49 (1958), p. 22.

Compare Spitz, *op. cit.* pp. 268–9.

[2] Little precise evidence, however, has been brought forward in demonstrating the influence of mysticism on Bucer. A critique of some points may be found in Heitz, Etude, pp. 40–3 and G. Itti, 'Dans quelle mesure Bucer est-il piétiste?', pp. 26–7.

Strasbourg had been an undoubted centre of mysticism and of the Friends of God (see, for example, James Clark, *The Great German Mystics*, pp. 9 and 95), and Alsatian piety in the fifteenth and sixteenth centuries seems to have reflected their influence.

[3] It is not clear how far the influence of Thomism is more than superficial, affecting Bucer's language rather than his fundamental understanding of the Christian faith. Koch, among others, argues for a Thomistic influence in *Studium Pietatis*, pp. 9, 12–13, 19, 70, and 80. Certain differences between Bucer and Aquinas may be seen in the presentation of the Thomistic position in Stanislas Lyonnet's article 'Liberté chrétienne et loi de l'Esprit selon Saint Paul' in I. de la Potterie and S. Lyonnet, *La Vie selon l'Esprit*, especially in the reference to *habitus* (pp. 192–3).

18

scripture. Thus, when deciding between differing views of holy communion, he assembled all the relevant biblical texts to see what view they pointed to. Moreover, when Christian doctrine had to be defined, he urged the importance of keeping to the words of scripture in the definitions.

The dominating role of the Bible in his work and thought shows itself in a wide variety of ways—in his stress on learning the biblical languages, in his considerable work as a commentator on the Old and the New Testament, in his use of biblical quotation and exposition in his varied writings, and in his constant reference to the Bible as the touchstone of Christian faith and practice.

The exposition of scripture marks the beginning and the end of his work as a reformer. At the beginning come his preaching from 1 Peter and St Matthew in Wissembourg in the winter of 1522 and the exposition of Paul's epistles in Strasbourg in the following summer. At the end come his lectures on Ephesians in the University of Cambridge. Moreover, his major works are biblically based, whether his great commentaries on the gospels, the psalms, and the epistle to the Romans, or his theological treatises, such as *Von der waren Seelsorge* and *De Regno Christi*, which lean heavily on the exposition of biblical texts. Equally, in his debates with catholics and radicals it is the Bible to which he appeals, urging its authority against the authority of the church or of private inspiration.

Other influences on Bucer are not to be underestimated. They determined in some measure his approach to the Bible and his interpretation of it. But he sought to test other views and insights by scripture. For him the truth was not to be found in the interpretation of men, however learned and godly, but in the Bible itself.[1] In striving to understand it, he sought the guidance of the Holy Spirit, who had inspired its writers. It is, therefore, by this twofold test of the word and the Spirit that his theology is truly to be judged.

[1] Compare 275.A.11–B.6; 171.A.2–15; 440.D.7, quoted on p. 136.

PART I

THE HOLY SPIRIT AND SALVATION

God's salvation of men can be viewed in several ways. In Bucer's theology the most satisfactory way is to distinguish the meaning of salvation from the means of salvation. The distinction is to some extent artificial, for the means and the meaning of salvation are inseparably joined. Christ is both the meaning and the means of man's salvation—and so, in a different way, is the church. Yet the distinguishing of the meaning and the means of salvation enables us to see more clearly the central issues in Bucer's theology and the points at which it conflicts with the views of his contemporaries.

At the heart of Bucer's understanding of salvation are the words of St Paul in Rom. 8:28–30:

We know that in everything God works for good with those who love him, who are called according to his purpose. For those whom he foreknew he also predestined to be conformed to the image of his Son, in order that he might be the first-born among many brethren. And those whom he predestined he also called; and those whom he called he also justified; and those whom he justified he also glorified.

It is this which offers the basis for our interpretation of Bucer's view of salvation as predestination, vocation, justification, sanctification, and glorification. Sanctification is not expressly mentioned in the Pauline passage, though Bucer does include it in the sequence on at least one occasion.[1] Bucer himself has various orders of salvation, and the five elements that we consider feature in them, though not necessarily all together.

The combination of these five elements does not precisely re-

[1] KR 2.197.10.

21

present Bucer's thought, simply because he does not express himself in a uniform way. It does, however, reflect the broad outline of his theology more adequately than any other scheme. The order of salvation, beginning in predestination and ending in glorification, represents not a chronological sequence, but a logical one, even though predestination clearly precedes the others, as glorification (in our use of the term) follows them.

1

PREDESTINATION

The doctrine of predestination or election is one that shapes the whole of Bucer's theology. Even where it is not expressed explicitly, its stamp is to be found. The centrality of this doctrine and the way Bucer interprets it distinguish him from Luther on the one hand, and from his catholic and radical opponents on the other.[1]

Predestination is mentioned in Bucer's earliest writings as a doctrine which he presupposes. Both *Das ym selbs* and the *Summary* refer to the elect and the damned (or lost, or reprobate),[2] but neither of them elaborates the doctrine of predestination, or relates it to other doctrines. It is not until the debate with Treger

---

[1] Failure to see the centrality of predestination in Bucer leads to a fundamental misunderstanding of his theology at a number of points. It is a mistake particularly characteristic of those who judge or interpret Bucer in terms of Luther. Thus Eduard Ellwein in *Vom neuen Leben* fails to understand Bucer's emphasis on sanctification, which is inextricably bound up with his doctrine of election (see ch. 4 on Sanctification and Glorification). Johannes Müller, though recognising the importance of election in Bucer, begins his exposition in *Martin Bucers Hermeneutik* with justification by faith and not surprisingly, therefore, fails to give full weight to election.

Koch (*op. cit.* p. 109) completely misunderstands Bucer's rejection of 'resignatio ad infernum' because of his failure to see the meaning of election for Bucer. For Bucer no one can be effaced from the book of life, for to be effaced from it means not to have been written in it. P 210.D.18-24. (The problem Bucer has here in expounding Ps. 69:28 was not new. See, for example, Thomas Bradwardine, 'The Cause of God against the Pelagians' in Heiko Oberman, *Forerunners of the Reformation*, pp. 157-8.) As early as 1523 he speaks of the zeal which makes a man, appointed by God, ready to risk his life and happiness for the sake of others. However, he rejects the idea that he can lose his spiritual life, on the ground that only those who sin against God are effaced from the book of life. BW1.51.39-53.16. See Strohl, *Martin Bucer—Traité de l'Amour du Prochain*, p. 41, n. 8 for a discussion of 'resignatio ad infernum'.

Jaques Courvoisier argues that it is precisely (though not only) in the doctrine of election that Bucer's originality over against Luther and Zwingli is to be found. *La notion d'Eglise chez Bucer dans son développement historique*, p. 61. See p. 24, n. 3.

[2] BW I.50.25-9, 88.6-11, 105.29-31, 109.28-31.

that the doctrine is developed and its formative influence on other doctrines is seen.

In *Against Treger* election is used to illuminate the doctrine of the church. For Treger the church is made up of the outwardly baptised. Bucer rejects this idea arguing that the baptised who are described as having put on Christ are not those outwardly baptised in water, but those who are inwardly baptised in the Spirit. Bucer argues that Paul is referring to these in Gal. 3, and he finds a basis for his argument in Paul's reference to those who are predestined in Rom. 8:28–30.[1]

From this point the doctrine of election plays a central part in Bucer's theology. Even when it goes almost unmentioned, it is the presupposition underlying his theology. There is at no point any fundamental change in his understanding of it, although it is considered in greater detail in the *Gospels* and *Romans* than elsewhere.

THE MEANING AND PURPOSE OF PREDESTINATION

Predestination expresses a division of men into elect and reprobate, an irrevocable division that rests on God's free decision. The division is so complete that the death of Christ can be said quite simply to be for the elect.[2]

This division, however, is not simply a statement of fact. It fulfils a role in Bucer's theology, as in the theology of the other reformers. Negatively it denies that man's works play any part in his salvation; positively it affirms that man's salvation depends totally on God's free election.[3]

---

[1] BW 2.118.29–120.18.   [2] BW 1.212.13–19, 215.10–13.

[3] See the discussion in J. I. Packer and O. R. Johnston, *Martin Luther on the Bondage of the Will*, pp. 40–61. It can be seen from a comparison of Luther's *The Bondage of the Will* with Bucer's writings after 1525 that Bucer is influenced by Luther's presentation of the issue. This is not to deny that predestination plays an important part in Bucer's writing before this date, and that the doctrine of election has a different role in Bucer's theology from the one it has in Luther's. For Luther it is linked with an insistence that salvation is of God. For Bucer it is linked not only with the source of man's salvation in God, but also with the goal of salvation in being sanctified and glorified.

St Matthew states that God's election of his sons is 'from the foundation of the world, before they had done good or evil'.[1] It is not dependent on works as the parable of the sheep and the goats might seem to suggest. For true works are a sign that a man has been blessed by God, and are only possible where God is at work. Moreover, this very parable speaks of the kingdom they receive, not as a reward but as 'an inheritance', and as having been 'prepared from the foundation of the world'.[2]

This same note is sounded in *Ephesians*. The doctrine of predestination not only affirms that 'everything depends on the free election of God',[3] but also excludes our merit, for it teaches that 'everything is to be attributed to divine goodness and nothing to our merit'.[4] Bucer stands with Luther in total opposition to any assertion of man's free will, as though men have in themselves any ability to do good.[5] For, until men receive the vivifying Spirit of God, they are unable to do good; they are quite simply dead.[6] Man's salvation comes from God, and to accomplish man's salvation God offered his Son. In this, however, he acted freely and was not stimulated to it by anyone else.[7]

The emphasis on election as the cause of man's salvation could easily lead to a by-passing of the part played by Christ in his incarnation, death, and resurrection. Particularly in *Ephesians*, however, Bucer stresses that election is bound up with Christ and his death. God is said to have elected us 'through Christ'.[8] 'He elected and predestined us in and through Christ before the foundation of the world.' This election, moreover, to be sons of God is 'by no merit of our own, but only by the merit of Christ's blood'.[9]

Romans gives the discussion a greater depth, though adding only one distinctively new point in relating election to man's being certain of his salvation. 'Therefore what you owe God first is to

---

[1] 204.A.24–B.5; 67.A.14–18; 169.B.22–170.C.2; and 248.A.3–8; 80.A.13–17; 203.B.8–12.   [2] 318.A.15–B.19; 184.C.16–D.3; 473.A.16–B.12.
[3] E5.A.12–16.   [4] E25.A.8–25.
[5] E39.A.3–12, together with the marginal note.
[6] E46.B.19–47.A.2.   [7] E32.B.8–17.
[8] E25.A.8–12.   [9] E30.B.20–5. Compare E3.A.9–12.

believe that you are predestined by him. For, unless you believe it, you imply that he is playing with you, when he calls you to salvation through the gospel.'[1] The giving of certainty is not, however, to be thought of as the sole purpose of God's election. This passage is rightly understood when it is seen that Bucer is opposing the setting of confidence in our mutilated righteousness and the setting of it in the promise and calling of God.[2]

Bucer's definition of predestination has two elements, the 'separation' of the elect from the reprobate, and the fact that this takes place before they are born. For him such a definition affirms that the source of predestination is God's goodness and that nothing that man can do can alter it.[3] God's free election is independent of works, both present works and future works.[4] There is quite simply no cause of God's mercy that lies outside God himself.[5] This does not mean that Bucer cannot speak of various causes of man's salvation (God's goodness in electing us, Christ's work as mediator and as expiator of our sins, Christian friends and parents, together with their good works, and our own good works performed through the gift of the Holy Spirit).[6] But other causes of man's salvation are dependent on God's election, so that, for

[1] R 411.B.9–11. Bucer refers warmly to Melanchthon's teaching in this section.
[2] 'But because all our righteousness is so maimed and mutilated that by its merit we can never be sure of our salvation (for it does not satisfy the law of God), certainty of our predestination and election is to be sought only in the promise and calling of God, and the mind must always be lifted away from our righteousness, which in the eyes of the Lord is in itself always an abomination, towards the promise of God.' R 412.D.16–E.1.   [3] R 409.C.1–10.
[4] R 527.A.15–18. Bucer thus rejects the scholastic idea that our future works can play a part in our election.
[5] 'Quid enim ex isto, Miserebor cuius miserebor, aliud accipias, quam misericordiae divinae nullam extra ipsam causam esse...?' R 452.D.3–8.
[6] R 114.E.19–115.C.1.
   There is clearly an ambiguity in the use of the word cause. Our friends and parents can be causes of our salvation only in so far as they are instruments used by God in our vocation. This is parallel to Bucer's speaking of preaching as a cause of salvation.
   Our good works are a cause of salvation in a different sense. They are part of salvation, in that God has created us for them. But they are good only in so far as they are the works that God has prepared for us and that he performs in us by the Holy Spirit.

example, it is not our parents' goodness or badness that determines our salvation, but God's sovereign choice.[1] Even the good we do is from God, for we can do no good of ourselves. The fact, therefore, that we do good in no sense denies that our salvation is all of God.[2]

The meaning of Bucer's doctrine of predestination is that man's salvation rests on the free sovereign choice of God, made before the foundation of the world. Its purpose, besides being an affirmation of God's sovereign love, is to deny to man any part in effecting his salvation and to offer him a sure ground for confidence (that is, in God, rather than in himself).

THE PROBLEMS RAISED BY PREDESTINATION

The problems raised by predestination are, for the most part, not germane to the discussion of the role of the Holy Spirit in Bucer's theology. They must, nevertheless, be touched on, lest the picture of predestination should lack the light and shade that Bucer gives it.

The basic scriptural difficulty that Bucer feels compelled to deal with is the frequent reference in scripture to 'all', which appears to deny a doctrine of predestination. Bucer takes 'all' to mean 'many' or 'all who are elect' or 'all kinds of people'.[3] In this he opposes the anabaptist or spiritualist view that takes 'all' to mean literally 'all'.[4] Their mistake is to think that to enlighten all, means to save all.[5]

---

[1] R 117.A.2–13 and 303.B.9–13.   [2] R 8.F.10–15.

[3] 203.B.4–14; 66.D.14–20; 169.A.17–23. 45.A.26–B.3; 95.C.21–4; 241.B. 12–16. 197.A.27–B.4; 72.D.8–13; 733.A.9–13. Compare P 102.B.20–C.3 and R 517.A.11–14, B.4–9.

[4] Compare Denck. 'You may say: Yes, he died indeed out of love, but not for all; rather, only for a few. Answer: Since love in him was perfect and (since) love hates or is envious of none, but includes everyone, even though we were all his enemies, surely he would not wish to exclude anyone. If he had excluded anyone, then love would have been squint-eyed and a respecter of persons. And that, (love) is not!' L.C.C. xxv p. 102.

Hubmaier distinguishes the secret and revealed will of God in election. God's secret will is, in effect, what he could do, his revealed will is what he does. He wills to save all, and only those who refuse are not saved. L.C.C. xxv pp. 132–4.

[5] 20.A.2–20; 7.B.18–C.15; 578.D.5–579.A.2. Compare H G.3.A–J.2.A.

Bucer, like Luther,[1] holds that the reason for election is unknowable, but that we shall have some understanding of it in the future, when we see God face to face. Meanwhile, however, we can believe God to be God and need not doubt that he is just.[2] Human reason, in any case, cannot grasp the purposes of God. Man, relying on his own reason, makes God a liar, rather than admit his own ignorance. Thus while Melchior Hofmann affirms that God does not demand what he does not give, Bucer, by contrast, argues that God requires faith from everyone, although faith is possible only where men have the Spirit, and God does not give the Spirit to everyone. Nevertheless, Bucer says, God does not wrong anyone, although he requires faith from everyone.[3]

It is in *Romans* that this problem is dealt with at greatest length. Bucer is well aware of the objections to the doctrine of predestination, not least those that derive from the analogy with a human father, who would save his son if he could, or indeed anyone, however ungrateful the person might be.[4] Bucer's reply to the varied objections involves an affirmation of God's justice and sovereignty and of man's having no right to question God. He allows that it may offend human reason that God judges those who can do nothing different. But he is content with the affirmation that God is just, even if inscrutable. '. . . the judgments of God are a great abyss, they are inscrutable but just. For the Lord is just in all his ways, even where to our reason he seems otherwise.'[5] As God cannot be unjust, his predestination of man before birth cannot be unjust. The commentary re-asserts Paul's 'Who are you, O man, to answer back God?'.[6] Although we cannot understand God's judgment, we are to live 'by faith in his promises and trust in his goodness'.[7] Bucer permits no questioning

---

[1] Compare Luther's light of nature, light of grace, and light of glory. W.A. 18.784-6 (Packer and Johnston, *op. cit.* pp. 314-18).

[2] 201.B.22-202.A.15; 66.B.13-24; 168.C.8-21.

[3] HH.3.A.4-10. Compare HJ.1.B.28-C.2.

[4] R 458.D.10-17.   [5] R 410.E.9-411.A.2.

[6] R 447.C.10-16, 448.F.12-16. Already in the *Apology* he has said that we have no other solution but the one that Paul gave. BW 3.243.15-29.

[7] R 525.B.4-11.

of God's action. All questions asking why God leads into temptation, or why he punishes some and not others, are brushed aside. They have only one answer: 'I will have mercy on whom I will have mercy.'[1] There is no cause for God's action outside himself.[2]

A further difficulty that Bucer faces is that of man's freedom, if he is predestined by God. The idea of free will is used in this context somewhat ambiguously. Man's free will is denied in the sense that man can do anything good of himself and so attain salvation. It is affirmed in the sense that man is not like a stone drawn on a piece of string; in other words, he is not coerced.

This discussion begins in *Psalms*[3] and is developed in particular in the *Gospels* (1530). Here Bucer makes the double point that we are not coerced, but that without the Holy Spirit we cannot choose or do good.[4] God gives light to all men, by which they see what is right, but this is ineffective in those who lack the Spirit of sonship. They are held captive by Satan.[5] At the same time, therefore, men may be said to be drawn by the Father, and to have free will, for 'the Father does not draw men to the Son as a man draws rock or wood behind him'.[6]

In the *Apology* Bucer develops this discussion of freedom. He quotes Bernard to show that free will does not mean the ability to choose good or evil, or else God would not be free, nor should we be free in the afterlife. Freedom of the will means, he says, acting without outward compulsion according to one's knowledge and pleasure, not choosing out of one's own strength. 'For no one can choose what he does not recognise as good, and no one can recognise what is truly good, unless he is enlightened by the

[1] R 465.C.1–7.
[2] '…hoc est, nullam aliam causam habeo meae misericordiae cuiquam impendendae, quam ipsam meam misericordiam, quia ita mihi visum est: est mihi pro ratione voluntas. Alterum oraculum est de induratione, cuius tamen causa adjicitur, glorificatio potentiae divinae.' R 448.D.1–4. Compare also R 452. D.3–8 (p. 26, n. 5).   [3] P 104.B.24–C.9.
[4] 130.B.27; 46.A.29–B.3; 676.C.5–10.
[5] 130.B.27; 46.B.4–14; 676.C.11–22. Compare 130.B.27; 45.C.10–12; 674.D.23–5.
[6] 130.B.27; 45.B.4–12; 674.C.13–23.

Spirit of God. Therefore, we also can choose the good, only when we are enlightened by the same Spirit.'[1] He has already quoted Augustine in saying 'Quite simply, if the Spirit of God is not there, you can do nothing good. Likewise, where the Spirit is, no one can leave the good undone, or not come to Christ.'[2] Man's good, therefore, is not something that he produces, but it is what God does in him.[3]

Essentially the same view emerges in *Romans*. Free will is asserted in terms of man's freedom to act without coercion,[4] not in terms of his acting without necessity.[5] Freedom does not mean freedom to do evil, and far from taking away freedom predestination gives it, for only those endowed with the Spirit of God can act in true freedom.[6] This point is made later in the lectures on Ephesians.[7]

THE SIGNS OF PREDESTINATION

If men are divided into elect and reprobate, then it is important to know whether there is any way in which they may be distinguished from each other. Bucer answers this with both a 'yes' and a 'no'. He distinguishes various marks that are characteristic of the elect and reprobate, and implies that some of these are clearly recognisable. At the same time, he accepts that appearances can be misleading.

Already in *Against Treger* he sees the difficulty of distinguishing elect and reprobate, when he says that Peter denied Christ and appeared to human judgment not to be a Christian.[8] But, at the same time, though the elect may remain in error in many things to the end of their days, 'they have always understood what is necessary for their salvation, namely that Christ is their Saviour'.[9]

St Matthew sees a distinction between the elect and reprobate even before the elect respond to the gospel and the reprobate

---

[1] BW 3.242.20–3.   [2] BW 3.240.31–3.
[3] BW 3.238.15–28.   [4] R 460.F.10–15.
[5] R 413.A.5–10.   [6] R 413.A.14–B.11.
[7] EE 28.B.1–6.   [8] BW 2.114.39–115.3.
[9] BW 2.108.26–31, 109.5–9.

reject it. '...even before their conversion, while their lives overflow with evil actions, some seeds of piety nevertheless frequently show themselves.'[1] Thus in Paul there was a zeal for the traditions of his people, and in others a latent love of what is just and right. The reason for this is that there is always 'some seed of God in the elect'.[2] The reprobate must, in some sense, be recognisable by their sin against the Holy Spirit, for we are forbidden to preach the gospel to those who commit this sin.[3]

In *Ephesians*, likewise, the sin against the Holy Spirit is regarded as a clear sign of the reprobate, but the example of the penitent thief is taken as a warning against rejecting any who do not commit this sin.[4] The fundamental difference between elect and reprobate is the gift of the Holy Spirit. The elect have the seed of God, that is, the Holy Spirit. From this comes a repugnance to evil and an impulse to good.[5] It is the Holy Spirit who distinguishes the elect from the reprobate, for the reprobate are without the Spirit and so unable to invoke God as Father and Christ as Lord. In their hearts they say 'There is no God' or 'Christ be cursed'. They are captive to the will of Satan and so follow the affections of the flesh. By contrast, the elect are impelled by the Holy Spirit; they always wage war with the flesh and with Satan, and, when they do evil, detest it.[6] The elect are, indeed, recognisable by the fruits of the Spirit.[7]

It is clear in *St John* that the division of elect and reprobate is

[1] 115.A.14–19; 37.B.13–15; 91.A.5–7.
[2] 'Nevertheless you may always discern some seed of God in the elect and a zeal for the truth, even at a time when they attack the truth, or are leading a life which undoubtedly conflicts with it. Thus Paul devoted himself to the traditions of his fathers more than his contemporaries did. And you may see some latent love of what is just and right in many of those who are living as though lost, [but] who are elect. Indeed, when they have accepted the truth, whatever sin they commit, the reason for their sin is that they are turned aside by the desires of the flesh, so that they do not strive towards the truth they know.' 131.A.23–B.4; 122.B.10–15; 308.D.24–309.A.4. Compare 15.A.20–4; 86.B.8–10; 218.C.11–13.
[3] 64.B.21–5; 101.A.3–5; 255.A.2–4.
[4] E 35.A.15–B.1.
[5] E 39.A.3–12.
[6] E 40.A.19–B.5. Compare 180.A.8–22; 138.C.3–11; 353.A.19–B.3.
[7] E 39.B.8–20.

not a division of good and evil, though ultimately only the elect are good and the reprobate evil.[1] Rather, it is the divinity of Christ that can be said to divide them,[2] or the ability to see the Holy Spirit. '...the world is not able to see the Holy Spirit; however, the saints see him because they have him continually indwelling them.'[3] The reprobate may, in fact, have the gifts of the Spirit. Thus Saul had the gift of ruling and Judas the gift of casting out demons, but they lacked the Spirit of piety.[4] Again, there are references to the seed of God, that is, the Holy Spirit, as present in the elect, as in Nicodemus, even before they have faith.[5]

The psalms often present a sharp distinction between good and evil, godly and ungodly, which Bucer echoes in his commentary, though with certain characteristic qualifications. Thus the sons of God, even while they are among evil men and are themselves evil, are distinguished from them by being sometimes displeased with evil, by desiring a change, and by having reverence for godliness and an admiration for those who are holy.[6] At the same time we are exhorted not to reject anyone, but, like Christ, to seek the one sheep that is lost.[7] For on earth men are mixed, and

---

[1] Lang curiously identifies elect and reprobate in Bucer with good and evil, regarding the distinction as moral or ethical, rather than as religious or dogmatic. For him the point of departure lies in what man does, rather than in what God does, so that the discussion is primarily about man rather than about God (see especially, *op. cit.* pp. 156–8 and 169). Quite apart from clear instances that show a religious rather than a merely moral distinction, there is the important fact that the first serious discussion of predestination (in *Against Treger*) is in a religious rather than a moral context. This is also true of the later discussions in the *Gospels, Ephesians*, and *Romans*.

[2] '*Schisma igitur rursum factum est.* Quo enim clarius divinitatem suam prodebat, eo magis et electorum atque reproborum revelabatur discrimen.' 178.B.24–6; 65.B.2–3; 715.B.14–15.

[3] 219.A.6–12; 80.B.3–6; 751.A.13–16.

[4] 205.B.24–206.A.11; 75.D.21–76.A.3; 740.C.5–17. See the discussion of the gifts of the Spirit on pp. 185–6.

[5] 70.A.4–8; 24.A.19–21; 619.B.18–21; and 106.A.13–B.5; 35.D.11–23; 650.C.24–D.14.

[6] P 3.A.27–B.7. Compare Z 65.A.15–23, where the elect show signs (*indicia*) of the Holy Spirit, even while they seem buried in error.

[7] P 3.B.11–18.

there is no telling who is elect and who is reprobate. Afterwards, some who seemed bad here will be seen to be good.[1] It is God who decides, and God alone who knows, who are elect and who reprobate. We may judge someone to be rejected by God, as David's sons judged him to be, especially after what Nathan had said. In the same way, it was possible to judge wrongly between the publican and the Pharisee.[2]

The same signs of predestination are present in Bucer's later writing. *Romans* regards the Holy Spirit as the sign of the elect, so that we may know that those who are led by the Spirit of God are sons of God. The Holy Spirit is 'the pledge and seal of our election'.[3] The sign of the reprobate is the sin against the Holy Spirit, though now the reprobate are described rather as those who reject the word either by contempt (swine) or by opposition (dogs). They are to be abandoned and the word is not to be preached to them again.[4] Here, however, the distinction is between the elect and reprobate, after they have heard the word of God. The idea of the seed (or root) of election is still present, but is used primarily in terms of the Jews whom God will one day restore.[5]

The varying marks and stages of the elect are insisted on in *Von der waren Seelsorge* on the basis of the various kinds of sheep in Ezek. 34. Otherwise the fresh emphases in the later Bucer are the insistence that there are more who are called than elect among the evangelicals[6] and that the reprobate are those who participate in the Holy Spirit, but without regenerating,[7] or justifying[8] faith.

It is important to see that Bucer's discussion of the signs of predestination is almost entirely limited to his commentaries, where he is expounding the text of scripture. The ambiguity of his position is due, indeed, to the ambiguity of the Bible itself. He regards the Holy Spirit as a mark of the elect, not, however, by his gifts, which the reprobate may share, but rather by his

---

1 P 3.B.23–6.   2 P 27.A.18–26.
3 R 381.C.1–7.   4 R 63.B.11–20.
5 R 429.C.4–6, 501.A.14–16, and 514.D.9–14.
6 DV 173.20–3.   7 TA 247.2–5.
8 EE 111.B.19–112.D.3.

fruits. In some measure these fruits may be discerned in the elect before they believe, though this idea does not seem to be expressed after the early commentaries. The only clear mark of the reprobate, on the other hand, is the sin against the Holy Spirit. However, even the reprobate may seem to embrace the truth and may, indeed, fight for it more fiercely than some who are elect. Nevertheless, they lack the Spirit of sonship and so their lives are never transformed.[1]

THE SIN AGAINST THE HOLY SPIRIT

The discussion of the sin against the Holy Spirit arises out of the biblical references to it, sometimes in sharp contrast with the anabaptist or spiritualist view.

From the first Bucer accepts that the elect sin. In *Against Treger* he speaks of God's allowing this, so that they do not become proud.[2] However, because they are elect, they cannot fall, but can only err for a time, 'for the gifts and calling of God are irrevocable'.[3] It is not, however, till the commentary on St Matthew that he distinguishes clearly between sin in the elect and sin in the reprobate.

There, in exposition of Matt. 12:22–32, he distinguishes sin against the Son of Man, which can be forgiven, because it is done out of ignorance, from that against the Holy Spirit which is not.[4] In this incident in the gospels Bucer holds that the sin was a sin against the Holy Spirit, because the Pharisees sinned knowingly, for they knew Jesus was working by the Spirit and they knew the Messiah would be endowed with the Spirit. Bucer even adds that if Paul had persisted in his sin after his Damascus road experience, he would have been guilty of the sin against the Holy Spirit. But he did not do so, because he was elect.[5]

[1] 131.B.7–23; 122.B.17–C.8; 309.A.7–B.5.
[2] BW 2.162.30–4.   [3] BW 2.107.5–10, 35–8.
[4] 128.A.11–24; 121.B.15–24; 306.D.1–10.
[5] 128.B.5–23; 121.B.28–C.9; 306.D.16–307.A.3. Compare 228.B.19–24; 84.D.8–11; 762.C.2–5.

Predestination

Those who sin against the Holy Spirit may be said to be convinced of the truth, but not persuaded by the power of the Holy Spirit, so that they are transformed and enabled to embrace it. The reason is that they are held captive by Satan. As a result, they know the truth, so that they cannot deny it, but they do not know it, so that they can embrace it.[1] Thus, Herod knew John to be just, but, being in the grip of Satan, he killed him.[2]

Bucer's understanding of the sin against the Holy Spirit separated him from the anabaptists, both in his assertion that there was a sin that could not be forgiven[3] and in his denial that any sin after baptism amounts to a sin against the Holy Spirit.[4]

In the *Handlung* Bucer interprets Heb. 6 as referring to the sin against the Holy Spirit. 'This is when...one is wholly aware of the truth of God, and yet out of pure evil sets oneself against it, blasphemes and persecutes it...'[5] He goes on to say 'it certainly does not follow from this that no knowing sins will be forgiven after receiving Christ—quite the opposite is expressed here. For the Lord himself says "All sin and blasphemy will be forgiven,

---

[1] 'For the godless man who has been rejected by the Lord is not under his own control (*sui iuris*), as has been said, but is held captive by Satan, and therefore he does indeed know the truth, yet he does not know it. He knows it, so that his mind can no longer deny it to be the truth, or invent anything to refute it, or prove that it is not the truth. Yet, on the contrary, he does not know it, because a captive of Satan cannot embrace it...Knowledge of the truth, therefore, among those who sin against the Holy Spirit is of this kind, that they are indeed convinced of the truth, but they are not persuaded of it, that is to say, they are brought to such a point by the power of the Holy Spirit that they have absolutely nothing whereby they can properly repudiate the truth, yet they are not transformed in mind, so that they can embrace it.' 130.A.6–12, B.12–17; 121.D. 24–8, 122.A.13–17; 307.B.25–308.C.5, 32–D.1. Compare 129.A.12–18, B.6–12; 121.C.19–22, D.5–9; 307.A.13–17, B.4–9; and 133.A.6–18; 122.D.7–14; 310.C.9–17.
Bucer distinguishes conviction from persuasion. Persuasion is a mark of the elect and is the work of the Holy Spirit.
[2] 152.A.9–17; 129.C.21–6; 330.D.3–8.   [3] BW 2.256.31–257.3.
[4] It was Hofmann's view, as Schwenckfeld's, that after regeneration the will is free, and therefore responsible for its decisions. As a result, all sin committed after baptism as a believing adult is a sin against the Holy Spirit and so unforgivable. Compare G. H. Williams, *Radical Reformation*, pp. 263 and 285.
[5] H J.3.A.21–3.

except the sin against the Holy Spirit".'[1] When Peter denied Christ, he knew that what he did was wrong and against his promise to Christ. However, fear had so taken possession of him that he was more taken up with his danger than with what Christ had told him. It is the same with all the children of God when they sin. Though they fall in love with temporal things, they recognise God's law as good and right, and themselves as bound to live by it. Whereas, those who sin against the Holy Spirit reject this, setting themselves against the Holy Spirit.[2] Bucer regards Hofmann's assertion that every sin after baptism is a sin against the Holy Spirit as removing 'the high comfort that in the Christian church we have forgiveness of sins'.[3]

This distinction between two kinds of knowing sin remains in Bucer's theology,[4] though it is rarely made explicit. It is true to his conviction that the elect sin, but are not themselves committed to sin (which is how he interprets the saying that those who are born of God do not sin). It is, however, in some ways a filling out of what he means when he speaks of the sin against the Holy Spirit as conscious and deliberate sin, in contrast to the sin of the elect as arising from ignorance and weakness.

[1] H J.3.B.13–17.
[2] 'Dermassen gehts in allen sunden der kinder Gottes/das sie Gottes wort unnd warnung ya wol wissen/auch bedencken/Aber/durch begyrd/oder schew der zeytlichen ding/nit dapffer vor augen unnd hertzen behalten/sonder vergaffen sich am zeytlichen/lassen die anschawung goettlichs willens/etwas hinfallen/ damitt thuond unnd lassen sie/das sie wissen unrecht sein...Nun aber/wie wol dem also/das die heyligen/Gottes gepott und willen/offt also auss vergaffen am zeytlichen/verachten und ubertretten/je doch kommen sie dahin nicht/das sie erst auch Gottes gesatz/und willen in yren hertzen/oder mit mundt/wissentlich widersprechen/oder lesterten/lassen Gottes gesatz guot unnd gerecht sein beken-nen auch sich dem selbigen zu geleben schuldig/unnd ubertretten doch. Die aber inn todtsunden/setzen sich auch wider den geyst Gottes/unnd seyn wort/ widerfechtens unnd lesterens/das sie doch Gottes willen unnd wort seyn/ erkennen/damitt machen sie es auss/und stürtzen sich in ewigen todt/laut der spruch vor eingefuert.' H J.4.A.1–19.
[3] H L.5.B.9–11.
[4] Compare V C.4.B.14–21.

Predestination

The use of Rom. 8:28–30 in *Against Treger* implies and expresses several elements in Bucer's thinking about the order of salvation. He is not there describing stages in the process of salvation, but rather stating that man's justification and glorification depend on his being elected.[1] Equally, man's election leads to his being conformed to the image of Christ, for this is the purpose of his election.[2] The elect may fall, yet they never fall from the gracious hand of God, but are led by God to attain the measure of the stature of the fullness of Christ.[3]

St Matthew has the same confidence, rooted in the fact of election. Those who have been elected are led by the Spirit, and will at their appointed time respond to the gospel.[4] Not only their coming to faith, but also their perseverance in faith, is certain. There is to be no anxiety about those who have not heard the gospel, for 'the Lord knows his own and is able to teach them about himself even without outward preaching'.[5] 'Therefore, since no one can snatch them from the hand of the Lord (John 10) and since he never rejects those who come to him (John 6), it follows that those who have at any time belonged to Christ will never be alienated from him.'[6]

In *Ephesians* a clear sequence is marked, though it is rather a logical than a chronological sequence:[7]

[1] BW 2.120.1–11.   [2] BW 2.120.12–18.

[3] BW 2.162.30–3.

[4] 235.B.7–12; 156.A.13–16; 404.C.25–D.4. Compare also: 'This persuasion, however, even in the preaching of the gospel, does not come to the elect at any time, but at a time fixed by God, nor does it come to them immediately in its complete form (*perfectissima*) but in the way which the Good Father has determined.' 24.A.23–6; 88.D.26–8; 224.D.10–12.

[5] 23.A.1–5; 8.C.22–5; 19.B.11–14.

[6] 204.A.24–B.12; 67.A.14–22; 169.B.22–170.C.7.

[7] Müller interprets it generally as a chronological sequence, *op. cit.* p. 24, n. 38.

Clearly election comes before the other elements in salvation, as glorification (in the sense in which it is used in ch. 4 on Sanctification and Glorification) comes after them. Moreover, in this quotation the fact that men are to see the good works of the elect suggests a further temporal sequence. For Bucer, how-

But the order is as follows (*notandus ordo*). First, God's election or predestination. Next, adoption as sons, which is also called vocation, since the Lord draws to himself those to whom he has given his Spirit, and gives them knowledge of himself for which he has destined them from eternity. Then (*demum*) in the third place come holiness of life and the duties of love, by which good works are produced. When men see them, they glorify the heavenly Father, from whose goodness they proceed. So that, fourthly, there is in the saints the glory of God, resulting from the righteousness, with which God has deemed it worthy to adorn them.[1]

This same sense of an order of salvation is expressed in *St John* (indeed the phrase 'order of salvation' is used this time), though now the fact of election is presupposed. The first point is the announcing of the gospel to the elect. Then they are given faith in it, so that in and through the gospel God is known. Immediately there arise confidence and love, from which come a zeal for holiness and the service of others.[2] The division here suggests logically, rather than chronologically, distinct stages.

The doctrine of election gives rise to two emphases in the understanding of salvation. The one is restrictive—it is only the elect who will believe. The other is forward looking—the elect will be called, justified, sanctified, and glorified. Self-evident as these two consequences of a doctrine of election may appear, they need to be stressed, precisely because they affect Bucer's total theology. The restrictiveness of the doctrine of election affects, for instance, Bucer's understanding of word and sacraments, and excludes the possibility that they can be automatic bearers of the Spirit and grace of God to all who receive them. The forward-looking note

---

ever, faith and love are inseparably bound up and the one cannot be present without the other. There is no need, therefore, to see holiness as a further stage in the order of salvation.

[1] E 26.B.16–25.

[2] '*Quia verba, quae dedisti mihi.* Hic vide ordinem salutis. Electis (1530 and 1536, primum) Evangelion annunciatur, tum datur eis illi habere fidem, deinde in illo et per illud, Deus cognoscitur, inde (1530 and 1536, hinc) continuo fidutia in eum, et amor eius nascuntur. Ex iis mox sequitur studium sanctitatis, et officiositas in fratres.' 239.A.18–23; 88.D.23–5; 771.B.9–11.

Predestination

implies a necessary link between faith and love, the new birth and the new life, imputed righteousness and real righteousness.

The restrictiveness of election is perhaps the less frequently mentioned of these two elements. It is, nonetheless, unquestioned. A person does not believe 'unless God has elected him to this from the beginning, for he calls and sanctifies those whom he has predestined...'[1] Similarly, men 'are not glorified unless justified, not justified unless called, and not called unless predestined'.[2] On the other hand, given that men are predestined, it is absolutely certain that they will be justified, sanctified, and glorified.[3]

It is 'impossible for the elect not to come to the Lord in the end'.[4] This depends on election, so that those who are sheep follow Christ and never perish.[5] Moreover, 'only those who are called and predestined are sanctified'.[6] The converse is also true, that those, who were rejected before the foundation of the world, will one day reject the offer of God's grace.[7] 'They cannot hear the teaching of Christ, that is, receive it with faith', whereas the elect 'cannot by any torture be torn from it'.[8] This is frequently, but not always, directly related to the presence and work of the Holy Spirit, who inspires the elect, leading them to faith and love.[9]

[1] 21.A.5–12; 7.D.13–18; 579.B.3–8.
[2] 128.B.3–14; 44.B.26–C.7; 672.C.12–19.
[3] Compare *Getrewe Warnung* where it is said that 'whomever God has ordained to eternal life, he will also call in his time and enable to believe his word'. BW 2.239.11–13. Bucer similarly insists that election implies a new life in conformity with the image of Christ. This is God's purpose in election and to this end he gives his Spirit. BW 2.249.21–39.
[4] 74.A.1–3; 25.B.10–11; 623.B.6–7.
[5] 179.B.15–17, 180.A.22–4; 65.C.5–6, 29–30; 716.D.1–2, 22–3.
[6] 206.A.11; 76.A.2–3; 740.C.24.
[7] 89.A.19–24; 29.D.27–30.A.3; 635.A.16–22.
[8] 170.B.22–7, 171.A.2–4; 62.B.19–22, 24–5; 706.D.2–5, 8–9.
[9] 'Now how does it arise that some are sheep, that is to say, some are able to receive the teaching of Christ, while others are not? Undoubtedly because the good Spirit of God has inspired the former, but not (1528 *minime*) the latter. For in 1 Cor. 2 Paul clearly attributes knowledge of divine things to those endowed with the Spirit and denies it to those who lack the Spirit as to unspiritual men (*animalibus*). But why then is it that the former are given the Spirit, and not the

The relation of the Holy Spirit to this whole process is clear in the *Psalms*. God is said to impart his Spirit to the elect today, as he imparted him in the past, 'for no other reason than that he elected and predestined them to this end before the foundation of the world'. The key text here, as often in this discussion, is Rom. 8:28–30.[1] In another place it is precisely those sealed with the Spirit, who cannot be lost in the end.[2] As vocation and justification indubitably follow election,[3] the use of outward means may in a given case be dispensed with. Bucer says, therefore, in expounding Ps. 1, that the Spirit can lead the elect into all truth without any outward teaching.[4]

The *Gospels* (1536) relates the Holy Spirit in particular to the act of believing in God. It argues that nothing is good unless it comes from the love of God, which is not possible unless one believes in God. This, however, happens only by the inspiration of the Holy Spirit, and only to those whom God holds as his own because of the merit of Christ through which their sins are forgiven. These are in fact 'those whom he elected to it before the foundation of the world'.[5] There is a sense, moreover, in which

latter? Surely for no other reason than that the former are appointed to life and not the latter, and that they are given the Son for their salvation, and not the latter. Let us therefore grant this glory to the Lord, that he himself gives his Spirit, assisted in no way by our works (and that he gives him without instruments that we might provide). But where he has decided to give him, then we ourselves can co-operate both to instruct and to guide, provided that he gives, by the same Spirit, a right understanding of what we say to those to whom we speak.' 179.B.21–180.A.7; 65.C.10–18; 716.D.4–12.

1 P 104.B.24–C.9.
2 P 232.B.5–8.
3 'Moreover, the book in which the elect are written is also remembered by Moses in Exodus 32. It is nothing other than the eternal election and predestination of God, which vocation and justification indubitably follow (Rom. 8). From this follows what I have said—that to be blotted out of this book is the same as to be rejected, so that it is clear that such people were never written in it. For whoever has once been written in it, that is, numbered among the elect, can never be removed from it. He has been given to the Son to be saved; and he rejects none of those whom the Father has given, nor is anyone able to snatch them from his hand...' P 210.D.18–24.
4 P 11.A.5–B.1.
5 187.B.18; 140.C.17; 364.C.6–14.

men's sins are forgiven and their regeneration confirmed at the same time as God elects them to life; yet it is necessary for them to receive these things through the ministry of the church.[1]

This picture is not developed any further in *Romans*, though the close link with the Spirit is maintained. '...God from the beginning chose this people from among all the peoples of the world so that he might impart to them his Spirit, and thence that they might live to his glory...'[2] The work of the Holy Spirit 'is to vivify his elect'[3] and to persuade those who are called.[4] He never deserts the elect, though the reprobate may be inspired by the Holy Spirit and then deserted.[5]

Bucer's fundamental understanding of the place of election in man's salvation is unchanged in his lectures on Ephesians. The cause of election is 'God's grace and Christ's merit'; the purpose (or final cause) is 'the sanctification of our life and God's glory', but chiefly God's glory.[6] It is precisely this twofold orientation of the doctrine of election in God's grace and Christ's merit, as opposed to anything that man is or does, and in man's living to the glory of God, knowing, worshipping, and loving him that offers one of the most significant clues in understanding Bucer's whole theology:

The purpose of election is that we may know, love, and worship God, and live lives that are pleasing to him. Paul, moreover, says that God elected us in him, so that we might not think that there was any merit in us. For in our election God had regard not to us, but only to himself and to his Son.[7]

---

[1] 'Ita apud Deum peccata hominibus remissa sunt, et regeneratio collata, simul atque illos Deus in vitam elegerit: ut autem homo haec apud se etiam vere percipiat et sentiat, eadem Ecclesiae ministerio percipiat oportet, postquam Deus in hoc ipsum Ecclesiae ministerium instituit.' 72.B.8–13; 24.D.19–22; 622.C.9–13. This statement is found only in the 1536 edition.

[2] R 193.B.13–17. [3] R 361.C.8–16.
[4] R 402.F.14–403.A.2. [5] R 61.C.1–13.
[6] EE 19.C.7–13. [7] EE 21.A.14–17.

2

VOCATION

There is no significant development in Bucer's understanding of vocation. Even to minor details, the commentary on St Matthew in 1527 presents his developed view of vocation. It therefore forms the basis of our exposition.[1]

VOCATION IN THE ORDER OF SALVATION

There are a number of dangers in presenting vocation as one element in the order of salvation. The main one is to see it as part of a chronological sequence, a part that can be clearly identified and separated from other parts. It is not this. It can certainly be separated from election and follows it in time. It cannot, however, be so sharply separated from justification, nor does it necessarily precede it. It can, nevertheless, be distinguished from justification logically, even if not chronologically.

For those who are elect God has an appointed time, at which he will call them and lead them to faith. This time is normally, thought not necessarily, to be identified with the announcement to them of the gospel. 'Therefore, whom God has fore-ordained to eternal life, he calls in his time, and gives him to believe his word. Romans 8:30 and Acts 13:48.'[2] For 'God sends those who announce the gospel', and then 'the Spirit persuades the hearts of the elect' 'at the time God has appointed for them'.[3] But the appoin-

---

[1] It is almost exclusively in the commentaries that Bucer considers vocation. The only point where there is any significant dicussion outside the commentaries, concerns the relation of vocation to the preaching of the word. This is dealt with in detail in ch. 10.

[2] BW 2.239.11–13.

[3] See 24.A.16–26; 88.D.22–8; 224.D.6–12; and 235.B.7–12; 156.D.13–16; 404.C.25–D.4. Compare EE 27.A.12–13, in which first there is election, and then effective and regenerating vocation.

ted time differs from person to person, and for that reason Christ can tell one man to preach and yet forbid another to do so.[1]

The fact that vocation is inseparably bound up with justification and sanctification is seen in the variety of names by which it is known. It is called adoption,[2] drawing or attraction,[3] illumination,[4] leading,[5] and conversion and grafting into Christ.[6] Although vocation in these various senses is primarily seen as the work of the Holy Spirit, it can also be ascribed quite simply to the Father[7] or the Son,[8] who are said to call men or to draw them.

GENERAL AND PARTICULAR VOCATION

It is especially the text 'many are called, but few are chosen', which leads Bucer to distinguish a general and a particular vocation. The general vocation is that by which all men are called, whether or not they be elect. This call discloses the truth of God. But many to whom the truth is disclosed 'are not changed by the Spirit, so that they follow God who calls them'. For this call is not the same as that in which God calls those whom he has predestined.[9] It is rather like the throwing of a net into the sea, which gathers bad fish as well as good.[10] To the problem that this raises (why God should command us to call to him those he does not wish to come) Bucer simply replies that it is for God to command and for us to obey. In any case, God wishes the reprobate to be without excuse —and this is as true of what he reveals through his word, as of what he reveals through creation (Rom. 1:19–20).[11]

Particular vocation is the vocation by which the elect are called. This is the strict use of the word vocation. Yet this vocation of the

[1] 42.B.17-27; 94.A.30-B.4; 238.C.18-24.   [2] E 26.B.16-20.
[3] 23.A.1-5; 8.C.23-5; 19.B.11-14.
[4] 76.B.10-15; 25.C.22-6; 61.A.14-19. Compare 126.A.19-24; 43.D.8-10; 670.D.11-13.
[5] 125.A.24-7; 43.C.2-4; 669.B.9-11.   [6] R 407.C.16-18.
[7] 126.A.19-24; 43.D.8-10; 670.D.11-13.
[8] 117.A.12-15; 38.A.18-20; 93.A.3-5.
[9] 244.A.6-10; 159.A.9-11; 411.B.1-4.
[10] 147.A.7-24; 127.C.24-D.4; 325.B.8-15.   [11] R 457.A.4-12.

elect corresponds, in a way, to a vocation of the reprobate. 'For God wishes himself to be preached to the elect for salvation, and to the evil, so that they may be convicted of their impiety.'[1] In this way the grace of God is offered to them. Thus the arrows of Ps. 45:5[2] are:

the power of the word and Spirit of Christ, by which, when the hearts of men have been touched by them, they are not able not to submit themselves, whether in love of him to their eternal salvation, or in total hatred to their complete destruction. For the gospel is the fragrance of death, to those destined to death, as it is the fragrance of life, to those ordained to life.[3]

True vocation, however, is not this negative vocation, but is the vocation to salvation. This true vocation is the beginning of all salvation. It is the gift and work of God, which he imparts to some and not to others. Those, to whom he imparts it, cannot but follow him when he calls them.[4]

THE WORK OF THE HOLY SPIRIT IN VOCATION

When vocation is viewed from the godward side, it is seen in terms of the contrast between election and reprobation; when it is viewed from the manward side, it is seen in terms of the contrast between the Holy Spirit and the natural man.

Man in himself, natural man, is unable to grasp the things of God. Left to himself, he is stupefied, unable to understand them or accept them:

[1] 87.A.21-3; 108.A.8-9; 273.A.8-9. Compare 297.B.26-298.A.11; 178.A. 16-23; 458.C.6-14.
[2] 'Thine arrows are sharp in the heart of the king's enemies; the people fall under thee.' (Ps. 45:5.)
[3] P 169.D.1-5. Compare P 333.A.21-B.3.
[4] 'For it is certain that obedience to God's vocation, which is the beginning of one's whole salvation, is the gift and work of God, which he bestows on some but denies to others. For he exercises suasion on the former, so that he persuades them, but he does not do so with the latter. And those whom he persuades cannot but follow the one who calls, but those whom he does not persuade cannot follow.' R 460.E.16-F.1.

Next, even this should not be overlooked, that the Galileans (let it be granted that they were Jews, and that beside the light of reason they had also the lamp of the law and the prophets) are nevertheless asserted by the evangelist to have sat in the darkness and shadow of death, before the gospel was preached to them. By this we are taught that all the while the human reason is blind and the letter of both the law and the prophets kills, until we are renewed by the gift of Christ, by faith in the gospel. Then at last the face is unveiled, and we ourselves, even we, see the glory of the Lord, and, like a mirror, reflect that glory to others. Finally, we are transformed into the same image, from glory to glory, as by the Spirit of the Lord (2 Cor. 3). For before we believe the gospel and are inspired by the divine Spirit, we are unspiritual (*animales*), and for that reason we are utterly unable to perceive the things of God (1 Cor. 2). Thus, all the wisdom, all the righteousness, which we possess in the absence of God's Spirit, are the darkness and shadow of death. And if we pride ourselves on these, then truly we shall sit in the darkness of death itself, as much strangers to the knowledge of God as also to life.[1]

Even the Jews, although there was no people more wise or holy than they, opposed Christ because they were not regenerated by the Holy Spirit.[2] It is only as God breathes his Spirit, that men are able to see that what appears as foolishness to the natural man is actually true and brings salvation.[3]

The work of the Spirit is not simply that of persuasion. Even before men hear the gospel, of which the Holy Spirit persuades them, the Holy Spirit is at work in their lives:

His principal work, in fact, is to make us inquisitive about and understanding of divine things, which the natural man neither cares about nor is able to receive. The result is that we thirst for the word of God, and that, when we have heard it, we receive it and keep it as the indubitable word of God, recognising in it that God is favourably disposed towards us through Christ and is a Father full of goodwill.[4]

---

[1] 107.A.23–B.14; 35.A.12–22; 85.A.11–22.
[2] P 14.B.4–11.
[3] P 9.D.3–11. As becomes clear in the discussion of the Bible and Preaching, the scriptural basis for this belief is found in such passages as 1 Cor. 2.
[4] 79.B.5–10; 26.C.6–9; 63.A.21–5.

In other words, there is a preparatory work of the Spirit in our vocation, that predisposes us to receive the gospel when it is announced. This work may be the negative one of making our lives disturbed and dissatisfied, or the positive one of making us eager to learn about Christ. For God gives his Spirit to the elect, precisely so that when the gospel is announced they may be ready for it. They are, as Bucer describes them in the *Berner Predigt*, the weary and heavy laden who are without rest or peace, because they do not please God, and who come to the Lord when he calls them.[1]

At the moment the Lord calls, the real work of the Holy Spirit in illuminating, persuading, and kindling takes place. The Holy Spirit is 'that sacred and divine energy and power, by which the mind is divinely inspired and renewed; that is to say illumined, so that it is able now to receive divine things, at which otherwise by nature it would be stupefied; then kindled, so that it burns for those things, which otherwise, by nature, it disdains.'[2] To the natural man the things of God are foolishness. They remain so until the Holy Spirit forms the heart,[3] testifies with our Spirit that God wishes to be our Father,[4] or persuades us of the truth of the gospel.[5]

Bucer links this convicting work of the Spirit with the outward word.[6] It is by means of the word that God himself penetrates the heart, persuading men of it by his Spirit. The outward word is ineffective until the Holy Spirit persuades the heart, but it is nevertheless through the word that the Holy Spirit works.[7] Nor-

[1] BW 2.285.16–287.7.
[2] 76.B.10–15; 25.C.22–6; 61.A.14–19.
[3] 120.B.6–7; 39.A.12; 95.B.16–17.
[4] R 30.E.1–7.
[5] 18.A.1–B.6; 87.A.11–B.7; 220.C.1–D.5.
[6] The exact relation of the Spirit and the word is considered in the chapter on Preaching. It is sufficient here to see that where vocation is interpreted in terms of convincing or persuading, it is closely related to the outward word.
[7] 'The certainties which are God's and which scripture predicates of God, the man who lives who according to his natural self (*secundum animam*) does not perceive. There is, therefore, need here of the inspiration of the Holy Spirit to persuade the hearts of the elect of the gospel. In this way as many as are foreordained to

mally references to being called, or drawn, or illumined, are immediately related to the hearing of the gospel. It is for that reason that men are commanded to preach the gospel to all people, with the exception of those who are incapable of being called because their lives show that they are among the reprobate.[1]

By whatever means vocation comes, it is always God's vocation. In calling men he certainly uses those who preach, and in *Romans* they may be spoken of as essential, but, without the inward vocation of God through the Holy Spirit, all their words are in vain. 'It is impossible to come to faith and eternal life unless you hear the gospel and that administered by a man...Yet the apostle knew, since he wrote such things, that God could call people without the ministry of men. He knew all teaching administered by men to be ineffective for salvation without God's giving all the increase.'[2]

life are at length called and drawn by the Father to the Son. And this is that hearing from which faith proceeds (Rom. 10). Even if an outward preacher of the gospel ministers, nevertheless, because planter and waterer are nothing, all preaching will be without effect, until the Holy Spirit has preached the gospel to the heart and has persuaded it. With the man in whom that persuasion has truly gained a hold, even if he knows [only] in part how good God is, yet he cannot but love and revere him and promise to himself the best from God, since he has faith in the gospel which proclaims him [God] in this way—this faith certainly follows, since our hope in God is not ashamed. Thus, after the election of the saints, the next thing is that God penetrates the hearts of his own by the word, of which, however, he persuades them by his Spirit. From this persuasion and the certain faith which they already have in his words, there follow trust (*fiducia*) in him, love for him, and a will ready to please him in all things.' E 20.B.4–25.

[1] Compare 249.A.5–10; 161.A.23–B.2; 416.D.16–20; and 57.B.1–7; 19.A.9–14; 607.B.24–608.C.3.

[2] R 488.F.11–17. Man's part in God's vocation is discussed in chs. 9 and 10.

47

3

JUSTIFICATION

That the order of salvation[1] in Bucer is not a chronological order is evident from the way justification cannot be separated from vocation or sanctification. For the sake of clarity they should be distinguished, as long as it is not assumed that Bucer's thought can be neatly schematised. There are some elements that belong clearly to justification (such as justification and faith), and some that belong to both justification and sanctification (such as righteousness and the law). The latter are treated in greater detail in the chapter on Sanctification, because that context illuminates more satisfactorily Bucer's particular understanding of them.

JUSTIFICATION

Justification is the element in Bucer's doctrine of salvation that has attracted most attention and most criticism.[2] Bucer uses justifica-

[1] Besides the description of the order of salvation that has already been given, Bucer can use other descriptions. For example, in the *Gospels* (52.B.23–5; 17.D.11–12; 42.C.9–23) he has the order:
  1. the mercy of God by which he saves us;
  2. the work of the Holy Spirit in giving us faith and love (for in baptism the renewal of the Spirit is offered and received);
  3. Christ, by whose merit and grace we are given the Spirit;
  4. our justification which is the work of the mercy of God, the renewing of the Spirit, and the merit of Christ; and
  5. eternal life.

[2] Apart from Lang, *Der Evangelienkommentar Martin Butzers*, on which most twentieth-century studies are dependent, the discussion in Otto Ritschl, *Dogmengeschichte*, vol. 3, pp. 141–52; Ellwein, *Vom neuen Leben*, pp. 63–6, 109–17, 132–3, 166–8, 209; Hans Emil Weber, *Reformation*, vol. 1.II pp. 207–10; Köhler, *Dogmengeschichte*, pp. 362–4, 418, and Müller, *Martin Bucers Hermeneutik*, pp. 16–40 should be mentioned. A weakness in many discussion is the failure to let Bucer's view speak for itself in the context of his whole theology. This feature, together with a sometimes unrepresentative selection of quotations, leads to such a judgment as Ellwein's that Bucer's theology is not truly that of the reformation.

tion ambiguously.[1] It means for him both to impute righteousness and to impart it. The two are distinguishable, and Bucer does distinguish them (at some points more clearly than at others); but he never separates them. It is not a question of one following chronologically upon the other, though this does happen, rather is the second necessarily involved in the first. God never imputes righteousness without also imparting it. He does not simply transform a man's standing in his sight; he transforms a man's life in his sight and in the sight of men. At the same time, no man is made righteous in this life in such a way that he does not always stand in need of the unmerited forgiveness of God.

This twofoldness, which runs through Bucer's writing, is present as early as 1523 in *Das ym selbs* where he says: '...if they believe in Christ, that is, wholly trust that through his blood Christ has placed them again within the grace of God and reconciled them to him, and that consequently, by his Spirit, Christ has made them again useful...to all creatures.'[2] This same link is expressed in the *Summary* where faith is shown to be active in love, for 'what Christ is, has, and does, is all theirs, because they are one with him, he in them and they in him'.[3]

It is precisely his concern to hold these two ideas together that seems to lead Bucer to use them almost indiscriminately. One moment justification can mean to impute righteousness or to forgive, another moment it can mean to impart righteousness or to renew. The grounds for this mixed use are varied. They may be the fact that with faith the Holy Spirit is given[4] or that the believer is in Christ and Christ in him.[5] They may be that faith leads to

Köhler rightly sees that Bucer's use of twofold or threefold justification was not determined by a standpoint alien to that of the reformation. He regards threefold justification as an approximation to Zwingli's view, and twofold justification as an approximation to Luther's.

[1] In fact the word is used less often than might be expected. The idea is frequently expressed either by the use of cognate words, like righteous and righteousness, or by the use of words like faith.

[2] BW 1.60.8–13.

[3] BW 1.92.4–5.

[4] BW 1.60.8–13. [5] BW 1.92.4–5.

love as a good tree to good fruit[1] or that it is for good works that God predestines, calls, and justifies a man.[2]

The looseness of his usage is shown in a passage in *St Matthew* where he moves from one sense to the other with little awareness of any apparent contradiction in what he says. In the 1536 edition he presents the idea of imputed righteousness more clearly, but even then adds a further comment to show that he also assumes that there is real righteousness as well.[3]

Although *Romans* shows a clearer distinction between the two, it does not show a significant change in Bucer's understanding of justification. Bucer does not give up the tension between the two ideas of justification; he simply seeks new and clearer ways of formulating it. Moreover, the distinction that he makes is also clear in some of his earlier works. In expounding Ps. 32 he affirms that it is to the man who recognises that he is not righteous that God does not impute his sins:

Now it is to be observed that he pronounces blessed not those who have committed no sins—for that is granted to no man—but those whose sins are forgiven and covered, so that the avenging eye of God should

[1] 187.A.23–B.18; 140.C.4–17; 363.A.22–B.12.
[2] 220.A.24–B.3; 71.D.7–11; 181.B.20–5.
[3] 'It is to be noted, however, that to be justified is here the opposite of to be condemned, in case anyone should think, from what has been said, that righteousness is acquired. For to be justified is here the same as to be pronounced just, not rendered (*reddi*) just. We are justified by faith, that is, we are made (*efficimur*) just; we are justified by deeds and words, that is, we are declared and judged just.' (1527 and 1530.) Compare this with the amended comment in the 1536 edition. 'It is to be noted...not rendered just. We are justified by faith, that is, we receive a justification that is freely given, by virtue of which the heavenly Father considers us just, and we receive a kingdom through Christ his Son. We are justified by deeds and words, that is, we are declared and judged just, both in our own eyes and in those of the rest of mankind, who are able to judge from [our] fruits.' 134.B.16–19; 123.B.3–5; 314.C.6–11.

Brecht discusses the correspondence between Melanchthon and Brenz which leads to a different formulation of Brenz's doctrine, more akin to Melanchthon's than to Luther's. Bucer's doctrine of justification is also more clearly formulated as a result of his contact with Melanchthon, but it does not become Melanchthonian, as does Brenz's. See Martin Brecht, *Die frühe Theologie des Johannes Brenz*, pp. 241–7.

not look upon them, from whom, so to speak, God has turned away his face. What Psalm 25 prays for is this: to whom God imputes no sins by taking away from them the punishment they deserve.

But whence [comes] this pardon for sins, whence such clemency on God's part, that not imputing sins he remits all the punishment? [It comes] if the spirit is void of guile and pretence, if a man does not seem just in his own eyes, since he is less than nothing, if he truly acknowledges his sins and consecrates himself to God in earnest.[1]

Although in the *Psalms*, almost more than anywhere else, he stresses the fact that God makes a man righteous, he always holds this with the idea of an imputed righteousness:

Thus they have sung appropriately: 'Thou shalt forgive the iniquity of thy people', which is then truly forgiven when it reigns over us no more. And when he clearly reconciles us to the Father, and makes us pleasing [to him], he truly covers our sins, lest he should ever see them to avenge them. Therefore it was also suitable to add this: 'Thou shalt cover all their faults'. Assuredly thou wilt have clothed them fully with thy Son the Lord Jesus.[2]

Likewise, in the *Bericht*, the two points go together but with a clear insistence on imputed righteousness. He affirms that however far we progress in godliness, which he regards as God's work in us, 'all our blessedness still consists in this alone, that God does not reckon our sins to us, that he accepts the death of our Lord Jesus as payment for our sins'.[3]

In *Romans* both ideas of justification are found, sometimes separately and sometimes together. Justification by faith is described as 'our believing on account of Christ, who died for this reason, that our sins are not imputed to us'. 'Our only righteousness is that our unrighteousness is forgiven.'[4] Most characteristically, however, the two are expressed together. By justification Paul is said to express first the remission of sins, but at the same time, however, the imparting of righteousness:

[1] P 129.C.12–27.   [2] P 238.C.17–D.1.
[3] BH O.3.A.25–30.
[4] R 5.45–50 (Preface). Compare R 8.54–8 (Preface).

Therefore, since Paul is accustomed to speak in this manner, and under the term justification first indeed to express the remission of sins, but at the same time always to signify that sharing of righteousness which God equally brings about in us by the same Spirit, by whom he renders us certain of the forgiveness of sins and of his own goodwill...'[1]

Precisely because we are given the Spirit, our lives display the righteousness of God which he effects in us.[2]

Bucer is at this point trying to do justice to the diverse testimony of scripture. He finds the word justification used in a variety of senses, and his way is not to choose between them, but to reconcile them. It is this that leads to his speaking of a twofold or threefold justification.

In the threefold justification the first is that which happens in our election to eternal life by the goodness of God and the merit of Christ. The second is that which we enjoy here in some measure and which is received by faith. It is again God's free gift, and is effected in us by his Spirit. The third is the full measure of eternal life. To this works make their contribution, but they are themselves the gifts and works of God's goodness:

Thus our justification is threefold, that is, God assigns eternal life to us in three ways. The first justification is that by which he destines eternal life for us. It assuredly consists solely in his goodness and in consideration of Christ's merit. The scholastics add the consideration of future merits, which no doubt God foresees in his own. But whence, I ask, does he foresee what no one ever has unless he himself gives it, which also he decided to give at the very time when he decided to give salvation? The second is that by which in some measure he now offers eternal life and grants enjoyment of it, having given his Spirit, in whom we cry 'Abba, Father'. This justification consists besides even in our faith, but this also God gives us freely out of his goodness, and brings

---

[1] R 12.51–6 (Preface).

[2] 'However great the righteousness which the Spirit of Christ without doubt works in us when we ourselves believe, yet that could never be enough for us to be reckoned righteous in God's sight by its merit, for we are unprofitable servants, even when we have done completely whatever he has commanded.' R 13.5–7 (Preface).

about in us by his Spirit. The third is when he at last offers in actual fact and fully eternal life, or even the good things which we enjoy in this life, but then not just in faith and hope. To this justification what we do is relevant, but what we do is also itself the gift and work of God's gracious goodness.[1]

A twofold justification is the distinction he most often makes. It is the justification of the ungodly (as in Paul) and the justification of the godly (as in James). Since all men are ungodly, none could be saved if God did not justify the ungodly here. On the other hand, God does not justify the reprobate, but is said to justify men according to their works.[2] The link between these two may be said to be the gift of the Holy Spirit to those whom God justifies. He turns the man whose ungodliness has been forgiven from his ungodliness and creates in him a new life of godliness:

First it is certainly necessary for God in his mercy to precede us and forgive all ungodliness. Thus he justifies the ungodly, but the ungodliness having been forgiven and remitted, and then the Spirit having also been given, who shrinks from all ungodliness and is zealous for godliness, so that in this way he pays us the benefits of his that follow, as if a reward and recompense for godliness, a godliness in fact given by himself. As the man whose ungodliness he does not at the same time both forgive and take away persists in his ungodliness, which cannot fail to be hateful to a just God, so he himself is also hateful to God on account of his ungodliness; and he necessarily pays him the penalty of his ungodliness at the time when he judges according to [our] works.[3]

For Bucer the forgiveness of sin is not simply an end in itself. It opens up a new relationship with God, the relationship of son to Father. It is God's intention by his Spirit to conform his sons to the image of his Son:

Here undoubtedly under the term being justified he included at the same time that righteousness which God works by his Spirit in those who believe in Christ, and which he wishes to be evidence that he has already remitted their sins, and holds them as amongst those whom he

---

[1] R 119.A.16–B.8.   [2] R 231.C.14–232.D.7.
[3] R 232.D.12–E.1.

has determined to justify, that is, to hold as amongst the just, not only by forgiving them wherein they have sinned, but also by conforming them to the image of his Son.[1]

This does not mean that the sons of God are not always in need of God's forgiveness, or that they somehow can start achieving something on their own account. Their relationship to God remains one of total dependence on him. It is for this reason that the righteousness of God is always both imputed and imparted.

The later Bucer keeps this notion of a twofold justification. He does not, however, relinquish the primary emphasis on justification by faith. In the *Bestendige Verantwortung* he says:

our true justification, whether it happens at the beginning of our salvation or after, always consists in God's graciously forgiving us our sins and granting to us and reckoning to us the righteousness of his Son, which we receive when we rightly believe.[2]

Justification is a gracious forgiveness of sins and the taking up into God's protection and the fellowship of eternal life in Christ our Lord.[3]

Of the justification of works his judgment is clear:

But this justification is rightly called God's justification, through which, when his own do right, he confirms their testimony and praise, and also richly rewards them. It is not, however, a justification of works as if the works made us righteous, for as the objectors admit they always lack something on our part.[4]

Man's confidence, therefore, is not in himself, but in God. It is the Holy Spirit, not his conscience or his works, who makes him sure of God's grace.[5]

In his writings in England, which show the renewed conflict with catholic opponents of the reformation, the insistence on justification is no less emphatic. The concern with good works does not prevent, but rather lead to, his affirming in *De ordinatione*:

[1] R 12.43–6 (Preface).   [2] BV 41.A.13–18.
[3] BV 41.B.3–6.   [4] BV 43.A.4–9.
[5] BV 43.B.32–44.B.9.

...it is necessary for us in the beginning, and always while we live here, right up to our last breath, to receive, embrace, and hold fast justification to eternal life, only by faith in the gospel, by faith in our Lord Jesus Christ, by which we know and apprehend him as the propitiator and propitiation for our sins.[1]

Ephesians (1550), with its specific denial of the scholastic doctrine of merit, adopts the twofold understanding of the word justification, already expressed in the *Bestendige Verantwortung*. Justification has two meanings, a forensic one which is the opposite of condemnation, and a further one, which is the equivalent of praise. In this second sense God is said to justify or praise the works of the regenerate. In the first sense it is the ungodly (*impii*) who are justified, in the second sense it is the godly (*pii*). The deeds of the godly which are justified and rewarded are not, however, perfect, but imperfect; and they are saved not because of their works, but because of the grace by which forgiveness is received.[2] The justification of a person's life must, of course, precede the justification of his works, for only from a good life do good deeds come.[3] The twofold justification (of faith and of works) is presented as the only way of preventing a contradiction between Paul and James. The justification of works, which means praising them and promising a reward to them, depends entirely on justification by faith.[4]

FAITH AND WORKS

The question of a twofold justification raises in acute form the question of faith and works. It is a question that Bucer deals with in a variety of ways from his first work to his last. As with the question of justification, he seeks to reconcile the apparently

---

[1] TA 246.43-7.
[2] 'There is also another justification of the godly, and proof of righteousness, albeit imperfect, on behalf of which God makes a pronouncement, which he asserts, which he also adorns and recompenses with a reward: see James 2 and the reference in St Matthew. "By your words you will be justified and by your words you will be condemned." You will be saved, not indeed because of what you have done, which is imperfect, but because of grace, by which we receive forgiveness.' EE 61.C.2-7.
[3] EE 61.C.11-62.D.3.   [4] EE 62.F.3-16.

diverse testimony of scripture about faith and works, not by discounting or by suppressing one of them, but by discovering a form that will embrace them both, and do justice to them both.

He accepts Luther's view that good works do not make a good person, but that a good person does good works. What a man does, therefore, depends entirely on what he is. By nature he is evil, and nothing he can do, can change this. But God can change it. In Jesus Christ he has forgiven men. If a man believes this and trusts himself to God, he receives the Holy Spirit, who renews his life, conforming it to the image of Christ. Thus man becomes capable of the good works which now flow from a good life, though ultimately it is not man himself who does them, but the Spirit of God in him.

It is in this context that Bucer considers the relation of faith and works, and God's promise to reward men according to their works. The first detailed discussion of this issue is in *St Matthew*. Bucer argues that salvation is by grace and through faith, 'but not so that we may do nothing good; indeed through this we are created for good works, but [only] for those which God has prepared'.[1] As a good tree produces good fruit, and not the other way round, so a good man produces good works. Works do not justify a man in the sense of rendering him pleasing to God, for man's whole salvation depends on God. A man, however, may be judged according to his works, in the sense of their being a testimony to the kind of person he is. Thus they can show a man to be a son of God, but cannot make him one:

Truly this saying is most frequent in the scriptures that in God's judgment 'it will be rendered to each man according to his deeds'. This is asserted in Ezekiel 18 and many other places. Flatterers of the Roman pontiff tear this asunder, wishing to prove from this, that we are justified and damned by our works, because, namely, we are judged according to them. The stupid men do not pay attention to the fact that a tree is also judged according to its fruit—however, not that the tree is such because of the fruit, but rather that the fruit is such

[1] 220.A.24–B.3; 71.D.7–11; 181.B.20–5.

because of the tree. When figs have been seen, that tree is indeed judged to be a fig tree. But it is not the figs that caused it to be a fig tree, but rather because the tree is itself a fig tree it has borne this fruit. Likewise in everything, what is done reveals something about the doer; yet it does not make the doer, but is made by him. In this way good works show a good man and a son of God; they do not make one. Therefore works do not justify (1536 adds: that is, make [us] favourable to God, upon which the whole of salvation depends), for, before you have become good through the Holy Spirit, such works cannot be anything but sins that damn you, because a bad tree cannot bear good fruit. But because each man is rightly judged according to what he is and as each man acts according to what he is, and what is done testifies about the one who does it, it is rightly said that judgment is made according to works or deeds, just as a judge judges by what has been proved by evidence.[1]

In 1536 the comment is developed and four causes of salvation are enumerated—God's free grace, Christ's merit, faith, and good works. But this faith is not man's contribution to his salvation, for no one is able to believe in God unless he is inspired by the Holy Spirit. The Spirit, moreover, is given only to those whose sins God has forgiven because of the merit of Christ. These are, furthermore, those who were elected before the foundation of the world. Man's good works are, similarly, not his contribution to his salvation, for they are the gifts of God's goodwill, the effect of Christ's merit, and the fruit of faith:

But God's spontaneous goodwill is the prime cause of his giving judgment in our favour and awarding us eternal life. Indeed his will is the prime cause of everything. Next is Christ's merit, for he died for the salvation of the world—but this itself is a free gift of the divine goodwill. The third is faith, by which we embrace and lay hold of this goodwill of God and of Christ's merit. For he who believes has eternal life. But this faith itself is also the work and gift of God in us, who is gracious now on account of Christ's merit. The last cause is good works, for everyone is recompensed in accordance with his works. But these themselves are also the gifts of God's goodwill, the effect of Christ's merit, and the fruit of faith. Indeed no work can be reckoned good in God's sight, which does not arise from love of and zeal for God. But there is no love of and zeal for God, except in one who believes in God. No one can truly believe in God who is not inspired by the Spirit of the sons of God. Now God gives him only to those whom he holds amongst his own because of the merit of his Son, those whose sins he has forgiven. But he does this only for them, and gives his Spirit only to them whom he chose for this before the foundation of the world. Thus everything pertaining to our salvation is a gift, even the work of God's free and spontaneous goodwill.[1]

Already, in *St John*, he has argued that our good works do not satisfy the law of God or expiate man's sin. They do not supplant what is our only hope of salvation, God's mercy and Christ's merit.[2]

Bucer's concern not to let works displace faith can be seen in his treatment of Matt. 25, which ascribes damnation to lack of love or mercy, rather than to lack of faith. In the *Catechism* he explains that 'as faith is always active in love, a failure of love always comes from a lack of faith'.[3]

In *Romans* there is a prolonged examination of the place of works in salvation. Bucer's view does not differ from that expressed in the *Gospels*. He accepts without hesitation the passages in the Old and New Testament that refer to God's promising a reward for good works. He explains reward, however, by analogy with the mother who promises her son something if he learns the Lord's Prayer. When he learns it, and she gives what she has promised, the chief thing is not his achievement, but the loving promise and goodwill of the mother. It is in this kind of way that God makes us co-workers in our salvation. It is, moreover, in this context that good works may be spoken of as causes of our salvation, but not as sole causes or chief causes. For not only are the exhortations to good works spoken to those who already be-

---

[1] 187.B.18; 140.C.17; 364.C.1-14.
[2] 6.B.23-7.A.3; 2.B.23-7; 564.D.13-20.
[3] GC E.7.B.11-22. Compare the treatment of this passage in *St Matthew* where the emphasis lies rather on our election from the foundation of the world. 318.A.15-B.4; 184.C.16-25; 473.A.16-B.2.

lieve in God and rely on his free grace, but also the good works themselves are entirely of God, for no one can do them without the inspiration of the Spirit.[1]

The reformation in Cologne and in England kept this issue to the fore in Bucer's later works and stimulated him to new formulations in his attempt to affirm the necessity of works and the supremacy of faith in salvation. In *Bestendige Verantwortung*, good works 'are the gifts of God and fruits of the Holy Spirit in the justified, whom God has taken up into his grace. They depend upon and follow justification... [but they are not] an essential part of justification, which is a work of God's pure grace in Christ and for the sake of Christ.'[2]

Ein Summarischer vergriff offers both a summary and a slightly different form of the relationship that Bucer sees between faith and works. He asserts that true faith always has a zeal for good works, but that because of sin our faith and, therefore, also our works are imperfect. We have always to pray 'forgive us our trespasses'. All the saints, therefore:

must regard the good that they have already done as nothing and as dung, and always reach forward to the appointed goal in Christ our Lord. They must strive to do better and must place all their comfort and hope of salvation uniquely, solely, and absolutely in our Lord Jesus Christ, who is alone the reconciliation of our sins, and who has been made for us by God, wisdom, righteousness, sanctification, and redemption.[3]

He goes on to affirm in the following article that God richly rewards men's good works, however slight and fragile they may be. This he sees as a comfort and as a stimulus to good works. However:

the reward which the Lord gives for their good works, he does not give because of their righteousness, but out of his pure free grace

---

[1] R 99–105. The reward, moreover, far outweighs the works, which are themselves God's work in us, rather than our work. R 496.D.14–18.
[2] BV 42.B.2–7.
[3] V B.4.B.12–C.1.A.2.

and for the sake of his dear Son, in whom he elected us to eternal life before the foundation of the world, and created us for the good works, which through him he effects in us and so richly rewards.[1]

In this context Bucer describes precisely those who do good works as unprofitable servants, who do not deserve a reward, but severe punishment.[2]

The sharpened conflict with his catholic opponents in England led Bucer to an attack on the scholastic doctrine of merit, both of merit 'de congruo' and of merit 'de condigno'. He does this in his exposition of Eph. 2:7 where he states that God is the unique cause of our justification, whereas in our pride 'we want to be as gods, our own saviours'.[3] The faith, moreover, by which we are justified, is not our work, but the gift of the Spirit. To talk of justification by faith, therefore, is to talk of being justified 'not by giving, but by receiving, not by doing, but by accepting, not by preparing God's goodwill towards us, but by taking it as something already prepared'.[4]

The good works that we do, spring from a life that has been justified by faith, for only such lives are capable of good works. These works are praised and approved by God (the second sense of justify in Bucer's later works), though they are nevertheless imperfect. In any case, God's kingdom is only for those for whom it has been prepared from the foundation of the world, in other words before they have done any good works.[5] Man does nothing

---

[1] V C.1.A.10–25.
[2] V C.1.A.16–18. In this context Torrance rightly affirms that Bucer's view is neither legalistic nor moralistic. He comments: 'It is this amazingly eschatological conception of love that is the most moving and characteristic element in Butzer's theology.' T. F. Torrance, *Kingdom and Church*, p. 82.
[3] EE 59.B.16–22.
[4] EE 60.E.3–10.
[5] 'The godly alone, being justified by faith, carry out the law, which they understand, remember, and have always before their eyes, which they exercise themselves to obey, and on account of this they are at length praised and approved by God (Matt. 25). Yet our obedience is always imperfect, and is [present] only in those who have previously been blessed by God, and for whom the kingdom has been prepared from the beginning, not after one has done good works.' EE 61.C.11–62.D.3.

for his salvation. Bucer rejects equally the scholastic idea of meritorious works before justification, as that of meritorious works, which are not the work of God but of man, done after justification.[1] Man's good works are never other than those that God has prepared. He prepares them by the vocation to which he calls us (which excludes papistical works, such as pilgrimages and celibacy), by the ability to fulfil our vocation, and by giving us both to will them and to do them.[2]

A further element that Bucer brings into this debate is the distinction between reward as a payment and reward as a gift. He argues that the second excludes the sense of merit, and that this second use is the one that scripture intends.[3]

This distinction is characteristic of the finer distinctions that Bucer makes in some of his later writings in the discussion of a twofold justification and the relation to justification of faith and works. At no point is it his intention to give up the idea that man's total salvation is from God. At the same time he seeks to do justice to the biblical use of the terms justification, faith, works, and reward. In different ways he safeguards the fact that salvation is entirely of God: by the doctrine of election (stressed as much in his last works as in his first ones), by the role of the Holy Spirit (in alone enabling men to believe and do good works), by the use of a twofold or threefold justification, and by the double meanings he gives to justification and reward.

The discussion is characteristic of Bucer's theological approach —his endeavour to be faithful to the total witness of scripture, his attempt to engage in a positive debate with his catholic opponents, and his concern to see the Christian life as a whole.

[1] EE 64.D.19–E.2, 65.B.6–11.
[2] EE 70.D.3–18.
[3] EE 69.B.12–16. Already in *Psalms* he has said that reward indicates something more than is deserved. P 82.D.11–13.

FAITH

The word faith is used somewhat differently by Bucer than by Luther. This may arise partly from Bucer's own experience of faith,[1] and partly from his method of arriving at the biblical meaning of a word.[2]

Faith for Bucer is primarily a confident conviction or persuasion.[3] This is his earliest definition,[4] and it remains the primary sense of the word. Faith in Christ is thus a confidence that he has reconciled us to God. It is through faith in him that we become children of God and receive the Spirit of sonship, and that our lives become available for the service of our neighbour:

It is clear, therefore, that by faith we become children of God and have the Spirit of children, who assures our spirits that we are children of God. Out of this it follows necessarily that just as through this Spirit we recognise and call on God as a Father, so also we recognise all men as our brethren and serve them. This especially pleases the Father,

[1] Müller contrasts Luther's experience of *Anfechtung* with Bucer's search for knowledge and the influence exerted on him by an intellectualist and Thomist view of man (*op. cit.* pp. 25–6). The contrast should not, however, be made too sharp. For example, Bucer, like Luther, could also regard faith as trusting God's promises, in spite of everything. P 128.A.15–19.

[2] The importance, for instance, of Heb. 11:1 in Bucer's definition of faith should be noted. His method of assembling all the relevant scriptural passages, before expounding a theologically important word, often gives to his definitions their own particular emphasis. His acceptance and rejection of the opposition of law and gospel arises likewise from his attempt to keep to what he sees as the usage of scripture itself.

[3] Müller distinguishes *persuasio* from *fiducia*, and regards the second as not identical with Bucer's use of the word faith. For this distinction he particularly draws on the references in *Ephesians*, which speak of *fiducia* springing out of *fides*. There is, however, a danger in making hard and fast distinctions between one word and another in Bucer, not least on the basis of a relatively small number of passages. There are a number of words and phrases (as, for example, *animus*, *mens*, and *cor*) which Bucer can at one moment apparently distinguish and at another use indiscriminately. Müller is himself aware of this difficulty (BW 1.60, n. 96), recognises that in Bucer *fides* and *fiducia* belong together, but insists that Bucer separates them (*op. cit.* pp. 28–9).

[4] 'believe in Christ, that is, wholly trust that through his blood Christ has placed them again within the grace of God and reconciled them to him...' BW 1.60. 8–10.

who created us for this and who has pointed us to this in all the law and the prophets. It is certain, therefore, that only faith can detach us from ourselves and lead us to consecrate ourselves to God the Father as children.[1]

Faith is related from the start to Christ's reconciling death, the gift of the Spirit, and the new life of love. Faith is also used in a more general sense, in terms of believing all the words of scripture;[2] but this is a derivative use and not the primary use. There is no doubt that Bucer is greatly influenced by Luther in *Das ym selbs*, and the influence is evident in his understanding of faith. But there is no reason to suppose that he later surrenders a view of faith, related to Christ and his death, for a more general view of faith as faith in God.[3] He does not see faith as some kind of general assent. In the *Summary* he insists that it is not enough to believe that God created all things, that Christ was born, died, and rose again, 'but we must believe that all this happened for *our* good, *our* redemption, and *our* blessedness'.[4]

It is, however, in *St Matthew* that there is the first sustained treatment of faith. It is an all-embracing discussion of the word, arising from its use in Matt. 8:10. It is expounded generally, in terms of faith in scripture[5] and faith in God and his goodness.[6] It is also expounded quite specifically as a faith related to Christ and his reconciling death:

From us comes nothing but sin, by which we all lack the glory of God, that is to say, true godliness, and in so far as it pertains to us, we are justified entirely by grace, by the grace of God alone, but through faith—whilst clearly [on his side] God by his grace and the merit and satisfaction of his Christ, gives us this conviction and undoubting confidence about his goodness towards us, by which we are certain that he wishes to forgive our sins and make us righteous.[7]

[1] BW 1.61.16–25. [2] BW 1.61.7–8.

[3] Itti wrongly regards faith in Bucer as not related to the forgiveness of sins until *Romans* (*op. cit.* p. 36). However, if the commentaries are read along with his earlier writings, this is seen to be a misunderstanding of what Bucer means by faith. [4] BW 1.90.26–7.

[5] 21.B.22–22 A.6; 88.A.25–31; 224.D.15–22.

[6] 19.B.7–21; 87.C.8–16; 221.A.9–19. Compare 20.A.17–19; 87.D.11–12; 221.B.10–11. [7] 20.B.9–16; 87.C.22–6; 221.B.22–222.C.1.

As faith in the Bible has both a general and a particular reference, so faith in Bucer's commentaries has both references. Not surprisingly, the reference to Christ and his death is more pronounced in *Romans*, where Bucer is expounding an epistle in which that is the primary reference of faith. Likewise, the general reference is more apparent in *Psalms* and in the *Gospels*. The contrast may be seen in the comments of Bucer on Ps. 113 and in his preface to *Romans*. In the former he writes: 'the whole of religion depends on faith in divine providence'. 'The beginning and sum of all salvation is to believe all things to be ordered and instituted by the one God.'[1] In the latter he speaks of an evangelical faith, that goes beyond a faith in providence. It is an assent 'to the promises of God about the salvation obtained for us through our Lord Jesus Christ'.[2]

In this context Bucer recognises many kinds of faith, but he does not fail to distinguish faith in Christ, which may be spoken of as justifying faith, from other kinds or levels of faith.[3] There is no doubt that in *Romans* he links faith more precisely and exclusively to Christ and his death on the one hand and to the forgiveness of sins on the other. 'Faith is the certain persuasion by the Holy Spirit of the goodness of God towards us and of his fatherly goodwill. It rests on our Lord Jesus Christ, who expiated our sins by his death, and by his life, in which he now reigns, he makes us participators in his righteousness.'[4]

No marked changes are to be found in Bucer's later writings, though certain further definitions in *Ephesians* (1550) may be noted. There, in a sevenfold description of faith, he gives as the heart of his definition 'that we know Christ the Saviour and in

---

[1] P 288.C.3–4, D.4–5. [2] R 15.61–16.9 (Preface).
[3] A discussion of faith in the Old Testament and among the heathen is to be found in ch. 5.
[4] R 6.15–18 (Preface). Compare R 12.27–31 (Preface). The growing contact with Luther and Melanchthon may have contributed to this, as is often alleged. Undoubtedly, however, the nature of the text that Bucer was expounding made the major contribution. In any case, we have seen that this was not a new feature in Bucer's thought, whose general definitions of faith ought not to be divorced from the particular references to justifying or evangelical faith.

him the Father, that is, we believe with certainty that through him
we have a God who shows favour to us'.[1] By reference to Rom. 4,
faith is described as the 'conviction of the expiation of sins and
the conferring of life through the death and resurrection of Christ'.
This faith, as in Bucer's earliest works, is linked with an assent to
the Bible and what it teaches about God and man.[2]

FAITH AND LOVE

Although faith is an abiding mark of the Christian on earth, it
does not stand alone. Real faith is always faith which is active in
love. Indeed, in Bucer the accent may seem often to lie on love
rather than on faith, though never on love as divorced from faith.
He rejects any idea that there can be true love without true faith
leading to it,[3] but his frequent concern is to insist on the love that
springs of necessity from genuine faith.

Strohl[4] notes that in *Das ym selbs* Bucer speaks of regeneration
before speaking of justification, placing the description of the
Christian life before it origin. He sees this concern with the new
life of love as characteristic of Bucer. It will be considered in detail
in the next chapter, but needs to be referred to here, for the close
relation between faith and love is closely parallel to the assertion
of a twofold justification and the double way[5] in which the role
of the Holy Spirit in justification is viewed.

The reasons for the link between faith and love are various.
With faith, we are sure of God as our Father and of his care for us;
therefore we need have no anxiety for ourselves and can think of
our neighbours' needs.[6] This comes about as automatically as the
bearing of good fruit by a good tree.[7] The reason for this is that
faith restores us to the way of life for which God created us and

---

[1] EE 33.C.12–34.D.11.   [2] EE 59.C.11–60.D.3.
[3] BW 3.236.5–14. Compare BW 1.59.30–60.1.
[4] Strohl, *Traité*, p. 7.
[5] I.e. in leading to faith, and in being given to those who have faith.
[6] BW 1.61.32–40, 62.11–16, 63.1–10.
[7] BW 1.62.27–30.

gives us his Spirit. As a result, we gladly act in love towards our neighbour.[1] Moreover, the man who knows himself redeemed by Christ will meditate on the life and example of Christ, and out of gratitude will be fired by this to a life like that of Christ, a life of self-emptying love.[2] In other words, 'true faith is that through which we come to live not for ourselves, but for others, to the glory of God, and are active in truly good work'.[3]

As faith is active in love it follows that where love is absent there faith is absent. Love is regarded as a sign of faith, but not as a cause of it, any more than forgiveness of others is a cause of our being forgiven. It is rather a necessary result of our being forgiven, and is made possible by the gift of the Spirit.[4]

THE PLACE OF THE HOLY SPIRIT
IN JUSTIFICATION BY FAITH

The Holy Spirit leads to faith and is given to those who have faith. The earlier writings of Bucer speak of the second of these rather than of the first. In them it is through faith that we receive the Spirit of sonship and are able to call on God as Father.[5] This remains an element in Bucer's thinking, but is soon dominated by the idea that it is the Holy Spirit who leads to faith, through whom alone faith is possible.[6]

In this it is the idea of faith as persuasion that is uppermost, a persuasion that is linked to the word of God, whether to the word preached or to the word of scripture. Bucer insists that faith comes

---

[1] 'Mer über das der glaub in uns uffricht das gaentzlich vertrawen in Christum, widerbringt und stellet er uns auch in die rechte und goettlich ordnung, in die wir geschaffen seind. die wir auch durch solchs vertrawen erlangen und entpfahen sein geist, der uns sichert, das wir gottes kinder seind. Daruss volget, das wir im gern in aller liebthot gegen unsern nechsten, das er am hoechsten von den seinen fordert, dyenen und wilfaren.' BW 1.63.1–7.

[2] BW 1.63.22–64.14.   [3] BW 1.66.18–20.

[4] 207.B.12–19; 68.A.8–12; 172.C.14–20.

[5] BW 1.61.13–23, 32–40, 63.1–5.

[6] 'Christus muoss zu vor kumen, vnss ein andern geist erlangen, durch welchen wir glauben, er hab das gesetz fur vnss erfult vnd von verdrueter vermaledyung erlöset.' BW 1.319.9–12.

from hearing,[1] and for that reason he does not allow that infants can have faith in Christ.[2] The word, however, does not automatically produce faith, which comes only when the Holy Spirit persuades and illuminates the hearer.[3] The work of the Holy Spirit is necessary, because the natural man cannot understand or believe the things of God.[4] It is, however, only to the elect that the Holy Spirit is given, so that they may believe the gospel. 'For to adults it is necessary, first, that the gospel is preached, then, if they are of the sheep, they are given the Spirit, so that they may have faith in the gospel...'[5]

The work of persuasion or illumination is variously described. It may be a persuading of the heart or the mind, or an opening of the eyes.[6] This persuasion is not a primarily intellectual persuasion, though this is an important element in it. Müller over-emphasises the intellectualism of Bucer, which he seeks to demonstrate by showing that for Bucer faith is *persuasio* rather than *fiducia*, that it is a persuasion of the mind rather than a persuasion of the heart, that it is conceived as knowledge, and that the will and the affections are subordinate to the reason.[7] In this Müller does not recognise that when Bucer talks of persuasion (as well as in other contexts) he uses *mens*, *animus*, and *cor* almost interchangeably.[8] However important the mind is to Bucer, it is never simply the intellectual part of man, set over against the heart or the spirit. It often means virtually heart and mind.

[1] 18.A.23–B.16; 87.A.26–B.7; 220.C.17–D.5.
[2] 235.A.8–25, B.19–23; 155.D.25–156.A.7, 20–4; 404.C.10–19, D.8–11.
[3] In the discussion of Preaching we see that Bucer makes faith, but not the Holy Spirit, dependent on hearing the word. The Holy Spirit brings men to faith when they hear the word, but men may have the Holy Spirit apart from the word. This is true not only of infants, like John the Baptist, who was full of the Holy Spirit from birth, but also of adults who only respond to the word, if beforehand (or perhaps more often simultaneously) they have the Holy Spirit.
[4] See the discussion in the previous chapter.
[5] 51.B.16–20; 17.C.3–5; 41.A.25–B.3.
[6] The illuminating of the eyes is the first of the seven marks of faith in EE 33.C. 12–34.D.11. This is then linked with the Spirit of wisdom and revelation.
[7] Müller, *op. cit.* pp. 25–9.
[8] In rapid succession Bucer talks of the Holy Spirit persuading the *mens* (17.B.4–9; 86.D.24–7; 219.B.12–26), the *animus* (19.B.7–21; 87.C.8–16; 221.A.9–

The work of the Holy Spirit is totally to persuade a man of the gospel, so that he accepts it and becomes a child of God. Such faith can be given only where someone has already been elected by God from all eternity. But even in the elect it does not happen automatically, but only through the Holy Spirit when the gospel is preached.[1]

The law, however, as well as the gospel, has its part to play in man's justification by faith, but again only where the Holy Spirit is present. Bucer's understanding of the law is not the same as Luther's, for Bucer sees it not only in contrast to the gospel, but also as standing for all the teaching which is given to man for his salvation. He regards the contrast of law and gospel as unscriptural. Paul, he says, sometimes understands the law as commandments, but not always. Moreover, he does not by the gospel mean promise, but the proclamation of redemption as promised and then accomplished by Christ. Bucer accepts, nevertheless, that what is taught by those who distinguish law and gospel is true. The law humiliates and beats us down, whereas the gospel raises us up. By the law we learn about ourselves, by the gospel about God. The law contains repentance, the gospel, righteousness. By the law the mortification of the old man is accomplished, by the gospel the creation of the new man.[2]

19), and the *cor* (24.A.16–B.19; 88.D.22–89.A.6; 224.D.6–24). There are instances when any two of the three are used in the same context apparently as virtual equivalents—*cor* and *animus* (242.B.1–9; 79.A.5–10; 199.B.16–22), *mens* and *animus* (17.B.4–9; 86.D.24–7; 219.B.12–16), and *cor* and *mens* (134.A.22–8; 123.A.18–21; 313.D.16–20). There are also some instances where there seems to be a distinction between them (266.B.3–26; 167.D.25–168.A.9; 433.A.4–20). This varied usage should make one hesitate before drawing over-firm conclusions about Bucer's intellectualism.

[1] Compare P 103.A.12–20.

[2] 'Some moderns distinguish between law and gospel in such a way that the latter contains only promises, the former solely precepts by which God exacts or forbids something. Yet these words are not used in this way either in the prophetic writings or even in the apostolic writings. Paul indeed uses law sometimes to mean precepts, but not always. Moreover, neither is the gospel for him a promise but rather the proclamation of redemption promised through Christ ... What those who divide scripture into law and gospel want to teach is in itself true. For whatever scripture contains that it sets before us: either what God re-

In *Romans* he accepts this distinction of law and gospel and sums up his understanding of the part played by law and gospel in salvation. In the law he sees what God commands to be done by us, in the gospel the mercy and goodwill which he shows to us in Christ:

> For in general the one is what God commands, and the other what he promises. By the commands sin is brought forth, by the promises a remedy is offered. By precepts righteousness is demanded, by the promises it is offered. By the former conscience is thrown down, by the latter it is raised up. But where the power of Christ is absent, by which faith in the promises of God is given, both law and gospel are the letter that kills and the certain administration of condemnation...apart from Christ there is nothing which is not harmful, law, gospel, or whatever God has given to us besides for our salvation...on the other hand, if Christ lays hold of us and imparts his Spirit, both law and gospel, and everything at which otherwise nature greatly trembles and which Satan contrives for our destruction, certainly work for our salvation, each one in its place.[1]

The role of the Spirit is here essential. Without the Spirit, that is, wherever faith in Christ is absent, the law increases sin and kills.[2] It is because of our corrupt nature that the law is the occasion of our sinning.[3] The law also exposes our sins and teaches us to hate them. But it does this only as we see the righteousness of God in Christ.[4] Furthermore, it drives us to Christ. It does this by terrifying us of divine judgment and making us despair of

---

quires of us (which they call law), or what he promises to give us (which they call gospel). And in these two all knowledge of God and godliness is contained. By the former one is cast down, by the latter raised up. By the former we learn to know ourselves, by the latter God. By the former penitence is established, by the latter righteousness. By the former the mortification of ourselves—that is, of the old man—is achieved, by the latter the life of the new man and certain happiness through the complete renewal of ourselves.' P 88.A.12–25.

[1] R 27.24–43 (Preface). See also R 27.11–24 (Preface). Compare for Luther, P. S. Watson, *Let God be God!*, pp. 152–60.
[2] R 360.F.14–15, 361.A.6–9. Compare R 350.E.5–8.
[3] R 24.6–12 (Preface). In EE 82.F.8–10 he says that the law in itself does not increase sin, but that this happens because of the weakness of our corrupt flesh.
[4] R 210.D.13–17, E.11–15.

salvation.[1] This implies the presence of the Holy Spirit, for without the Holy Spirit the despair is a despair that leads to death and not to life:

> If, however, the Spirit of Christ is present, that death, by which we die through the sin brought to life in us by the law, leads to this saving death, by which we die to sin as also to the law. For those in whom this Spirit is lacking, sin, stirred up by the law, destroys eternally. They are driven to desperation, which is what happened to Cain and Judas. Thus sin, brought to life by the law, always slays. But some it slays for their salvation, so that, as they flee for refuge to Christ, they die to sin and the law, and live to God; while others [it slays] for their eternal destruction, when, in their ignorance of Christ, who alone sets men free from this death, they are driven to desperation by the terrors of divine judgment roused by the law.[2]

This is, therefore, the Holy Spirit's use of the law: to show a man his true self, to show him that he can do nothing to help himself, and to point him to Christ. This use of the law is totally different from man's use of the law as a way to God, a means of securing some hold on God. Such a use Bucer rejects, as obliterating the grace of Christ.[3] It is opposed to faith in Christ and thus leads away from justification by faith. By contrast, the Holy Spirit uses the law precisely to bring men to that faith by which they are justified. For those whom the Lord casts down by the law, he inspires by the Spirit to hear the gospel, so that they may believe it and be justified.[4]

---

[1] R 350.F.1–4.

[2] R 356.F.12–357.A.3. Compare R 349.B.10–C.13.

[3] 119.A.13–18; 38.C.23–7; 94.D.6–10.

[4] '...while he offers and promises the gospel in our Lord Jesus Christ, the Lord at once inspires by his Spirit to hear the gospel those whom he has thus justly cast down and made anxious by his law, so that, having faith in him, they trust themselves wholly to him and do not in any way doubt that they have been reconciled to God through him and have been fully justified.' R 291.C.6–10.

4

SANCTIFICATION AND GLORIFICATION

SANCTIFICATION

At the end of his life, in his lectures on Ephesians, Bucer describes the purpose of election as our sanctification and God's glory.[1] This stress is, in fact, common to every period of his life, and without it election, vocation, and justification are not to be understood. God's purpose for man is that he shall live the life of a son of God, and to this end everything is directed. It is quite false to see Bucer as starting with a question like 'How does one come to a life that corresponds to the divine will?'[2] He begins rather with God's purpose in creation and redemption, which he sees as men living the lives of sons of God.

THE PURPOSE OF GOD IN SALVATION

The order of salvation which Bucer describes in *Ephesians* in 1528[3] is already apparent in *Das ym selbs* in 1523. Election is

---

[1] 'The final causes are the sanctification of life and the glory of God. For it is not the sanctification of our life, that is the chief purpose of our election, but the very glory of God. It is on account of this and for this that all things were created and that we have been regenerated.' EE 19.C.10–13.

[2] Koch's over-emphasis here (*op. cit.* p. 99) on Bucer's humanism leads to a total misunderstanding of Bucer's view of the Christian life. The varied influence of humanism on Bucer is not to be denied, but it is not through humanism that he gains his fundamental theological insights. A concern with 'recht glauben und fromm leben' he held in common with Capito and Oecolampadius (see Pierre Scherding, 'Un Traité d'exégèse pratique de Bucer', *R.H.P.R.* 26, p. 35). Indeed it may be argued that Bucer is here an interpreter of Luther (see Strohl, 'Bucer, interprète de Luther', *R.H.P.R.* 19, pp. 225–45). Whatever the influences on him, Bucer would consider that he was simply faithfully presenting the teaching of scripture, and it is by that, that his teaching must ultimately be judged.

[3] Election, vocation or adoption, sanctification, and the glory of God. See E 26.B.16–25.

mentioned only occasionally, but it is presupposed. Vocation is also there, though it is seen chiefly in terms of adoption; while sanctification is held before our eyes as the vision of what God intends the life of a man to be. The Christian is said to be created for good works as a bird for flying, or a fish for swimming.[1] Such a life becomes possible to men through the Spirit by whom they again become useful to all God's creatures.[2] It is faith that opens the door to this life,[3] a life which Bucer sees from first to last primarily in terms of a true love to God and to man.

The stress that *Das ym selbs* gives to sanctification by its presentation of the life of love for which God has created man and redeemed him, is expressed (especially in the commentaries) in the use of the word righteousness. For Bucer the righteousness of the Christian is never simply an imputed righteousness, the forgiveness of his sins; it is always as well imparted righteousness, a sharing in the life of God. In commenting on the Marburg articles in the preface to the *Gospels* (1530), Bucer refers to those who are not godly, and who have no love for godliness, but who think they are saved by Christ's righteousness. On their account, he says, he and others are accustomed

to add the reason why we are freed from sin and given the righteousness of Christ. Namely, when the Spirit of Christ has been given to the elect, just as he enables them to consecrate themselves to Christ, and through him to call on God as Father, so also he at once represses in them sinful desires and daily transforms them to the image of Christ. Their redemption from sins will be complete in the future, when, with all sin purged away, they fully express his image. Our salvation and our happiness is indeed nothing but complete (*solida*) righteousness.[4]

---

[1] BW 1.66.8–12. Compare Z 75.A.3–11: 'If indeed we are made to live not for ourselves, but for our neighbour, yet is our nature so depraved that in everything we seek only our own advantage. Therefore we must apply ourselves with our whole strength, so that we may purge out immediately the remains of sin in us, that is, of self-love. For our salvation is nothing other than being conformed to Christ, that is, our entire selves given in love to our neighbours. In this both the whole law is accomplished, and the work of God in us consummated, and his image restored.'

[2] BW 1.60.8–13.   [3] BW 1.63.1–7. Compare BW 1.59.30–60.1.

[4] 7.B.1–7 (1530 Preface).

It is not that a real righteousness in those who are justified is something added on after they have been justified. It is there in the moment of justification, for justification is not an objective event in a law court, in which a judge pardons the guilty, imputing righteousness to the unrighteous. It is an act in which the guilty trusts in and is united to Christ:

For the man who comes to have faith in the gospel has already been grafted into Christ and has become a partaker of his fruitfulness in good works. From being a sterile and completely dead piece of wood, he has become a tree that is unable not to produce fruit in its season. He has been dedicated to a heavenly master, to be fashioned for godliness of every kind—a master who cannot teach him in vain.[1]

In this union with Christ the Christian shares in the life of Christ and in the Holy Spirit, who accomplishes in him what he accomplished in Christ. God wills men to be righteous 'not only by forgiving them their sins, but also by conforming them to the image of his Son'.[2] This is especially the work of the Holy Spirit who is imparted to those who believe.[3] Sin, indeed, is only truly pardoned, for Bucer, when it no longer lords it over a man.[4] There are many other grounds given for linking real and imputed righteousness (for example, that a zeal for righteousness becomes possible when we are justified, because we are sure of God's grace, and, therefore, are relieved of anxiety for our own salvation),[5] but they are all ultimately linked to the gift of the Spirit, for only the Spirit can do what is righteous.[6]

There are a number of other ways in which sanctification is seen as the purpose of salvation. It is described as the purpose of Christ's

[1] E 54.B.22-7.   [2] R 12.43-6 (Preface).
[3] R 50.F.14-51.A.8.
[4] 'Commodum igitur succinuerunt: Condonabis iniquitatem populi tui, quae tum vere condonata est, dum non dominatur amplius nobis...' P 238.C.17–D.1. Compare p. 51.
[5] R 18.2-5 (Preface).
[6] Compare 144.B.12-15; 47.A.9-17; 115.B.20-116.C.4. There is, moreover, a necessary connection between the Holy Spirit and real righteousness, just as there is between faith and real righteousness, so that the one implies the other, as fire implies heat. R 13.49-55 (Preface).

death, resurrection, and ascension. 'Indeed he died, so that he might expiate your sins and destroy the power of Satan in you... He ascended into heaven, so that inspired by his Spirit he might restore you fully to his image.'[1] It is also described as the purpose of Christ in calling us. In expounding Matt. 11:28–9 in the *Berner Predigt* he says:

> Therefore, with these words the Lord wishes nothing other than, come to me and receive me as your Lord, your master, and your teacher: be my subjects and my disciples. What does he command us now? What does he teach? Why does he wish to rule over us? Only to save us (*selig zu machen*). He commands nothing else, wishes nothing, but that we acknowledge him as our only Saviour, and love one another. That is his new and only command, teaching, and yoke.[2]

At every point it is the Spirit who is the key to the doctrine of sanctification. It is not only that sanctification is peculiarly the work of the Spirit,[3] but also that the peculiar work of the Holy Spirit is sanctification. This is implied by the name of the Spirit as holy; as we shall see, it is implied equally by the fact that the Spirit in Bucer is undoubtedly referred to more often in this context than in any other. The Spirit's work belongs to vocation and justification. But it always leads on to sanctification. 'Indeed the Spirit of Christ is one. He persuades [men's] hearts of the truth; he sanctifies by faith; he makes [men] fruitful in good works.'[4]

THE ROLE OF THE HOLY SPIRIT IN SANCTIFICATION

There are a variety of ways in which the centrality of the Holy Spirit in sanctification is evident. The names by which the Spirit is known relate primarily to sanctification. His presence in men's lives is seen as leading to sanctification. Moreover, sanctification is spoken of as the work of the Spirit, and not the work of man himself.

---

[1] R 482.F.2–7. [2] BW 2.287.9–16.
[3] 'Our sanctification is attributed to the Holy Spirit...' EE 27.C.13–17.
[4] P 108.D.11–12.

The Names of the Holy Spirit. Quite apart from the various names given to the Holy Spirit, there is the name holy by which the Spirit is known. This, Bucer says, expresses the fact that his work is to make men holy, to sanctify them.[1] However, the names given to him express this even more clearly. They are enumerated in *St Matthew* in the first sustained discussion of the Spirit to be found in Bucer's works. The names Bucer especially mentions are water, fire, spirit, anointing, paraclete, and finger of God.

In the reasons he gives for the use of these names can be seen significant pointers to his understanding of the Spirit. 'The Spirit is in truth called water because he makes minds, which would otherwise be barren, fecund to bring forth the fruit of piety.' This idea is developed with a series of biblical references, showing the Spirit as the source of true life within the elect.[2] 'Further, he is called fire because of his strength and power; for indeed he transforms the whole man, burns up the filth of sin, and makes him absolutely ardent and invincible in promoting the glory of the Lord.'[3]

The description of the Holy Spirit as Spirit refers to his power, like the wind, a description borne out by what happened at Pentecost.[4] The use of the term anointing refers to the way kings and priests were appointed to their office and declared fit for it. 'Thus through the Spirit of God the elect are appointed to live for God and to glorify him, and are not only declared but also made fit (*idonei*) for it.'[5] The word paraclete means that the Holy Spirit is not only comforter, but also advocate and protector, sustaining Christians not least as they witness to a hostile world.[6] Finally, the Spirit is called the finger of God, that is the power and potency of God.[7]

[1] 'Sanctus est, quia a sancto venit, et sanctificat...' P 181.C.15. Compare BW 2.238.1–5.
[2] 76.B.15–77.B.16; 25.C.26–26.A.2; 61.A.19–62.C.5.
[3] 77.B.16–22; 26.A.2–5; 62.C.6–10.
[4] 78.B.1–5; 26.A.25–7; 62.D.6–9.
[5] 78.B.25–79.A.2; 26.B.10–13; 62.D.22–5.
[6] 79.A.11–25; 26.B.18–C.2; 63.A.6–16.
[7] 79.A.25–7; 26.C.2–3; 63.A.16–18.

The variety of these names is accounted for by the variety of the Spirit's work.[1] It involves enabling men to understand and respond to God's word. Then follow setting them on fire to proclaim the glory of God, transforming them so that they seek the good of others, rather than their own, and conquering in them all that is opposed to God:

> Next, he inflames us, so that we value nothing more highly than to preach and advance the glory of God and the grace which is ours in Christ, being terrified by the loss of nothing, not even of life. Then he transforms us to such an extent that we who formerly sought only our own advantage in everything, having denied ourselves, seek the advantage of others, and in sincere love dedicate ourselves as slaves to all men, but especially to those who are of the household of faith. Lastly, he subdues whatever in us fights against these things, as indeed our whole nature, which in the scriptures is called flesh, is opposed to the divine will. These things, indeed, the Holy Spirit works in all who are Christ's.[2]

The Effects of the Spirit. In almost everything that he wrote, Bucer refers to the effects of the Spirit in the lives of the elect. It is the Spirit who purges, liberates, redeems, renews, and conforms men to the image of God. The rich variety of this work can only be hinted at, but it can be seen to cover every aspect of sanctification.

Thus, as happened with John the Baptist, the Spirit may be said to be given, so that a man may 'excel in real (*solida*) sanctity';[3] or, as with Zachariah and Elizabeth, 'to live blamelessly in the commandments and ordinances of God' may be said to come from the possession of the Spirit of sonship.[4] The fact that a holy life is seen as the necessary outcome of the presence of the Holy Spirit testifies to the view that a holy life is pre-eminently the work of the Holy Spirit.

---

[1] 'Tam multis autem nominibus, haec Dei virtus appellatur, quod quae infra in electis efficit, satis nobis exponi nequeunt. Nec enim tot nomina habet, quin plura in nobis operetur et efficiat.' 79.B.3–4; 26.C.4–6; 63.A.19–21.

[2] 79.B.10–20; 26.C.6–15; 63.A.21–B.7.

[3] 10.A.7–13; 214.C.1–5; 532.D.24–533.A.2.

[4] 12.B.20–5; 217.A.16–19; 540.C.3–6.

His work is both negative and positive. It is the negative one of purging or mortifying sins and of liberating from the power of Satan. For Christ 'gives the Holy Spirit, by whom he redeems from the power of Satan and the corruption of sin, purging away their sins'.[1] When the Spirit of Christ is present 'sin is dead, so that its fury is destroyed day by day'.[2]

Alongside this work is the positive one of transforming the lives of the elect, to make them conform to the image of God. This work is equally diverse. It means replacing self-love by love of one's neighbour, filling the heart with a desire for those things that please God, producing the fruit of good works, and transforming the whole man:

> For those elect to this from all eternity, whom this renewing power of God inspires, he so renews, so transforms, so makes them despise carnal things and admire things celestial, so strips away their self-love and fires them with love of their neighbour, that they are a source of wonder to men of this age...[3]

> From these words (Isaiah 32:15) we perceive that no one comes into the kingdom of Christ or remains in it, unless he is inspired and renewed by his Spirit. For before we are inspired and renewed, we are like a rough desert, producing nothing but thorns and briars, that is, works harmful both to ourselves and others. But when our king has sent his gospel and has poured on us from heaven his Holy Spirit, then we, who were before like a barren and thorny desert, now bear a plenteous harvest of all good works, like a cultivated and fertile field...[4]

The Holy Spirit is the sanctifier,[5] the author of holiness.[6] At our baptism, when we are baptised into the name of the Holy Spirit, it is so that we may receive 'the one who forms and renews the whole of life'.[7] Thus it is that a man becomes like a tree planted by streams of water (Ps. 1). For 'the elect are planted in heavenly

[1] E 30.A.23–4.   [2] R 366.E.18–19.
[3] 70.B.18–26; 24.A.15–21; 620.C.24–D.7.
[4] OB 15.26.17–26.   [5] R 15.A.19–B.7, 16.E.15–18.
[6] R 11.A.12–14.   [7] 49.B–50.A; 16.D–17.A; 39.B.14–15.

soil, where the sap of the divine Spirit never fails them'. Therefore, they cannot but bear the fruit that God intends, both in word and deed.[1]

The Work of the Holy Spirit. Although Bucer affirms that man co-operates with God in a way that God has appointed, he nevertheless sees the work of sanctification as the work of the Holy Spirit, and not as man's work. Bucer sounds the Pauline note that we are to work out our salvation, but he adds no less emphatically than Paul that it is God who works. Even in the passages where exhortation is strongest, the insistence on the work of the Holy Spirit is uppermost. Men are indeed to crucify the flesh, but they do it by the power of the Spirit.[2]

To affirm that this work is man's would be to affirm some inherent ability in man that he does not have:

For true repugnance to evil and the impulse to good is the work of the Spirit of the sons of God (Gal. 5). Besides, every thought of the human heart is evil from a man's youth (Gen. 8).[3]

Nothing pleases the Lord, that does not proceed from a willing love. Such a love is not my work or yours, but the work of the Holy Spirit...[4]

Truly nothing of good can come from us, unless the Spirit of God effects it in us. He, however, dwells only with those who believe...and forms them to the image of Christ, in which love has the primacy.[5]

THE REALITY OF SANCTIFICATION AND
THE REALITY OF SIN

Holiness was not for Bucer only a matter of faith, but in a measure also a matter of sight. In affirming its reality he was clearly influenced by the confidence of the saints of the Bible in their being

---

[1] P 4.D.21–5.A.2.   [2] PR A.4.A.3–20.
[3] E 39.A.3–12.
[4] 192.B.25–193.A.7; 71.B.24–C.3; 729.B.12–18.
[5] 176.B.7–11; 137.C.5–8; 350.D.12–14.

righteous and holy men. This they tempered, as did Bucer, with an awareness that they were sinners, unworthy to stand in the presence of God.

The Reality of Sanctification. It is especially in the psalms that we read of the confidence of the saints in their righteousness. This Bucer notes in his commentary. In his comment on Ps. 17:4 he refers to David's confidence of his righteousness over against his enemies, and his confidence therefore that God will vindicate him.[1]

For Bucer it would be a denial of God's goodness, if a man were not to acknowledge his righteousness, for God's gifts are to be acknowledged:

Who does not know, whether he fears God, whether he desires to live according to God's will, whether he wishes approval by his neighbour? If he has these things, he has them from God, and he has them, so that others may know and perceive it. For God does not light a lamp, so that it may be covered over.

Bucer is well aware of the dangers of glorying in oneself, but he does not think the dangers should hinder us, for our action is not, like that of the Pharisee, done in pride, despising other people, but rather for the glory of God and for the salvation of our neighbour.[2]

Bucer realises that men may deceive others and that some who are impious may seem to be pious.[3] Nevertheless, there is a difference between the elect and the reprobate. Ultimately indeed it is the Holy Spirit that distinguishes them. In the elect the Holy Spirit produces faith in Christ and wages war on the flesh. By contrast, the reprobate say that Christ is anathema, and follow the desires of the flesh, because they are held captive by Satan.[4] In particular, the fruits of the Holy Spirit may be evident in some, as they were

---

[1] P 75.C.13–19.
[2] P 25.B.11–26.A.2. Compare BW 2.117.22–30, where the fact that the righteous man falls seven times in a day does not alter the fact that he walks in love and controls the flesh.
[3] BW 2.116.11–22. [4] E 40.A.19–B.5.

in the apostles, whereas the works of the flesh, which are the fruit of a devilish spirit, are evident in others.[1] True love, which is a fruit of the Spirit, is something that cannot be simulated in Bucer's judgment. In this it differs from the gifts of the Spirit which anabaptists, papists, Jews, and Mohammedans may have.[2]

A text that is often referred to is Matt. 5:16. It affirms that men will see the good that the disciples do, and will glorify God. Bucer takes this quite seriously as one of the ways God has of bearing testimony to himself. When men see those who are endowed with his Spirit, they will be led to believe in him:

> Come therefore, lest you be disposed to respond too little to that great esteem which I have—or rather my Father has—for you, and you receive such grace in vain. But exert yourselves to this end, and mortify yourselves to this extent, that your light may shine before men, and that it may be clear to all that you are endowed with my Spirit. By this means others may also be attracted and desire to believe in me and be written down as citizens in my kingdom—people who will glorify not so much my Father, as your Father, who has finally visited the human race with such great kindness, stirring it up to what is good and heavenly.[3]

It is indeed because the righteousness of God shines forth in their lives, that the Holy Spirit is able to convict the world of its unrighteousness. 'Therefore it was then that, in the apostles, the Paraclete convicted the world concerning righteousness, that is, proved it openly to be destitute of righteousness, since a righteousness that was truly real and divine shone in those who believed.'[4] A demonstration of this may be seen in the fact that the fruits of the Spirit were so evident in the early church at Jerusalem, confirming the word of the gospel, that all the ends of the earth began to trust in God.[5]

[1] BW 1.87.21–9. Compare BW 1.97.1–10. See also BW 1.342.13–14: 'Aber wo der geist ist, da spurt man auch seine frucht, alss da sind lieb...'
[2] E 26.A.19–27. See the discussion of the gifts of the Spirit (pp. 185–6).
[3] 138.B.20–139.A.3; 45.B.11–16; 111.A.21–B.2. Compare E 36.B.19–23.
[4] 233.B.19–25; 86.D.21–4; 766.C.25–D.4.
[5] P 199.D.8–22.

Thus Bucer regards the new life that the Holy Spirit effects in the believer as something of which he can be aware himself and of which others can be aware. In this he was not insensible of the self-deception from which men suffer, nor of the power of sin.[1] He was aware rather of the undeniable testimony of scripture and the power of the Spirit that he saw as the source of a genuinely new life.

The Reality of Sin. However confident the saints may be of their righteousness, they are at the same time conscious that it is nothing compared with the righteousness of God.[2] Therefore, even though David was more righteous than his enemies, that would not save him, if it were not that God's righteousness means his mercy, not his judgment:

...it does not mean the severity of God, by which some people say that they are summoned to his mercy. Righteousness is the highest goodness. It is therefore in accordance with this and not in accordance with [God's] severity that this holy man prays that he may be judged. For even indeed compared with his enemies, he would not have been able to endure this. For even if it had been right for him to receive less punishment, yet, with God judging severely, it would have been right for him to receive so much, that it would infinitely have surpassed his strength.[3]

For even in the saints the flesh and its fruits are present, helping them to realise that whatever righteousness or salvation they have is not theirs but God's.[4]

Bucer's use of the word flesh is ambiguous, as indeed the biblical use is. Sometimes it is used in the sense of men's living in

---

[1] Müller (*op. cit.* pp. 34–5) holds that Bucer is not as aware as Luther and Melanchthon of the subtle and pervasive power of sin. This is almost certainly true, but it is perhaps just this that enables him to do greater justice to the reality and transforming power of the Holy Spirit.

[2] P 42.C.20–3.   [3] P 142.A.10–15.

[4] 'The flesh always clings to the saints, while they live here, and to that extent it also produces its fruit at the same time. By this the saints are warned that whatever righteousness and salvation they have is of God, and not of themselves.' Z 71.A.2–5.

the flesh or in the body, sometimes of man's being sinful, of his living according to the flesh. The opposition of flesh and Spirit is primarily the opposition of man's sinful nature to the Holy Spirit. It is not the opposition of a lower part of a man (his body) to a higher part (his mind and spirit). There is in the Christian an ongoing battle between the flesh and the Spirit.[1] The Christian, however, can be said to live according to the Spirit, because his life is above all ruled by the Spirit, even though he does evil. On the other hand, those who live according to the flesh are those in whom 'the flesh has primacy'.[2]

If the reality of sin is less strong for Bucer than for Luther, he is, nevertheless, aware that the saints on earth are never without sin. In this he is opposed to the anabaptists. Among them were those who held that the Holy Spirit prevented the saints from sinning, and that the petition 'Forgive us our trespasses' in the Lord's Prayer was given to the apostles and prayed by them, only before they received the gift of the Holy Spirit.[3] For him there is no doubt that we always sin and that we always have to seek forgiveness.[4]

He explains the apparent contradiction between the fact that the saints are said not to sin and the fact that they do sin, in two ways. First, the godly are not committed to sin, but rather to God, so that they sin unwillingly. Second, their undoubted sins are not sins, as they are not imputed to them, just as debts that are remitted are not debts.[5] It is the first of these that is normally stressed and it

---

[1] R 96.E.5–13. Compare BW 2.286.7–22.
[2] R 376.F.5–16.   [3] Z 76.A.26–B.10.
[4] 199.A.5–28; 65.C.8–21; 166.C.4–19.
[5] 'Therefore to this extent a godly man is not able to sin, because he is not able to be given over to iniquity and sins in the way that the ungodly are wont to be. But in his mind he will continually delight in the law of God, because God's seed, his Word and the Spirit of the sons [of God] dwell with him, and he is born of God. At the same time, however, since he has nothing good in his flesh, he does many things that he hates, and that are truly sins. Yet since he does not delight in them in the inward man, and is dedicated to Christ in his mind, and desires above all to correspond to his [Christ's] image, and does not doubt that in the end, by Christ's merit, everything will be forgiven him, and that he will arrive at that image, there will be no condemnation for him, albeit a sinner, for thus

is used to reconcile the passages in 1 John (1 John 1:8 and 3:9), where all are said to sin and yet those born of God are said not to sin. They do not sin, in the sense that they do not yield themselves to sin.[1]

One of the reasons why they sin, although they do not wish to, is seen in Peter's denial. The power of the Holy Spirit was absent, and therefore, to save his life, Peter followed his senses and his corrupt nature rather than the will of God.[2] A further factor is ignorance or a lack of conviction about the will of God.[3] What Bucer never speaks of, on the part of the elect, is a calm, deliberate intention to sin, but he allows that they can be aware that what they are doing is wrong.[4] God, indeed, permits even those dearest to him to fall, so that they may be mindful of their weakness and may pray more diligently for his Spirit.[5] This same Spirit, however, never deserts the elect and never lets them give themselves wholly to sin.[6]

THE CHARACTER OF SANCTIFICATION

If the characteristic mark of Bucer's view of sanctification is love, it is not the only one. There are others that need to be underlined because of their affinity with or their difference from the views of his contemporaries. They do not give a total picture, but they offer complementary glimpses of the whole.

Continuing Renewal by the Spirit. The new life of the Christian never reaches its goal on earth. The Christian is always on the way and never at the end of the road. His life is always being made holy,

---

assuredly he dwells in Christ (Rom. 8). Since indeed God will not impute sins to him, therefore they will not be sins, just as debts, which a creditor has remitted, are not debts, even though you have really contracted them and yet have not fully paid them.' 243.A.10–25; 79.A.27–B.5; 200.C.16–D.1.
[1] P 82.B.3–18. [2] R 368.D.3–9.
[3] 21.B.22–22.A.6, 131.A.17–B.6; 88.A.25–31, 122.B.6–16; 222.D.15–22, 308.D.19–309.A.6.
[4] See the discussion of the sin against the Holy Spirit, especially p. 36, n. 2.
[5] R 43.A.11–15. [6] R 61.B.11–C.13.

it is never completely holy. He is not like a pupil who, when he graduates, becomes independent of his teacher; rather he lives his life in constant need of the Holy Spirit.

This note is vividly expressed in the *Handlung* where Bucer writes:

God's working in us does not mean that he gives us the ability to know and will the good and leaves us the same for us to use or not, earnestly or not. In other words that he would no longer work, like a man who teaches another a trade, which afterwards, when he no longer sees his master, he uses or not according to his pleasure. But as in the world the sun gives and produces the day, so God gives and produces (*würket*) piety. The sun must shine for ever and ever, so the children of God must for ever be led and impelled by the Holy Spirit (Rom. 8), that is, taught and inclined and made ready to do good. Hence Paul says: 'I live, yet not I, but Christ lives in me' (Gal. 2).[1]

Bucer sees the Christian life as one of constant dependence on the Holy Spirit. Man does not acquire some ability to live independently of God and, in that sense, to build his own life or achieve his own righteousness.[2] Bucer's doctrine of election could have led him to stress men's perseverance in salvation, without at the same time stressing that only the Holy Spirit makes this possible. It did not. Man's perseverance as a Christian, as his growth in holiness, is in total dependence on the Spirit who 'illuminates us and who holds us in the contemplation of the truth'.[3] The work of the Holy Spirit is one that goes on daily without ceasing. Daily

---

[1] H G.2.A.10–23.

[2] This is a point that Prenter (*op. cit.* p. 79) makes about Luther, though, unlike Bucer, Prenter can talk of a real righteousness that man can have apart from being in the Holy Spirit, even though he would not allow that it would carry weight at man's judgment (*op. cit.* pp. 104–5). For Bucer the Christian certainly co-operates in his salvation, for God has willed this. This does not, however, mean that man does anything apart from the Holy Spirit. He, on the contrary, does everything that is necessary for our salvation, but he has chosen to make us co-workers in this. 'For even though the Spirit of Christ alone achieves in us everything pertaining to salvation, still he thinks fit to use our will and zeal as well to that end. In that way he restores us to the divine life, by using our strength and all our members, like instruments, for the life of God.' R 320.D.10–14.

[3] R 368.E.5–8.

our sins are put to death by him.[1] 'Daily he transforms us more
and more to the image of Christ.'[2]

The renewing of the Christian is not something that happens
apart from the church and the means of grace that God has
appointed in the church. In particular the Holy Spirit uses the
word, the sacraments, and the discipline of the church:[3]

He still daily works this holiness in those who believe in Christ, but not
without means. In this he uses his word and his holy sacraments, just
as he himself says to the Corinthians: 'I have begotten you etc.', that
is, I have preached the word among you and administered the holy
sacraments, by which you have been born again, for God has indeed
added the growth. Thus through the ministry of Saint Paul the Corinthians were sanctified, were born again, and became Christians. So high
is the honour God gives to his own, poor worms that we are, whom he
raises up and appoints as his own instruments.[4]

This is notably expressed in *De Regno Christi* where it is ascribed
to Christ ruling in his kingdom:

And those incorporated in this way he himself rules and governs, by
purging them daily more and more from their sins, and by instructing,
forming, and perfecting them to all godliness and righteousness, indeed
to eternal life, using for this the dispensation of his word and sacraments through suitable ministers, in public, in private, and in the home,
and also the vigilant administration of his discipline, both of penitence
and ceremonies, and of the whole of life.[5]

The Guiding of the Spirit. The continual dependence of the Christian on the Holy Spirit is particularly evident in what Bucer has to
say about the leading or guiding of the Spirit. His views are
presented chiefly in the exposition of biblical texts which refer to

[1] 65.B.21–5; 22.B.16–19; 52.D.21–3.
[2] 71.B.12–18; 24.C.20–4; 621.A.9–12.
[3] This is a note more characteristic of the later Bucer, but, from the first, a genuine
reading and hearing of the word is regarded as leading to a growth in piety.
[4] ZP 204.30–7.
[5] OB 15.55.5–11. The references to Christ's sanctifying us are almost all linked to
the work of the Holy Spirit. For example, it is by the Holy Spirit that Christ
puts to death men's sins.

the leading (as in Rom. 8) or guiding (as in the gospel injunction about flight in persecution) of the Spirit. Of Simeon's entry into the temple he writes: 'Therefore, warned by the Spirit, he came into the temple, even as the sons of God are always led by the Spirit...'[1] He affirms that being led by the Spirit is a mark not of a few, but of all the sons of God.

It is, however, especially where he considers the examples of flight that he refers to guidance, linking it to prayer. It is alone the Spirit who can show whether or not one should flee; therefore the Christian is to pray for his direction.[2] This guidance of the Holy Spirit is not like some kind of superior system of espionage, which can tell the Christian whether he will be safer escaping or facing the enemy. It is concerned rather with what will serve God's glory, and this is something that God alone through the Spirit can tell him.[3] There is a sense, therefore, in which this is a particular expression of the role of the Holy Spirit as teacher. He alone understands the mind of God and he it is who leads into all truth.[4]

The guidance of the Spirit covers the whole of the life that a Christian has to lead,[5] but it does not exclude the use of the ordinary means of arriving at decisions:

Here you see that help and alliance are sought. Nevertheless, the Lord ordered Judah to go up, and not Simeon, and he gave the land into the hand of Judah, not Simeon—yet Judah admitted Simeon into an alliance. From this we learn that, although we must rely solely on divine

---

[1] 23.B.21–3; 219.A.24–5; 545.B.7–8.

[2] 104.A.13–17, B.11–15; 34.B.18–21, C.8–11; 83.B.3–6, 19–22. Compare 83.A.2–7; 106.D.9–12; 270.C.3–6.

[3] '...it is allowable for us to flee if that is to God's glory, and not allowable if it is against it. This the Spirit of God alone will teach. He will also cause us at the right time to recognise danger, just as Christ [while] here recognised his danger at the right time. Therefore, we must always pray for the counsel and guidance of the Spirit.' 99.A.9–14; 33.C.30–D.3; 645.A.1–5.

[4] 68.A.26–B.5; 23.A.9–13; 617.A.22–B.1.

[5] In what is perhaps the first instance, in the *Verantwortung*, the reference is to the stewardship of possessions. However, it is not certain that the reference here goes beyond the guidance that one has from the Holy Spirit in the Bible. BW 1.166. 5–9. For Bucer, in any case, the guidance of the Holy Spirit inwardly should always be tested by the word of scripture (see the discussion in ch. 10).

help, yet we must not spurn any ordinary means. Although we must be led only by the Spirit of God, yet we must use reason as well. But we must test the lawful and ordinary means which are divinely appointed, when they are at hand, and also temper them to the Spirit of God, otherwise we should be putting God to the test. Indeed, when some function is enjoined on someone, all the means that pertain to its being duly and rightly performed are also enjoined on him at the same time. But if he neglects them, he puts God to the test...[1]

Moreover, where there is no particular call of the Holy Spirit (as there was with Samson to use the jawbone of an ass), we should use our common sense and the ordinary means that God has placed at our disposal.[2]

Bucer does not set prayer for the guidance of the Spirit over against the divinely given ways of discerning God's will, in particular the Bible. Prayer is, moreover, not simply additional to an understanding of the Bible, but is necessary for such an understanding, for the will of God in the Bible is not discerned other than by the Spirit of God, who gives understanding of it. The stress on the guiding of the Spirit expresses the view that the whole life of the Christian is to be lived in dependence on God, that the discerning of God's will is possible only through the Spirit of God, and that there is no situation in which God cannot reveal his will to those who, being children of God, are led by his Spirit.

Prayer in the Spirit. Bucer's sustained discussions of prayer arise in particular contexts in *St Matthew, Psalms,* and *Romans,* and the contexts account in different ways for what he says and why he says it.[3] In ignoring the context in *St Matthew,* Lang arrives at an exaggeratedly spiritualist view of Bucer's understanding of prayer, for he fails to see that the stress on the inwardness of prayer is set over against the mechanical outwardness in prayer that Jesus was deploring.[4] In this Bucer uses an opposition between prayer as

[1] J 474.21–8.   [2] J 511.23–6.
[3] In *St Matthew* the context is Matt. 6:1–13 and 8:1–4, in *Psalms,* Ps. 5 and 6, and in *Romans,* Rom. 8:26–7.
[4] See Lang, *op. cit.* pp. 127–9.

spiritual and our words as carnal, which he later changes.[1] This opposition is not his real concern. He is primarily concerned to point to prayer as a 'colloquy with God'[2] or 'the elevation of the mind to God' or 'the speaking of the heart not of the mouth'.[3] This does not require outward words, but only inward words, the inward word of the heart, for God has no need of words.[4] Prayer is, in other words, a matter of the heart or mind, not of the mouth.[5]

True prayer is not something that man does, but is the work of the Holy Spirit, moving and impelling him to pray.[6] Precisely because it is the Spirit who drives the Christian to pray, he is able to pray with confidence, just as the leper did, who prayed for healing. This confidence comes from the Spirit who knows what God's will is, and who enables men to pray according to God's will. Such confidence is seen in the leper who had heard of the power of Christ and believed that Christ would heal him.[7] Similarly, when a Christian prays for outward things, he should not pray for them unconditionally, unless he is certain that what he

[1] 'But why do I waste words about this? Real prayer is too spiritual a thing to be able to be delineated, much less expressed, in carnal words.' (1530 and 1536 use 'our' instead of 'carnal'.) 191.A.13–15; 63.A.20–1; 157.B.12–14.

[2] 191.A.22–4; 63.A.26–7; 157.B.19–20.

[3] P 33.B.12. Compare EE 31.B.3–7.

[4] 191.A.16–24; 63.A.22–7; 157.B.15–20. Bucer would have in mind not only the 'vain repetitions' of the heathen, but also the vain repetitions of his own day.

[5] 'Prayer, as we said, is the work of the mind (*mentis*), not of the mouth, and therefore it is not in any way dependent on words. And we are not taught here in what words to pray, but what to seek with the desires of the mind (*animi*).' 194.B.3–6; 64.A.18–20; 162.C.11–13.

In *Psalms* he quotes Augustine and Aquinas in making the same point that prayer concerns our inward thoughts and affections, not our outward words. P 34.C.22–33.

[6] 'For what else is praying without longing, or giving thanks without a sense of benefit, than rejoicing without joy, grieving without grief? Now who will put within us even the very longing for spiritual things, who will determine the form of the longing, except the Spirit? Thus it will be for him alone to move [men] to pray and to determine the form of the prayer, because whatever attempt mortal men make, it will render hypocrites hateful to God, and not make those who pray pleasing to God.' 192.A.6–14; 63.B.19–24; 158.C.21–D.1. [7] 3.B.5–12; 82.D.29–83.A.2; 209.A.2–7.

asks is to God's glory. Such certainty the Holy Spirit alone is able to give. Therefore in such prayers the godly man will add 'nevertheless, Father, not my will, but thine be done'.[1]

Bucer sums up his exposition of the prayer of Christians in four points:

First, they are impelled to pray by the Spirit. Second, through him they will be certain, that what they pray for is to the glory of God. Third, persuaded by the same Spirit, they will not doubt, that they will be granted what they pray. Fourth, impelled by the same Spirit and after pondering their lowliness and God's majesty, they will pray with great humility and resolution, however much they are certain that God will gladly give, what they pray for; nor will they pray for something, unless they believe it would be most pleasing to God to give it.[2]

The role of the Spirit in prayer is taken a stage further in *Romans*. There the context speaks of men's weakness and inadequacy, indeed of the times when the weight of temptation is so great that they cannot pray. In that situation, in spite of their failings and preoccupations, the Spirit prays within them.[3] Moreover, God knows and grants this prayer, because it is the prayer of his own

---

[1] 'But no one ought to make private requests (which is the sort of thing the healing of this leper was) absolutely, unless he is certain that these things, if he obtains them, will be done to God's glory. This no one can teach, except the Spirit in the heart. Wherefore in all prayers for outward things, the godly man will add: "Nevertheless, Father, not my will, but thine, be done. If thou knowest that thou wilt do it to thy glory, heal me..."' 3.B.21-7; 83.A.8-12; 209.A.14-18. Compare 4.A.16-B.21; 83.A.22-B.9; 209.B.5-24; and 45.A.1-20; 95.C. 6-18; 241.A.20-B.8.

[2] 5.A.11-23; 83.B.20-6; 210.C.11-18. In *Romans* Bucer argues that imprecations belong as properly to prayer as the punishment of the impious belongs properly to God. R 499.A.11-15.

[3] 'But although the Spirit cries so plainly here that he is heard in the heavens, yet so great is the tumult in the flesh, arising from the tortures and torments by which it is harassed, that the saints do not hear this cry of the Spirit within themselves. So they pray, but do not know they are praying—or rather the Spirit of Christ himself prays in them, the Spirit with whom they are sealed, in whom they live, by whom they are led. They themselves indeed do not feel it. They are gripped by grief. They are seized by complaints and laments. He intercedes, therefore, for the saints with unutterable groans.' R 398.D.12-18. Compare R 398.E.15-F.8 and 399.A.19-B.12.

Spirit.[1] The way the Spirit takes control and prays in the Christian in his helplessness, may even be compared to the way sin is said in Rom. 7 to be at work in us, so great is the Christian's helplessness.[2] Whatever may oppress the Christian, his life is lived in the Spirit and is sustained by him, for God is a loving Father and the Spirit that he has given Christians 'will never desert them'.[3]

In *Psalms* there is equally an emphasis on the role of the Spirit in inspiring true prayer, but there is at the same time some particular counsel about prayer. Bucer commends the use of the scriptures, the psalms, and the prayers of the saints as a help to prayer. However, he seeks to prevent this from becoming something done mechanically, by reference to Paul's saying about singing and making melody in one's heart.[4] In expounding Ps. 143:8 he urges the morning as the best time for prayer, saying that the most ardent prayers are usually made in the morning. It is also the time when God answers his people more openly and when the mind is ready to receive his answer.[5] In *St Matthew* he has already spoken of the importance of solitude for prayer.[6] This advice, based on scriptural example, about the time and place of prayer and the use of the Bible and the prayers of others in praying, is a far cry from the one-sided spiritualist picture presented in Lang.[7]

The prayer of the Christian is always prayer in the Spirit and prayer for the Spirit, for the Christian's life is possible only in the Spirit. But prayer in the Spirit is not opposed to outward prayer,

---

[1] R 398.E.3–5.

[2] R 400.E.11–17.

[3] R 398.D.8–11. Compare R 401.A.19–B.5.

[4] P 33.B.14–18. Compare 191.A.22–B.7; 63.A.26–B.3; 157.B.19–158.C.3.

[5] 'He burns with the same passion in the eighth verse also. For he seeks that God should cause him to hear his goodness early in the morning, either saying this instead of soon, or signifying the morning time, which is particularly consecrated to sacred prayer. This is because more ardent prayers were wont to be made in the morning time, and at scarcely no other time was the Lord wont to respond to his own more openly, as likewise at no other time is the mind equally fit to grasp God's answers.' P 325.B.5–10. Compare P 31.C.23–D.6.

[6] 158.B.12–15; 131.C.1–3; 335.A.21–3.

[7] Lang, *op. cit.* p. 128.

only to merely outward prayer which is a matter of the mouth, not of the heart. In other words, it is opposed to prayer that comes from man and not from the Spirit of God.

Love—the Fruit of the Spirit. Love is the characteristic mark of Bucer's understanding of sanctification. This love is made possible by faith and is the expression of a living faith.[1] It expresses the total intention of God for man, for love is the fulfilling of the law.[2] It is not a work of man, directed ultimately to winning the love of God for us; on the contrary, it is the fruit of the indwelling Spirit, arising out of the love of God for us, which we can never win.

The love which characterises a Christian's life is a love that takes him out of himself and turns him towards his neighbour. Our good works are not to be ones that we think up ourselves, but those which God has prepared for us. 'They are the works of brotherly love, which we are to do to people, not to God, nor to the saints, nor to the dead.'[3] For the Spirit of God leads men away from a concern with their own needs. He does not cause men to withdraw from others, but rather to live for them. 'In reference to which, take note that all the works of the Lord in men are of such a kind, that from them some benefit reaches their neighbours. Therefore the Spirit of the Lord is not one who withdraws men from public, so that looking after their own concerns they are of use to no one else.'[4] That man was made for the loving care and service of others is as much a mark of Bucer's last works as it is of his first. In *Ephesians* (1550) he speaks of the greater gifts that God gives one man as a reason for him to serve others, not for him to be served by them.[5]

Love can take many forms. Bucer insists that it should not be judged from outward circumstances, but from the heart. The

[1] The relation of faith and love is considered in ch. 3.
[2] Some consideration of love as the fulfilling of the law is given in the following section.
[3] BW 1.318.10–14.   [4] 29.A.14–18; 90.B.9–11; 228.C.13–14.
[5] EE 178.E.3–11.

anointing of Jesus was open to misunderstanding, judged outwardly. Jesus, however, judged it inwardly, knowing the heart
of the woman who had poured out her love in the anointing.
'Since therefore the heart, on which the goodness of what men
do depends, is unknown to us, let us not easily condemn.'[1]

One of the chief faults that Bucer found with many of the radicals was their lack of love, and indeed a spirit not only lacking in
love, but also displaying a divisive arrogance and self-indulgence.
The fruit of the Spirit, he says, is, as in Gal. 5:22–3:

...love, joy, peace, patience, friendliness, goodness, faith, gentleness,
and self-control. It is not to separate oneself from the fellowship of those
who have a sincere zeal for the Lord, scorning and avoiding them,
falsely blaming them, believing and passing on all kinds of untruth
about them, pleasing oneself, being envious, spiteful, selfish, and often,
under the guise and boast of a higher spirit, falling into wild licence,
as nevertheless daily manifests itself in such a gross way with the miser-
able separatists.[2]

Bucer not only opposes any so-called leading of the Spirit which
is out of keeping with the fruit of the Spirit, but he also insists on
the subordination of the gifts of the Spirit to the fruit of the Spirit.
Without the fruit of the Spirit (to be found only in the godly) the
gifts of the Spirit (to be found also in the ungodly) are of no value.[3]
This he urged against the anabaptists, who were sometimes strong in
the gifts of the Spirit, but who were often manifestly without love.[4]

The love that a Christian shows to his neighbour is so much the
expression of God's love, that there is a sense in which a man is
God to his neighbour:

Man is God to [his fellow] man, that is, you could be and ought to be
a benefactor to your neighbour. In this way God has willed to test your
dutifulness towards himself and equally has willed to accept whatever
you do to your neighbour, as if you had done it to him. In short, it is
about these things alone that God has given us commands, for Paul says

---

[1] 324.A.12–27; 187.C.7–15; 480.C.12–21.
[2] BW 7.97.20–9. [3] See pp. 185–6.
[4] 22.B.18–23.A.23; 88.B.23–C.16; 223.B.6–25.

that the whole law is fulfilled in this one word alone 'You shall love your neighbour as yourself'. Consequently whether you chastise your body, or pray, or preach the gospel, or bless God, or whatever else you do, if it is not undertaken for the benefit of your neighbour, it is not a good work. It is for that reason that God has made you good, that is, giving his Spirit, he has given you to be salt, so that you may bring a true savour to others, and to be light, so that you may be light to other men, and by your goodness help those whom it is permitted to help. If, therefore, you chastise your body and subdue it to the Spirit, you ought to have regard to this: that the Spirit is able to use it all the more easily for the salvation of your neighbour.[1]

Indeed, the more a man is conformed in this way to the image of Christ, the more he may be said to possess divinity.[2] For to share in the life of God is in some sense to share in his nature.

THE HOLY SPIRIT AND THE LAW

Bucer speaks of the law with a characteristically different accent from Luther. He is aware of Luther's position and in many fundamental points shares it; but, significantly, whereas a discussion of law in a study of Luther would be part of the discussion of justification, with Bucer it belongs properly to the discussion of sanctification.[3]

The Law. The opposition of law and gospel is one that Bucer allows, but does not regard as strictly scriptural.[4] For him the law is the teaching of God, contained in the Bible, and given to men

---

[1] 114.B.12–25; 47.A.9–17; 115.B.19–116.C.4.

[2] 'Sicut autem homines, aliis creaturis plus divinitatis possident, maxime sancti, ita ii rebus aliis expressius Christi in se imaginem exhibent.' 307.A–B; 203.C.2–3; 521.B.1–2. Compare Luther's comment: 'quilibet Christianus debet se agnoscere magnum esse, quia propter fidem Christi, qui habitat in ipso, est deus, dei filius et infinitus, eo quod iam deus in ipso sit.' W.A. 4.280.3–5.

[3] This does not mean ultimately that Bucer's position is wholly different from Luther's; but it is different. One of the important influences in Bucer's understanding (and not his alone) is unquestionably Augustine's *De spiritu et littera.* Certain similarities with Aquinas may also be noted. See the discussion by Lyonnet in *La Vie selon l'Esprit.*   [4] See pp. 68–9.

so that they may live a godly life. It has three elements: faith in and love of God, love of one's neighbour, and whatever concerns our bodily needs.[1] He understands 2 Tim. 3:16–17 of the law, and therefore regards the law as instructing to salvation and to every good work.[2]

The law is in no sense to be opposed to the Spirit, any more than faith is to be opposed to works. They belong together; and the law, when not separated from the Spirit, can be said to be given for salvation.[3] The law may properly be spoken of as spiritual, for

it teaches and requires the things which are of the Spirit, that is, living faith in God, sure love of one's neighbour, and all such things, which belong to the new life of the Spirit. Nor does it only teach and require these things, but even in its way (*suo modo*) confers them, when it has been administered by the Spirit of God and written in the heart, and when it is not received from the letter alone, by a mind not yet renewed by the Spirit of Christ—for in this way it kills.[4]

The law in this sense (as given by God to lead to a godly life, when it is joined with the Spirit) is clearly not something that the saints dispense with, but something that they meditate in day and night. The law presents God's will and therefore it shows the saints both what pleases and what displeases God. It shows them where they have fallen short and what they have to do. In this there is some change between the 1527 edition and the 1530 and 1536 editions of *St Matthew*. In 1527 Bucer allows that the righteous need the law, as they are not free from sin in this life; the law, moreover, leads them to embrace Christ the more eagerly.[5]

---

[1] 149.A.10–25; 48.B.15–24; 119.A.23–B.12.   [2] Compare P 87.D.6–13.

[3] 'His law God gave to his people for their salvation, and by it, along with his Spirit, he approves of works, but [only] those born of faith, and not those done indeed without faith...But because there were those who exalted the law without the Spirit, works without faith, the ministry of Moses without the grace of Christ, Paul disjoined these things, so that it might be apparent that whatever in the law at any time brought salvation was of the Spirit...' 53.B.20; 18.A.14; 46.D.20–1, 24–47.A.1.   [4] R 363.B.7–C.3.

[5] 'On account of the unrighteous, to wit, as I said, the disobedient, the ungodly, and sinners, and the rest of this sort, the Lord gave his law, so that they might— even if only to a small extent—be restrained from their shameful deeds. Then,

Later this is omitted and the stress is placed on the Holy Spirit as taking the place of the law, though there is still some reference to the use of the law for the righteous, because they are not wholly righteous.[1] *Romans* certainly sees the law as of use to the saints, for it shows them what sin is, stirs up their sense of and sorrow over sin, and their fear of judgment, and leads them away from trust in themselves to consecrate themselves to Christ.[2]

The Spirit does not only use the law to show men where their lives fall short; he also uses it to show them what God wishes them to do. The law is, therefore, a sure guide to men, when they might otherwise be led to serve God according to their own mistaken idea of his will. This happens with many so-called good works. In the *Bestendige Verantwortung* Bucer argues 'we are not to do God's service and work according to our own thinking, without God's command. Therefore Christ says: "in vain do they honour me with human commands".'[3] God's primary command is to love one's neighbour. This command will demand, as Ambrose had asserted, that men feed the poor and liberate those who are captive before they adorn churches, although in principle Christians may properly share in adorning churches.[4] In his service of God the meditation of God's law helps the Christian to a true obedience, for it enables him to distinguish between divine and human commands.

Freedom from the Law. For Bucer the Christian is set free from ceremonies and from all external things that do not help faith and love.[5] In this he is no doubt influenced by Erasmus' opposition to

---

since a great deal of unrighteousness clings to all of us as long as we live here, to that extent there is for us also a use of the law for this end, that we may know all the more fully that sin that lies hidden in us, and for that reason also may all the more eagerly embrace Christ the physician.' 157.A.27–B.7; 50.D.25; 126.C.12.

[1] 157.B.7; 51.A.22–6; 126.D.12–17.
[2] R 283.B.5–13. Compare R 351.B.16–20 and 366.D.5–18.
[3] BV 46.B.30–3.   [4] BV 49.B.27–50.A.3, B.11–30.
[5] 154.A.27–B.11, 9.B.15–10.A.2; 50.A.1–8, 84.C.27–D.7; 123.B.15–23, 213.A.25–B.10.

ceremonies and his understanding of the law (from which the Christian is free) as the ceremonial law. The positive side of this, however, is the stress on faith and love, which Bucer sees as summing up the whole law.[1] With this principle he regards what concerns faith and love as what is permanent and binding in a command of God, and what concerns the outward details of time and place as temporary.[2] It is only from this second, from the external details, that men are free.

There is also a freedom from the law of God in particular instances, where God, so to speak, himself overrules a command he has given. In *Judges* there are a number of examples of this. Thus God reveals secretly to Samson that he is to marry a foreigner, which is forbidden by the law.[3] Similarly God can make use of the jawbone of an ass, which is impure and therefore against the law,[4] and he can allow Samson to lie, though this would also be against God's law.[5]

Besides these two restricted senses in which a Christian is free from the law, Bucer can speak broadly and generally of a Christian's freedom from the law. He does not easily find a form of words that satisfies him. In 1527 and 1530 he says that the Christian is freed but not loosed (*solutus*) from the law; in 1536 he says that he is freed and loosed, but not estranged (*alienatus*) from it.[6] This general freedom is not a freedom to live contrary to the law, but a freedom to live according to it in the power of the Spirit.[7] It is in this sense that the Christian may be said to be free from the

[1] This is discussed in the section on the interpretation of the Bible, see ch. 6.
[2] 73.A.1–74.A.25; 103.D.27–104.B.14; 262.D.10–263.B.19. Compare EE 90.E.15–F.10.   [3] J 506.48–57.
[4] J 511.23–36.   [5] J 513.55–8. Compare EE 167.C.9–10, 168.D.
[6] 'Atque ita nos quidem lege liberasse, sed non solvisse, hoc est, effecisse ut illa quidem nobis neque molesta sit, neque condemnet, nos tamen amemus illam et meditemur in ea die et nocte.' 158.B.15–19; 51.C.10–13; 127.B.9–11.

In place of 'Atque...illa' 1536 reads: 'Atque ita puto constare, nos per Christum lege quidem esse liberatos, et solutos sed non alienatos (1530 has: liberatos, sed non solutos), hoc est effecisse illum, ut ea...' Compare 155.A.4–6; 50.A.20–1; 124.C.12–14.
[7] EE 82.E.8–18 (quoted on pp. 97–8). The Christian is also free from the condemnation of the law because of the forgiveness of Christ.

law, not in himself, but in Christ, just as he is dead to the law, not in himself, but in the body of Christ. 'So that he might show that he did not say that we are in ourselves free from the law, but [only] in Christ, he did not say simply that we are dead to the law, but that through the body of Christ [we are dead to the law].'[1]

The Holy Spirit and the Law. The freedom of the Christian is a freedom that he has in the Spirit. Possessed by the Spirit, he has no need of the law to instruct him, as the Holy Spirit is a better teacher: for he not only teaches the will of God perfectly, but also gives the desire and ability to do what he teaches:

Therefore those who believe are not under the law, because they have the Spirit within, teaching them all things more perfectly than the law, and impelling them much more powerfully to do them. In other words he moves the heart, so that for their part they wish to live by those things which the law commands. But this is what the law could not do.[2]

Christ, therefore, fulfils the law in us daily by giving us his Spirit.[3]

In other words, the law is replaced by the Holy Spirit. Because of the presence of the Spirit the law is not abrogated but fulfilled. It is obeyed not unwillingly, but gladly and spontaneously:

They are, however, set loose from the law, not so that they may live contrary to it, but so that they may serve God in the newness of the Spirit. Therefore we must always work to fulfil the law with our whole strength, just as likewise the righteousness that is taught in it is to be promoted, always voluntarily and not by compulsion. For we are now free, but not free in an absolute sense, so much as free in a qualified sense. We are free from its censure and condemnation, free from the accusation of sin and concupiscence and so on. However, if you understand [the matter] correctly, we are free from it even in an absolute sense. If you have the Spirit of Christ and are led by him, you are free from it even in an absolute sense, and yet you love and embrace what is commanded in it, out of love. Just as there are two ways of serving,

[1] R 345.A.12–14.
[2] 155.A.19–23; 50.A.30–2; 124.C.22–5. Compare 156.B.25–157.A.3; 50. D.15–17; 126.C.2–4.
[3] 153.B.14–16; 49.D.6–7; 123.A.11–13.

against one's will and of one's own accord, so the things which belong to the law come about in two ways, against one's will and of one's own accord. If we have the Spirit of Christ, [we fulfil the law] of our own accord, not against our will.[1]

There is no need of external commands,[2] for the commands of God are obeyed automatically. 'It is necessary to love one's neighbours in deed and in truth. Where that is present there will be no need of other commands about works of mercy. Sincere love will never neglect its duty. But this is nowhere present, except where there is faith and the Spirit of the sons of God.'[3]

The prophecy of Jer. 31, which speaks of the law being written in the inward parts, is fulfilled for Bucer in the gift of the Holy Spirit, for the Spirit does what the law could not do. He works inwardly, transforming men into sons of God who understand and desire the will of God. He is also the source of true liberty in the sons of God, the liberty to do good not by compulsion, but by our own inward desire.[4] Since 'the Spirit acts by teaching what is truly good and inflaming [our desire] for it', so that 'we do and are zealous for those things that become the children of God', we may say 'where the Spirit is, there is liberty'.[5]

GLORIFICATION

To represent the future and, as yet, incomplete element in man's salvation by the word glorification, is not entirely true to Bucer's use of the word. He uses it and its cognates for events in the past, the present, and the future.[6] It is, however, used by him to describe

---

[1] EE 82.E.8–18. Compare R 336.F.3–8.

[2] Bucer was not unaware of the obvious contradiction between this idea and his affirming that the Christian, as he was sinful, was always in need of the law. The contradiction corresponds with the contradiction in the life of the Christian himself, who is led by the Spirit and yet nevertheless sins.

[3] 283.B.7–11; 173.B.11–13; 446.C.12–14.

[4] 168.A.6–8; 61.C.10–11; 704.C.14–15.   [5] R 381.C.7–15.

[6] He almost passes over the word in his exposition of Rom. 8, but does refer briefly to it on a number of occasions. The varied use of the term may be seen in comparing two quotations from succeeding pages.

the completion of salvation, and in our presentation of his theology is more suitable for this purpose than for any other. In *De ordinatione* he writes: 'However, regenerating faith is different. By it those, to whom it is given to believe, have eternal life, and thus are justified by God, even those foreknown and predestined, and are called according to the immutable purpose of God, so that undoubtedly they may at length even be glorified.'[1]

What is important for Bucer is that those whom God has predestined will one day be perfectly conformed to his will, reflecting his glory, and that this will not happen in this life. There is an unbreakable link holding together predestination, vocation, justification, sanctification, and glorification, so that for anyone to whom one of these words applies, the others apply as well.[2] Election is meant to lead, and will lead, to the glory of God in the lives of those whom God has elected.[3] It is for this reason that the elect perseveres in the faith. His final glorification is God's declared intention in electing him, which God cannot break without being untrue to himself.

The completion of God's purpose lies beyond this life. It belongs to the last day. 'This communion in Christ and full enjoyment of him is not yet complete here. Then it will indeed be complete, when all sin has been destroyed in us by the Spirit of Christ, and God will be all things in us (1 Cor. 15).'[4]

'When here the apostle especially resolves to strengthen the saints and harden them against adversity, he speaks of that conforming of us to the image of Christ, by which alone we shall be glorified with him, by which also we shall attain fully to the likeness of his resurrection, and for which we have been grafted into Christ...' R 406.E.5–8.

'He repeats what he had said about the predestination of the sons of God and explains in greater detail, moving choicely from step to step. In truth, what he wished to show is that those who have already been glorified in the sight of God, that is, who have with certainty been destined for the glory of the sons of God, are those whom God had foreknown to be among his own, and had already fore-ordained.' R 407.C.8–11.   [1] TA 247.4–8.

[2] 'Ex his quis non clare videat Paulum haec, diligere Deum, et esse secundum propositum vocatos, praescitos, praedefinitos, vocatos, iustificatos, glorificatos, haec ita eisdem tribuere, et ea adeo inter se connectere, ut indubitatum haberi velit, cui unum ex his competat, ei competere etiam reliqua?' R 405.C.4–8.

[3] E 26.B.16–25.   [4] 132.A.18–21; 47.B.4–5; 678.D.18–19.

The accomplishing of this task is the work of the Holy Spirit. He brings the elect to the point where not a single good work, for which God has created him, is lacking.[1] He will make us finally blessed, and may be described as 'a never failing spring, because he never deserts those whom he inspires'.[2] 'For he who trusts in him and hangs on him in sure confidence, however much a sinner he is, will not be condemned, but one day will be fully liberated from all his sins through his Spirit, and will be given true righteousness.'[3] The forward-looking note is a constant one. The Christian waits for his full redemption in which he will be perfectly renewed in the image of Christ, liberated from sin and death, and blessed with all good things. Then he will know God, even as he is known.[4] The goal, which is a life in which we love and worship God, has nothing to do with our merit, for it stems from God's election.[5] This expectation is enjoyed by those who have received the first fruits of the Spirit, and who await the glory of the sons of God:

He heightens the effect of the groaning with which the sons of God long for glory, so that he may show how great this longing of the saints is, and from this how great is that glory of theirs for which they groan and sigh so much...This blessedness of the saints, then, is very great. Yet, however truly great it is up till now, even so it cannot be compared with that future glory of the sons of God about which the apostle speaks here. Why should those who have with certainty embraced the promise of this, because of it and from the very taste of it which they enjoy in advance, not groan and sigh continually for that glory, even indeed from the depth of their heart, that is, within themselves?...It is about this completion of our blessedness that the apostle speaks here, calling it the vivifying, the inheriting, the glory, and the adoption of the sons of God.[6]

---

1 'Von dem aber, das wir guotte werck verwerfen, sein wir souer, das wir frey bekennen, das der mensch nymmer mer ganntz selig werden mag, er seie dann durch den gaist Cristi dahin bracht, das ime ietz vberall kains guotten wercks mer mangle, deren nemblich, zuo wöllichen in gott beschaffen hatt.' BW 3.60. 11–15.

2 98.A.21–B.2; 33.C.4–9; 644.C.22–D.3.

3 75.B.14–17; 25.D.11–13; 624.D.22–4.   4 E 28.A.4–10.

5 EE 21.A.14–17.   6 R 390.E.6–F.10.

PART II

THE HOLY SPIRIT AND THE WORD

The relationship of word and Spirit was a focus of debate and division in the sixteenth century. The reformers argued with each other, as well as with their catholic and radical opponents. Their debate concerned not only the audible and visible words of preaching and sacrament, but also more fundamentally the incarnate and written word. We must, therefore, consider the word in its varied forms—the incarnate Word and the written word that bears witness to him, the people, the ministers, and the servants of the word, and the audible and visible words of preaching and sacrament.

It is in his understanding of word and Spirit that many have seen a change in Bucer's thought from an early period, influenced more by Zwingli and the spiritualists, to a later one, influenced more by Luther. This alleged change in Bucer's position demands a treatment of his theology, in which any change or development may be seen. For that reason Bucer's thought is presented in the chronological order of his works, so that change or development can be manifest.

5

CHRIST—THE INCARNATE WORD

In considering the Holy Spirit and Christ, we must leave on one side the relation of the Holy Spirit to the birth of Christ[1] and the role of the Holy Spirit in the life and ministry of Christ.[2] It is not there that the primary interest lies. It lies rather in discussing how far, and in what sense, the Spirit in Bucer is the Holy Spirit who proceeds from the Father and the Son.

This issue has been raised in a variety of ways in the discussion of Bucer's theology. From Lang's *Der Evangelienkommentar Martin Butzers* to Müller's *Martin Bucers Hermeneutik* it has been argued that the Spirit is far from closely linked to the incarnate Christ. Lang refers to Bucer's spiritualism and the secondary role of Christ's death, especially in the early Bucer.[3] Köhler understands Bucer as ascribing the Spirit to all men.[4] Bornkamm sees Bucer's Christ as no more than a name for the universal divine Spirit,[5] whilst Müller sees Bucer's theology as fundamentally unhistorical, not to say unchristological.[6]

---

[1] In this Bucer constantly affirms that Christ was conceived by the Holy Spirit without the participation of a human father, and so was without sin. It is because of this that redemption was possible. BW 1.111.24–9. Compare 13.A.15–B.3; 215.C.7–16; 535.B.18–536.C.6; and also GC A.8.B.19–25 and OB 15.47.28–9.

    In this matter Bucer shared the Aristotelian–Thomist view that the male seed was alone formative—see G. H. Williams, *Radical Reformation*, p. 325.

[2] Christ is spoken of as anointed with the Spirit so that we may all receive of his fulness. 9.B.26–10.A.17; 4.A.22–B.3; 8.D.17–9.A.2.

    'The Father gave and anointed him with the Holy Spirit above all others who shared in the Spirit, so that he might be the Saviour and Lord of all.' 126.A.5–9; 43.C.27–30; 670.C.11–14.

[3] Lang, *op. cit.* pp. 127 and 324.

[4] Köhler, *op. cit.* p. 89.

[5] Heinrich Bornkamm, *Martin Bucers Bedeutung für die europäische Reformationsgeschichte*, p. 28.

[6] Müller, *op. cit.* pp. 65–8, but also pp. 70–1 and 248.

These judgments are not lightly to be dismissed, but they do scant justice to Bucer's theology. They are unduly influenced by a refusal to see him except through the eyes of Luther, Zwingli, or Erasmus. For all that, they suggest a concentration on three issues: the relation of the Holy Spirit to the incarnate Christ, the relation of the Old Testament to the New Testament, and the relation of Christ to the Gentiles. The aim, however, in presenting Bucer's thought in these three ways is not primarily to refute one or other of these views, but to show the way Bucer himself sees the relationship.

THE RELATION OF THE HOLY SPIRIT TO THE INCARNATE CHRIST

Bucer's earliest writings exhibit a close relationship of the Holy Spirit with Christ that has been overlooked. The Holy Spirit is spoken of not as leading to faith in Christ, but as proceeding from faith in Christ. This is, indeed, the only way in which the relationship of the Holy Spirit with Christ is mentioned in *Das ym selbs* and the *Summary*. It is through faith that we become children of God and receive the Spirit of sonship. Then it is that the Holy Spirit testifies that we are children of God.[1] It is, furthermore, those who 'have believed the word of his grace' who are spoken of as having received the Holy Spirit whom 'the Father sends in the name of our Lord Jesus Christ'.[2] Not until *Dass D. Luthers Lehr* is the Holy Spirit described as leading to faith in Christ, rather than as proceeding from faith in Christ, and then the link with Christ is kept. 'Christ must first come and obtain for us another Spirit, through whom we believe that he has fulfilled the law for us and redeemed us from its threatening curse.'[3]

---

[1] BW 1.61.13–23, 32–40; 63.1–10.

[2] BW 1.82.20–6. It is in this context that all men are said to have the Holy Spirit to understand the scripture as far as is necessary for faith. It is only those who are Christ's who have the Spirit. Having the Spirit they are spiritual men, and so are able to judge spiritual things. BW 1.83.12–17.

[3] BW 1.319.9–12.

The Holy Spirit, who is given to men as they believe in Christ, has been gained by Christ through his death. He is not spoken of as present apart from Christ, blowing where he wills, but as being specifically obtained for us by Christ through his death. In other words, our receiving of the Spirit, though not the existence of the Spirit himself, is dependent on Christ's death. Thus, in *Grund und Ursach*, it is said that 'Christ, by his suffering, has earned and gained for us the Holy Spirit'.[1] In the *Apologia* we are told that it is thanks to his reconciling death that we are given the Spirit of sonship.[2] This same note is sounded in *St Matthew*. It is by his death that he expiated the sins of the elect and earned the giving of the Spirit by the Father.[3] *Ephesians* affirms that Christ as mediator gained the Holy Spirit by his blood.[4] In the *Berner Predigt* we read: 'It is Christ Jesus alone who has satisfied the Father on our behalf and gained a good Spirit, who will change us and make us like him...'[5]

In his exposition of Ps. 65 Bucer speaks of the mercy of God in forgiveness in these words:

For it is in his blood, as St Paul proclaims everywhere with such clarity, that true expiation of sins consists and real redemption from the wrath of God; whilst by the merit of his death we are given that Spirit who not only makes us certain of the full remission and purification of our sins, but also implants in our minds both a hatred of what is evil and a love and zeal for what is good.[6]

Not only is the Holy Spirit related historically to the death of Christ, but he is also spoken of as given to men specifically by Christ. In other words, he is not the possession of all men everywhere. On the contrary he is possessed only by those to whom Christ gives him. This conviction is true of Bucer's earliest writings, as it is true of the commentaries on the gospels. Thus he comments

---

[1] BW 1.258.11–13.   [2] AP 11.B.9–23.
[3] 15.B.9–18; 5.D.17–23; 12.D.20–13.A.1. Compare 190.A.9–16; 141.D.13–17; 367.A.16–21.   [4] E 25.A.26–B.6.
[5] BW 2.286.7–9.   [6] P 199.C.23–8.

in *St Matthew*: 'Christ, having received power from the Father, by right dispenses the Spirit of the sons of God.'[1]

In the *Getrewe Warnung* it is the Father who is said to give the Spirit because of the Son:

Just as the prophets and apostles teach, so we preach concerning Christ: namely that through his blood he has so redeemed and reconciled to the Father all the elect (who by nature are totally corrupt and cannot will or do anything good), that he will remember their sins no more (Jer. 31). (Otherwise it would not be true reconciliation.) And he will give his Holy Spirit, through whom they are purified, trust in him as their God and Father...[2]

The *Berner Predigt* says that Christ alone can give the Holy Spirit without whom all divine things are foolishness.[3] The same assertion that it is the Son,[4] indeed only the Son,[5] who gives the Holy Spirit, is to be found in *St John*. In the 1536 edition of the *Gospels* it is again only from Christ that the Holy Spirit comes.[6]

It is not in some vague religious activity that the Holy Spirit engages. His work is specifically related to God's revelation in Christ. This is affirmed in the *Preface*, where the Holy Spirit 'teaches, illumines, and inflames us by his testimony and that inward teaching by which he leads us into all truth, so that we truly know the Father through the mediator, Jesus Christ...'[7] It is expressed clearly in *St Matthew* where it is said to belong to Christ to give the Holy Spirit, by whom men know that he is in

[1] 80.B.11-15; 26.D.12-16; 64.C.14-18. Compare 9.B.26-10.A.17; 4.A.12-B.3; 8.D.17-9.A.2; and also 49.A.4-11; 96.C.22-6; 243.B.14-19.
[2] BW 2.250.19-25.
[3] BW 2.284.14-17.
[4] 26.B.22-5; 9.C.8-9; 583.B.23-4.
[5] 'But it is from the Spirit of God alone that we know God, are made certain of his goodness towards us, and moreover (*tum*) are eager to reproduce it towards [our] neighbours. Now this Spirit Christ alone gives to his own. Therefore everything depends on faith in him. For that reason not only here but also elsewhere Christ exhorts [us] to this above all.' 159.A.23-B.3; 57.A.6-10; 695.B.12-15.
[6] 53.B.3; 18.A.14; 47.A.11-20.
[7] PR A.3.B.20-4.

the Father, and the Father in him.[1] He brings to mind the sayings of Christ, and so bears testimony to him.[2] In *St John* it states that 'he glorifies Christ by alone giving the mind to confess Christ as Saviour'.[3] Indeed, 'it is not possible to know Christ except through the Holy Spirit bearing witness to him'.[4] He, moreover, binds the disciples to Christ, and prevents their being torn from him.[5]

Nor does the Holy Spirit add new revelations of his own. Rather he brings to remembrance what Christ has already said, especially those things which the disciples could not perceive in Christ's lifetime.[6] 'For as I also have done, he will not say anything of himself, but he will speak only what he hears. Whatever he brings to mind, will be my word and my Father's...'[7]

Finally, the Holy Spirit is said to be in the place of Christ, or, alternatively, Christ is said to work by his Spirit. Thus Christ, at the right hand of God, 'accomplishes salvation in the elect by his Spirit',[8] and 'by his Spirit he daily mortifies sins in us'.[9] 'He is invisibly present with us through the Holy Spirit to the end of the world.'[10] *St John* says of the Holy Spirit that he 'succeeded to Christ present in the flesh, by whom Christ himself, for it is his power and secret strength, is more perfectly and divinely present with his own than when he was present in the flesh'.[11] We preach

[1] 104.A.2–B.6; 113.B.7–26; 286.C.16–D.11. Compare 369.A.20–6; 202.A.20–4; 518.C.18–23.
[2] 79.A.11–25; 26.B.18–C.2; 63.A.5–16.
[3] 229.B.1–6; 84.D.32–85.A.3; 762.D.2–6.
[4] 230.A.3–4; 85.A.21–2; 762.D.26–763.A.1. Compare 164.A.1–4; 59.B.17–19; 701.A.16–18.
[5] 215.A.12–16; 79.A.15–17; 748.C.13–15.
[6] 220.A.3–10; 80.C.8–11; 751.B.22–6. Compare 229.A.12–B.6; 84.D.20–85.A.3; 762.C.15–D.6; and 232.A.22–5; 86.B.29–C.2; 765.A.23–5; and also 220.B.22–221.A.13; 80.D.5–15; 752.D.2–12.
[7] 233.A.4–6; 86.C.22–3; 765.B.19–20.
[8] AP 16.A.21–3.
[9] 65.B.21–5; 22.B.16–19; 52.D.21–3. Compare 2.A.25–B.2; 1.D.18–20; 3.A.5–8; and 45.B.15–18; 15.D.4–5; 35.A.23–4.
[10] BW 2.244.10–11.
[11] 229.B.22–4; 85.A.15–17; 762.D.21–3.

that 'Christ went away in the body so that he might be present to his own in a better way, in other words that he might be present by his vivifying Spirit'.[1]

It should be noted that the primary reference throughout is to the incarnate or glorified Christ, not to the pre-existent Christ, though there are some references to the pre-existent Christ as the eternal Word of God.[2] The fundamental importance of Christ, and of his death, is a marked feature of Bucer's early writings. The cross may not be the central and determinative element in Bucer's theology, but its importance should not be ignored. For Bucer it plays an indispensable part in the salvation of mankind.

In *Grund und Ursach* he opposes a false understanding of baptism as leading to 'a belittling of the death of Christ'.[3] *St Matthew* asserts that it was 'necesary for him to die so that the indignation of God might be removed from us and sin in us perish...'[4] *Ephesians* frequently refers to the essential role of the death of Christ in man's salvation. Our receiving forgiveness of sins through Christ is specifically related to his death for us.[5] Likewise, his death was regarded as necessary for the gathering of the sons of God who were dispersed abroad.[6]

This picture of the relation of the Holy Spirit to Christ has been deliberately limited to the period up to 1530 (with occasional references to the 1536 edition of the *Gospels*) for two reasons. First, this is the period in which Bucer's theology has been regarded as more spiritualist[7] or less Lutheran.[8] Here, therefore, the divorce between the Spirit and Christ might be expected to be most evident. Second, the development which is described in the next two sections will cover the rest of Bucer's writings. It should,

---

[1] 231.B.14–16; 86.B.9–10; 765.A.7. Compare 234.A.18; 87.A.4; 766.D.19–23.
[2] 36.B.24–37.A.9; 12.C.4–11; 591.A.24–B.6. Compare P 9.C.6–10.
[3] BW 1.254.22–30.   [4] 369.B.5–8; 202.A.27–9; 518.D.1–3.
[5] E 30.A.17–28.
[6] E 34.A.24–B.4. Compare E 4.B.18–21.
[7] Lang, *op. cit.* p. 325.   [8] Lang, *op. cit.* pp. 89 and 103.

however, be added that the picture so far presented is confirmed not only in the *Gospels* (1536) and *Romans*, but also in Bucer's later works.

The relationship of the Old Testament to the New Testament was one of the issues which divided the reformers from the radicals. For Bucer, as for the other reformers, the contrast between the Old Testament and the New Testament was not one of letter and Spirit or law and gospel. They held that the people of the old covenant shared in the same God and in the same faith. The important questions to which this view gives rise are: In what sense and to what extent did the people before Christ share in his righteousness and his Spirit? On what ground can they be said to have done this? In Bucer's answer three elements in the relationship of the Old and the New Testament must be noted: their fundamental unity, their contrast, and the relation of this unity and contrast to Christ and his death.

Bucer's answer can be found even before the period of the commentaries in the *Apologia* and the *Preface*. In comparing the symbols of the Old Testament and the New Testament (the frequent context of this discussion) he argues the likeness of the one to the other. The difference is simply that in the New Testament more is revealed, the knowledge of Christ is more open, and there is a freer worship of the Spirit (as against a worship in ceremonies).[1] The *Preface* affirms that God circumcised people in the Old Testament by his Spirit, and, by his Spirit, impelled them to consecrate themselves to him a living sacrifice. The basis for this was not the external acts themselves, but the future sacrifice of Christ, which circumcision and sacrifices adumbrated. It was because of this that God made a covenant with the elect who were circumcised, and was placated by their sacrifices:

[1] AP 22.A.3–9.

So also circumcision was once called a covenant between God and [his] people, and sacrifices a propitiation of God, since they indeed signified those things, but they nonetheless signified them in such a way that it was with the elect who were circumcised that the Lord really made a covenant, and by them when they sacrificed that he was truly propitiated. It was not indeed because of outward circumcision or sacrifices, but on account of that future sacrifice of Christ which they foreshadowed—it was with regard to this that, being propitious to the elect, he circumcised them by his Spirit, and impelled them to consecrate themselves completely to his will as a living and holy sacrifice, so that what was done outwardly really represented what was inward. From this it was truly the case that the men of old were part of the people of God and had a propitious and propitiated God.[1]

Almost everything that Bucer is later to say is found in these two brief passages. They represent his fundamental answer to our two questions. However, as he wrestles with the biblical text in his commentaries, especially in *Romans*, and as he tries to understand the meaning of the sacraments, there come into his presentation both a greater subtlety in expression and a greater detail in exposition.

The similarities and difference between Old and New Testament are developed in *St Matthew* and *St John* without any significant development in between. They affirm a fundamental unity between the Old Testament and the New Testament. The people of the Old Testament had the same Father, Son, and Holy Spirit,[2] indeed some may be said to have been more richly endowed with the Spirit then, than we are now.[3] This advantage of some in the Old Testament over some in the New Testament seems newly expressed in *St John*.[4] The reasons for asserting the similarity of

[1] PR A.8.B.18–B.1.A.4.
[2] 35.B.26–36.A.13; 12.A.30–B.7; 590.D.15–24. Compare 150.B.21–5; 48.D.12–14; 120.D.21–3; and 177.A.17–22; 57.A.13–16; 142.D.3–6.
[3] 35.B.26–36.A.13; 12.A.30–B.7; 590.D.15–24.
[4] This point is also made in *Zephaniah*, where the fact that some were given a richer, fuller Spirit in the Old Testament is held not to invert God's order, any more than the fact that some boys are wiser than old men! Z 71.A.5–18. Bucer, moreover, makes the contrast between the people of the two covenants as a whole, allowing that some individuals may be exceptions. Z 69.B.4–70.A.1.

the Old Testament and New Testament are directly or indirectly biblical. Moses, Elijah, and others show evidence of the Holy Spirit, for they are different from what men naturally are.[1] Moreover, Christ's statement about believing Moses implies a possible possession of the Holy Spirit, as only by the Spirit of God is the word of God believed.[2] Therefore 'whoever from the beginning of the world has believed in God, has had the Spirit of God but not so richly, plentifully, or efficaciously [as since Christ]'.[3]

The dividing point between the peoples of the Old and New Testament is placed not at the incarnation,[4] but at the glorification of Christ. It is then that the Spirit is given in that greater measure, which is the chief distinguishing mark between the Old Testament and the New Testament:

... this covenant is marked by the remission of sins and the fulness of the bestowing of the Spirit upon all the elect, so that they may know the Lord from the least to the greatest, having the law of God written in their hearts. The saints of old were also sharers in this covenant, but with less revelation and a less powerful Spirit than when Christ was exalted.[5]

The differences between the Old Testament and the New Testament are variously described but amount most frequently to an opposition between those who are children and those who are adults in the Spirit, the first needing the law as a tutor, and the

[1] 'The Spirit inspires whom he wills and you rightly sense his power in all whom this Spirit inspires. For who does not see in Moses, Elijah, and innumerable other saints the divine strength and the celestial Spirit? Who does not sense them to be other than what everywhere men are like and are born like, and also other than they themselves were by natural birth?' 70.B.13–18; 24.B.12–15; 620.C.20–4.

[2] 'The word of God is believed by the Spirit alone. If therefore they had believed Moses, they would have had the Spirit, who searches the depths of God, and, relying on him, they would not have been able not to recognise that God was offering himself to be known in Christ much more splendidly than in Moses.' 120.B.8–12; 40.D.16–18; 663.B.4–7.

[3] 159.B.27–160.A.3; 57.A.25–6; 696.C.6–8.

[4] 35.A.21–B.1; 12.A.11–15; 590.C.20–4 is not to be interpreted in that way.

[5] 329.A.1; 188.D.21; 491.B.19–23. Compare 219.A.19–22; 80.B.10–12; 751.A.21–3.

second having the Spirit himself. It is not simply that the Old Testament was marked with more ceremonies,[1] though the picture of the three ages of man emphasises this. Indeed, there is an opposition between worshipping God in the Spirit and worshipping with ceremonies and sacrifices.[2] We are described as living in the middle age, which is not completely spiritual, for we still use the outward word and signs. It is a more spiritual age than the period of infancy (in the Old Testament) which had a great number of signs. But it is not as spiritual as the third period when we shall be fully adult in heaven, needing no outward forms.[3]

Bucer here seems guilty of some confusion between outward forms, as the necessary form of worship of those whose life is an outward, bodily life, and outward forms, as giving an incentive to those who are weak in the Spirit. This confusion lies behind much of his discussion of ceremonies, which can be used in two opposed ways—as they are given by God (that is, in the Spirit, and not as a means of binding God to us or securing his favour) or as distorted by man in his sin (that is, not in the Spirit, but as a means of binding God to us and securing his favour).

The distinction of the Spirit of fear and of adoption is the one that Bucer uses most frequently. The Spirit of fear is marked by

[1] 151.A.17–B.7; 49.A.5–15; 121.A.11–22.

[2] '...he will send the Holy Spirit to his own and bring it about that the elect everywhere will worship the Father in Spirit and in truth, having removed that outward worship which consisted in bodily sacrifices and oblations.' 302.A.6–11; 179.B.5–8; 460.D.24–461.A.3.

[3] 'But the middle age which is governed by the word of the gospel, though it is more spiritual than [the age of] infancy, yet it is not entirely spiritual as the completely adult age, the life of heaven, will be. Accordingly it makes use of the outward word and for this reason also the outward fellowship and on account of this especially the two signs, the one by which we enter into that fellowship and the other by which we renew and confirm it.' 49.B.6–11; 16.B.5–8; 601.B.1–5. Compare 85.A.15–18; 28.C.20–2; 631.B.18–20.

Psalms speaks of a growing freedom from ceremonies as we come nearer the life of heaven. P 178.B.18–C.7. They are regarded as having been deliberately used by God to separate Jews and Gentiles, until the more adult Spirit, that came with Christ's glorification, was given. P 155.B.16–C.2.

Erasmus regards ceremonies as necessary and valuable for babes in Christ, see, for example, Spinka, *op. cit.* p. 339.

the tutorship of the law.[1] Under it man is servile. He does not know the reason why something is commanded, nor does he act with freedom and spontaneity.[2] By contrast, the Spirit of sonship means the Spirit who makes us certain that God is Father, and who impels us by love to do his will.[3] For those with the Spirit of sonship the Spirit may be said to have taken the place of the law, for the law as a tutor is not needed by those more fully endowed with the Spirit.[4] The Spirit is now said to be possessed more 'richly, plentifully, and efficaciously' than before.[5] Moreover, the Spirit in the New Testament is not limited to one people, but is given, as the gospel is given, to all nations.[6]

The relation of all this to the incarnate Christ is considered more fully in *Ephesians*, whereas the similarity and contrasts of the Old Testament and the New Testament are scarcely touched on there. On the basis of Eph. 2:11–12,[7] the Jews are said to have had Christ (that is, they believed in the prophecies of the Messiah and ex-

---

[1] In *Psalms* it is also linked to death, of which people in the Old Testament were afraid, whereas we are not, as we know more about God's goodness. P 39.B.3–6. This is not in the 1529 edition (51.A.23).

[2] Compare here the passage in Zephaniah (see pp. 150–1) which speaks of those who are slaves of the outward letter, and those with the Spirit of sonship, who understand both the outward letter and why it was given. Z 8.B.6–9.B.11. In the infant state the law is observed without knowing the reason. It is obeyed in fear, not through one's own judgment.

'In puerili ergo illa aetate, ut iam ex Paulo adduxi, spiritu servitutis ad timorem duntaxat fuit Ecclesia praedita, eo Sancti, tanquam servi huc agebantur, ut praescripta sibi observarent quidem, haudquaquam tamen rationem cur ita observanda essent, agnoscerent: eoque ut sine proprio iudicio, ita citra singularem amorem et animi voluptatem, non aliter atque pueri initio ad mores decentiores et studia literarum, solo fere timore, nullo proprio ipsorum arbitrio, atque ideo citra ultroneum affectum, impelluntur et aguntur. Id autem de populo hoc, non de singulis affirmo...' Z 69.B.4–70.A.1.

[3] The contrast is worked out in 26.B.22–27.A.15; 9.C.8–22; 583.B.23–584.C.12. See also 39.A.12–B.5; 13.A.26–B.9; 593.A.20–B.7.

[4] 198.B.6–199.A.16; 73.A.16–B.11; 734.C.2–D.3. See also 151.A.17–B.7; 49.A.5–15; 121.A.11–22.

[5] 159.B.27–160.A.3; 57.A.25–6; 696.C.6–8. See also 200.A.6–11; 73.C.10–14; 734.D.19–22; and 53.B.27–54.A.7; 18.A.18–22; 42.D.19.

[6] 35.A.24–B.1; 12.A.13–15; 590.C.22–4. Compare 198.B.6–14; 73.A.16–22; 734.C.2–9; and also 200.A.6–11; 73.C.10–14; 734.D.19–22.

[7] E 56.B.4–12.

pected his coming), in contrast to the Gentiles, who are said to be without Christ. The death of Christ, however, removes the middle wall of partition between Jew and Gentile both internally and externally—internally by gaining for them the Holy Spirit by whom they may know and worship God, externally by abolishing rites and ceremonies.[1]

As the incarnate Christ by his death affected the relation of Jew and Gentile historically, so, in a way that includes but goes beyond the historical, his death affected the situation of the Jews of the Old Testament. 'The saints are written in the book of the sons of God before the foundation of the world by virtue of Christ's blood which is one day to be shed. For all things are present to God.'[2] His death is necessary for man's salvation, but as all things are present to God Christ's death can be effective beforehand.[3] This is related to Christ as the eternal Word of God:

He rightly preached about himself that no one could come to the Father but by him, nor could the Father be known by anyone apart from his revealing him. Therefore, those who at any time from the foundation of the world have known God, or will in the future know him, and hence have been made sharers in righteousness, or in the future will be made sharers, have been, or will be, given the Holy Spirit through Christ the eternal Word of God...[4]

In this twofold way Bucer seeks to affirm both the necessity of Christ, and in particular the necessity of his death, for man's salvation, and the fact that men were saved before his death. They were saved by his death because all things are present to God. Therefore, his death was valid with God before it happened historically in the world. Moreover, Christ the incarnate Word is no other than the eternal Word of God. All that is known of God, in whatever time or place, is known through him and him alone.

The controversy with the anabaptists provoked a number of references to the relation of the Old Testament and the New Testament, but little that is new. That the two peoples are funda-

---

[1] E 59.A.18–25.   [2] E 25.A.26–B.6.
[3] E 28.B.2–9.   [4] E 28.A.14–24.

mentally the same is affirmed in the *Schweinfurt Confession*[1] and
Quid de baptismate[2] in a discussion of the sacraments of the Old
Testament. Their differences are also recognised—the Holy Spirit
is spoken of in *Tetrapolitana*[3] as being given to us 'more richly', in
Quid de baptismate[4] as being a 'more adult Spirit', in *Dialogi*[5] also
as being 'given more richly'. The Gentiles now share in the Spirit,[6]
ceremonies are fewer and men are no longer sons under a tutor
(to be compared with slaves) but grown sons, acting freely and
with understanding.[7] More significantly, the *Bericht* insists that
the opposition is not between the letter and the Spirit,[8] a point of
fundamental disagreement with spiritualists and anabaptists. The
third aspect of the problem—the relationship to Christ and his
death—is also considered. The *Apology*[9] speaks of Christ's merit
as always being present to the Father, while the *Bericht* affirms that
the merit and death of Christ help all who have faith before and
after Christ's incarnation.[10]

[1] J. V. Pollet, *Martin Bucer—Etudes sur la Correspondance* 1.70.28–71.21.
[2] QD B.7.A.3–B.12.
[3] BW 3.160.28–9.
[4] QD B.5.B.20–6.A.3. Compare B.3.B.11–4.A.22.
[5] D O.3.B.23–32 and Q.3.A.7–12.
[6] BH M.2.B.22–3.A.5. See also D O.3.B.23–32 and Q.3.A.7–12.
[7] BH M.2.B.22–3.A.5.
[8] 'Now some see these words of Paul in such a way that they understand Paul to
grant the Spirit, faith, and a piety that is from the heart only to those who believe
in our Lord after the revelation of the gospel. They see all the people of old as
having been only slaves of the letter, with their piety as having consisted only in
ceremonies, their calling also as having been only to a temporal promise. In a
word, what Saint Paul allowed to those who place the works of the law before
the grace of Christ, that they grant to the whole people of Israel before the
incarnation of Christ. Thus they make them wholly fleshly, with nothing but
the letter, and us entirely spiritual, possessing the power of the law. [Likewise]
with them everything was shadowy and figurative, with us everything is truth.
God also had with them no covenant other than one directed towards temporal
piety and bodily goods, but with us it is all directed towards the Spirit—and
from this they presume to conclude that we are so entirely different a people
that ours is so completely a spiritual existence, that it can in no way be proper for
us to observe how the people of old with their fleshly sacraments acted. Circumcision was a sign and sacrament of the fleshly covenant. We have a spiritual one.'
BH M.2.A.12–B.1. Compare BH M.4.6.A.6–13.
[9] BW 3.261.26–32.   [10] BH AA.2.A.23–B.1.

It is, however, in *Romans* that this question receives its fullest discussion and definitive form. Here there is a richness of detail and argument that makes the exposition of the earlier commentaries seem nothing but a sketch or outline. It is not that Bucer's position has altered. Rather it has gained in perspective. This can be seen as in turn we consider his treatment of each of the three elements in the relationship—the fundamental unity between the Old Testament and New Testament, the contrast between them, and the relation of this unity and contrast with Christ and his death.

In a variety of ways and places, Bucer asserts the fundamental unity of both the Old Testament and the New Testament. There is 'one nation of saints' before and after Christ.[1] The Jews are said to have 'had Christ' before his incarnation.[2] By the Holy Spirit they were 'fruitful in all good works'.[3] Those who lived before Christ are described as not 'destitute of the grace of Christ' and as not 'having nothing of liberty from the law'. 'For, indeed, the saints of old lived by the same Spirit of Christ as we, and there is one mediator between God and all who are saints.'[4] The Jews were saved by Christ,[5] indeed, whenever God acts in the Old Testament, there is Christ:

It is not, therefore, in those few places which are usually quoted that scripture speaks about Christ, but everywhere it makes God and his works known to us. 'For God is in Christ', says Paul, 'reconciling the world to himself.' Moreover, God is by nature one. 'In him dwells the fulness of the Godhead in bodily form', that is to say, the Godhead itself, full and complete. Therefore, he is God himself, the true God, yet at the same time the only begotten of God, the everlasting Word that was with God, having at the same time distinction of person from the Father and the Holy Spirit, and identity of substance.[6]

[1] R 245.C (margin).   [2] R 194.E.18–F.6.
[3] R 194.E.1–4.   [4] R 350.F.8–13.
[5] 'For if the men of old also were saved by him, without doubt they were partakers in that same spiritual food and drink which is Christ. Nevertheless satisfaction had to be made in our flesh once, and in consideration of this sacrifice all the saints from the beginning of the world received remission of sins and the benefits of God.' R 26.D.14–17.
[6] R 23.A.16–B.2.

Jehovah in this sense stands for Christ.[1] Their ceremonies, and not simply circumcision, had in them 'the promise of the divine covenant'.[2] Their sacraments are like ours. In them they shared in Christ the spiritual rock.[3]

Two kinds of arguments are given for affirming this fundamental unity. The one is direct. It concerns passages which state or imply that the Jews were endowed with the Holy Spirit:

But they are proclaimed blessed in the psalms and elsewhere in the divine scriptures who walk in the ways of the Lord, who observe the law of the Lord, who fear the Lord, and so on. But because no one does any of these things except it come from the good Spirit of God, who is the pledge (*arrhabo*) of justification already given, it is necessary for them, by faith, to be already justified and blessed, who wish to fear God, listen to his voice, and walk in his ways.[4]

The other is indirect. It refers to the fact that the apostles proved from the Old Testament the incarnation of Christ, his expiating death, and his resurrection leading to a new life in which men participate by his word and Spirit.[5] Christ may therefore be said to have been present in the Old Testament. This is seen as confirmed by the way people accepted various Old Testament quotations as referring to the Christ.[6]

In pointing the contrast between the Old Testament and the New Testament, Bucer insists that it is not a contrast of flesh and Spirit.[7] The Old Testament is not carnal, mere letter, over against the New Testament as Spirit.[8] Such a distinction he regards as the

[1] R 23.B.4–8, 204.F.4–8.   [2] R 156.E.11–F.1.
[3] R 152.E.14–F.15.   [4] R 225.C.2–7. Compare R 508.F.1–9.
[5] R 202.E.6–F.8.   [6] R 203.B.5–10.
[7] R 197.B.8–C.11.
[8] 'Thus when they read that the Old Testament and the New Testament, the letter and the Spirit, the flesh and the Spirit are to be contrasted with each other, they understand these things, as if where the Old Testament was, there was nothing of the New, and on the other hand where the New is, there is nothing of the Old, where the letter is, nothing there of the Spirit, where the Spirit is, nothing of the letter, and so on. That is not the teaching of Paul, but the blasphemy of the Manichees, who urged in this way that what was given to the people of old by Moses was fleshly and brought death, so that they rejected the whole of the Old Testament.' R 137.B.9–15.

error of the Manichees. Both the Old Testament and the New Testament are letter, where they are without the Spirit. Where the Spirit is present both are spiritual.[1] The difference between the two is one of degree, not one of kind. The Spirit is now given more fully, is given to all nations, and is more efficacious.[2] The passage which refers to the Spirit as not yet given because Christ has not yet been glorified (John 7:39) is said to employ a characteristically biblical way of speaking, whereby something is described as not given, when it is not yet fully given. It does not mean that the Spirit was not there in the Old Testament, rather that the Spirit has been much more richly received since Christ's glorification.[3]

The basic contrast remains that of the Spirit of fear and the Spirit of adoption—a contrast that is worked out in detail in the exposition of Rom. 8. In the Old Testament there was the Spirit of fear. Men were not renewed by the Spirit in mind and judgment, so that in themselves they approved what God approved and commanded. Their depraved desires often prevailed. They did the evil they detested. They loved things, because they knew God desired them, but also because they feared God's enmity.[4] In the New Testament there is a more adult Spirit. He recreates us so that we revere God more and more in gratitude, avoid evil and seek good. He gives us God's nature so that we approve what God approves. Yet we are still moved by fear and our zeal and love are not complete. In us there is a battle between the flesh and the Spirit, that will not end until the flesh is abolished with the resurrection.[5]

The two states are likened to the state of those who are sick. Those with a servile Spirit are like those who detest their medicines, but who do so less, because they are persuaded that the doctor and their friends are offering what is for their salvation. Only because of their authority and their own fear of death do

[1] R 137.B.5–C.11.　　[2] R 65.B.18–C.9, 112.F.12–113.A.7, 153.B.2–16.
[3] R 196.E.18–20, 196.F.15–197.A.6.
[4] R 382.D.4–E.9.　　[5] R 382.E.19–F.10.

they take them. Whereas those with the Spirit of liberty and adoption, for the greater part desire and love health. They ask for the remedies without needing to be persuaded or urged. Their desire is not total, for in sickness true judgment is never achieved, but their contrary feelings are weaker. They are not yet wholly healthy because of the flesh; but one day God will be all in all.[1]

This distinction, however, between fear and adoption does not correspond absolutely to the distinction of Old Testament and New Testament. For the adult Spirit was given to some before the gospel, while by contrast not all those who truly believe the gospel are strong in the Spirit. But 'publicly and for the most part (*epi to polu*), that Spirit of fear was given to those who believed under the law, and this Spirit of adoption is given to those who believe under the gospel'.[2] These latter know and sense themselves sons of God, have confidence in him, and dare to call him Father.[3]

In considering the relation of the Old Testament to Christ, Bucer views the issue from both God's and man's point of view. Christ's death is regarded as a cause of our redemption because God appointed it to be. Christ was destined for this long before he came in the flesh and redeemed us by his death.[4] Moreover, as all things are present to God, including future events, the death of Christ was also present to him.[5]

On the other side, the Jews' faith was in Christ who was to come. Indeed, their faith can be described as faith in the birth, death, and resurrection of Christ, for without such a faith no one can be saved.[6] The same is true of the sacraments of the Old Testament. They adumbrated the death of Christ.[7] 'They signified the Saviour who was to come, those of the New Testament signify the Saviour who has come.' Therefore, those who partici-

---

[1] R 382.F.10–383.B.6.   [2] R 383.B.6–17.
[3] R 383.B.17–C.4.   [4] R 189.A.11–17.
[5] R 323.B.13–C.14.
[6] R 199.C.10–200.D.6 (see p. 126, n. 9) and 201.A.11–13. Compare R 122. D.17–E.1.
[7] R 204.F.12–14, 208.E.4–10.

pated in faith participated in Christ who was to come, and it is by this faith that they were justified.[1] Thus, whereas the Old Testament sacraments gave salvation 'by promising the Saviour',[2] the New Testament ones give salvation, 'already perfected by Christ in the flesh'. 'This the Old Testament sacraments could not yet give, but only promise, just as in the New Testament sacraments salvation in a regeneration [still] to be completed is only promised, not offered.' The sacraments of the Old Testament and the New Testament impart the Spirit according to the measure in which the promise of salvation has been revealed. In the Old Testament this revelation was more obscure and the Spirit not so full. However, 'the Old Testament sacraments conferred grace, and did not only signify the salvation of Christ, but also, in their measure, by signifying it, offered it'.[3] The effecting of this in the past is in some sense attributed to Christ as the eternal Word (for Christ did not begin his existence in the incarnation), from whose fulness Moses and the prophets received. Christ is the one mediator between God and man, therefore whatever truth and grace there is comes from him.[4]

The same understanding of the relationship between the Old Testament and the New Testament exists in the later works of Bucer.[5] In particular, he insists that the distinction between them is not one of letter and Spirit.[6] The Old Testament was the letter only for those who 'wished to find their consolation only in the outward letter and ceremonies'.[7] Moreover, the gospel itself is

---

[1] R 323.C.14–324.D.17.
[2] Augustine had said that 'the New Testament sacraments give salvation, the Old Testament ones promised a Saviour'. R 324.D.17–E.1.
  'This is the teaching of all schools in scholasticism. The Sacraments of the Old Testament are held to be effective on grounds of the faith of the recipient in the expected Messiah (*ex opere operantis*), the Sacraments of the New Testament function on grounds of the accomplished messianic task of Christ (*ex opere operato*).' See Heiko Oberman, *Forerunners of the Reformation*, p. 277.
[3] R 324.D.17–F.3.
[4] R 198.E.12–16, 18–19, F.6–14.
[5] BV 28.B.37–29.B.7, 32.B.5–8. See also TA 247.24–34 and EE 75.C and 76.D.
[6] BV 28.A.15–27.   [7] BV 28.B.37–29.A.6.

letter, 'if you do not embrace Christ, who is promised in the gospel', whereas 'if the law is read and received in faith, it is the ministry of life'.[1] This does not mean, however, that Bucer saw the distinction between the Old and New Testaments in terms of law and gospel, as these words were used by Luther.

Bucer's positive evaluation of the Old Testament rings strange in ears accustomed to the sharp distinction that modern historical scholarship makes between the Old Testament and the New Testament. It stands, nevertheless, in a long tradition of Christian interpretation of the Old Testament, beginning with the New Testament witness itself. His position cannot be described as an unhistorical levelling of the two. It is from the start related primarily to the incarnate Christ and his death, not to Christ as the eternal Word, though the two are not to be separated. It is because the saints of the Old Testament shared in Christ that they also shared in the Spirit, though less fully than the saints of the New Testament. At the same time, the possession of the Holy Spirit by the Old Testament saints is argued on the simple ground that they are said to have had the Spirit or that they lived in a way that for the Bible betokens the presence of the Spirit.

THE RELATION OF CHRIST TO THE GENTILES

The relation of Christ to the Gentiles in Bucer is misunderstood if the accent is placed chiefly on the discussion of philosophy in the preface to *Romans*. This emphasises unduly the static comparison of platonic thought with Christian doctrine. It also ignores the context which Bucer's earlier writings provide.[2]

References to the Gentiles and God's revelation to them are not common in Bucer at any point in his career. The first important references are in *Ephesians* and *St John*, and they arise naturally in the course of exposition. Commenting on Eph. 2:11–12 Bucer

---

[1] EE 84.E.8–12, F.4–7.
[2] A discussion of the immediate historical context of *Romans*, in particular the defence of humanist study in preparation for the founding of a humanist college in Strasbourg, can be found in Strohl, *Bucer, humaniste chrétien*, pp. 17–35.

describes the Gentiles as destitute of the laws by which the Jewish nation alone was rightly governed. They had not heard of Christ. They had no covenant, no promises, no hope. They were without God and plainly impious. What, he adds, could be more wretched than to be without God, without hope of a better life, without expectation of a saviour?[1] Such a sombre picture of the Gentiles Bucer instantly corrects by saying that God illuminated some Gentiles by his Spirit, so that he might be known as God of the Gentiles as well. By the Spirit they had faith in Christ and expected him. Of such men the Bible gives many examples, Jethro being one.[2] Here, as with the centurion in the gospel,[3] Bucer contents himself with biblical references to Gentiles who in some sense believed.

In *St John* the discussion goes a little further. Here, in a comment on John 4:35–8, he hopes that the reader will not be offended if he considers 'the work of philosophers to have been of benefit to the gospel'.[4] The ground he gives for this is that 'all truth is of God',[5] and that there is 'a great deal of truth in the writings of the philosophers and poets'. Their work is thought of as preparatory: 'they drew the minds of men to God and thus prepared them also for the gospel'. This preparatory work is then related to the doctrine of election by a reference to the seed of God.[6] Bucer argues that those who have the seed of God (by which he generally means the Holy Spirit) become displeased with themselves, the more they learn about piety, for they see themselves as unlike God and devoid of true piety. They respond eagerly 'when afterwards Christ is proclaimed to them as the righteousness of God and the true redeemer from sins'.

Apart from this, *St John* speaks of those who have believed in God from the beginning of the world as having had the Spirit (for

[1] E 55.A.21–56.A.2.   [2] E 56.B.13–57.A.1.
[3] 14.A.18–20; 86.A.7–8; 21.A.23–4.
[4] 106.A.13–B.5; 35.D.11–23; 650.C.24–D.14.
[5] Compare P 11.A.22–B.13, B.33–C.14, where Bucer says that whatever is true is of the Holy Spirit.
[6] 106.A.13–B.5; 35.D.11–23; 650.C.24–D.14.

belief is possible only with the Spirit),[1] and of there having been an expectation of Christ among the Gentiles.[2]

In the *Apology* and the *Handlung* there are two references which may be noted and which are taken up again in *Romans*. In the first, the presence of Christ and the Holy Spirit in the Gentiles is deduced from their doing good. Their obedience to the inward law is the work of the Holy Spirit.[3] In the second, Gentile baptism and sacrifice are linked to the Holy Spirit and to Christ. The one shows that 'the beginning of the worship of God and our righteousness must come from God's forgiving our sins, and washing and purifying us with his Holy Spirit...' This was 'promised and offered' in Gentile baptisms. The other shows that 'we have God's grace and eternal life, and that we share in the true sacrifice of Christ'. This was 'offered and promised' in Gentile sacrifices.[4] Bucer has adduced all this in a context where he seeks to show the pious Christian what sacraments are and why they are appointed.

What Bucer has argued in these writings is developed in *Romans* and in particular applied to the question of Greek philosophy. His concern is not only with Greek philosophy, which is discussed in detail in the preface, but also with the general relation of the Gentiles to Christ.

The general relation of the Gentiles to Christ is considered at various points. In the preface there is reference to Christ as the mediator between God and man, who has taught men about God through the creation, through miracles, and through messengers. (The reference is to Christ as the eternal Word.) 'Moreover, in order that the elect might rightly understand this proclamation of the deity he always imparted to their minds at the same time of his heavenly light.' Without this light men cannot perceive the things of God. By this light God is discovered to be the greatest good, the greatest power, and so on.[5] Here there may be said to

---

[1] 159.B.27–160.A.3; 57.A.25–6; 696.C.6–8.
[2] 170.B.9–12; 62.B.10–12; 706.C.15–17.
[3] BW 3.244.3–10.   [4] H K.1.B.18–2.A.19.
[5] 'Iam Deum nemo vidit unquam, qui in sinu eius est dominus noster Iesus Christus Verbum aeternum, et unus mediator Dei et hominum, variis iam inde ab initio

be a general revelation (the phrase should not be overpressed) of God, by Christ, the eternal Word, through the Holy Spirit.

Two of the other main passages concerning Christ and the Gentiles affirm that some Gentiles shared in God's righteousness before Christ's incarnation. Bucer says both that 'before Christ was revealed among the Gentiles, there were those to whom God breathed the Spirit of true righteousness' and that 'it was given to some Gentiles to believe in Christ before his incarnation'.[1] In this assertion he leans on the one hand on Chrysostom and Augustine, and on the other on the interpretation of the inward fulfilling of the law in Jer. 31, as the token of the presence of the Holy Spirit. For him this cluster of ideas hangs necessarily together. Where there is true righteousness, there must also be faith and the Holy Spirit, for true righteousness is possible only by faith and through the Holy Spirit. They were, however, present to a different extent before Christ's incarnation.

A further treatment of this relationship develops the idea sketched in the *Handlung*. Citing, among others, the example of Naaman, he argues that justification was offered to the Gentiles and that there was absolution of sins in Gentile baptisms.[2] In spite

rationibus de patre nobis enunciavit, tum machinae mundialis tam mirificae ostentatione, tum miraculis et memorabilibus facinoribus, quae subinde edit, tum verbis sacrorum vatum, tam illis quos Gentibus, quam quos Iudaeis inspiratos, inde a primordio humani generis misit. Hanc autem divinitatis praedicationem, ut rite intelligerent electi, mentibus illorum semper de luce sua caelesti simul impertivit. Ea enim ab ortu vitiato caligo obfusa nobis est, ut citra infusum e supernis novum lumen, eorum quae Dei sunt, nihil possimus percipere. Hinc ergo a contemplatione tam admirandi opificii caeli et terrae, praeclarisque providentiae factis, quae quotidie exhibet, atque ab oraculis, quae omnibus et gentibus et seculis impertita sunt, ac deinde aliis ab aliis per manus tradita, affulgente iuxta luce superna, homines primum didicerunt Deum esse, id est, esse summam potentiam, summam bonitatem, summam potentiam, a qua omnia ut ficta sunt, ita etiam conservantur, esse numen quod moderetur universa, cui robur sit, et bonitas, ut rependat cuique secundum facta sua. Huiusmodi Dei cognitione et admiratione iam imbutis, si qua Deus praeterea revelaret, hominum ad id vel Angelorum usus ministerio, aut alias instinctu arcano, suum pondus illa, suam autoritatem, ut pronis animis susciperentur, habebant, et fidem inveniebant. Nam simul suo spiritu, quo illi agnoscerent Dei sermonem sibi adferri, in cordibus eorum irradiabat.' R 15.1–18 (Preface).

[1] R 112.E.10–F.10. Compare R 132.D.7–18.   [2] R 323.A.1–B.8.

of superstition among the Gentiles God granted to Gentiles who used baptism and sacrifice piously those things for which they were divinely instituted, just as he did to the Jews.[1] The ceremonies of Jew and Gentile are linked to the Christ who is to come. Those who participate in faith share in him, and by faith in him they are justified.[2] Here, where Bucer again makes use of Augustine, the link with the incarnate Christ is made clear and the effectiveness of his death before it happened is related to the doctrine that all things are present with God.

From this general consideration of the relation of Christ to the Gentiles (where the discussion has been anticipated in his earlier writings), we turn to the specific discussion of Greek philosophy in the preface. Here the Gentiles are non-biblical;[3] elsewhere they are more often biblical. Here the treatment is systematic; elsewhere it is more incidental. Here the concern is primarily with doctrine; elsewhere it extends more generally to doctrine, worship, and life.

Bucer compares what is taught by Greek philosophy with what Paul teaches, and finds extensive agreement. In the former he finds, among other things, that God created the world by his goodness and rules it by his providence, that he attends to man's salvation and requires from him righteousness, that man is depraved and is not able to become like the image of God without God's inspiration, that virtues are the gifts of God, and that the chief virtue is to love one's neighbour.[4] Bucer can even say that all that was necessary to salvation was revealed to the Gentiles.[5] Behind this concern to reconcile philosophy and theology lies the conviction that 'God is the God of the Gentiles'[6] and that some of the Gentiles, precisely in Athens, had worshipped (the unknown) God in the midst of idolatry. Underlying his positive evaluation of philosophy are the axioms that whatever is true is

---

[1] R 324.F.3–15, 325.A.12–16. [2] R 323.C.14–324.D.17.
[3] In R 29.39–46 (Preface) the dispersion of the Jews is mentioned as a cause of the bringing of truth to the Gentiles.
[4] R 29.10–37 (Preface). [5] R 33.52–34.2 (Preface).
[6] R 29.5–10 (Preface).

from God (for man is a liar and incapable of the truth) and the constant emphasis on a godly life as being both God's will for men and a sign of God's activity in men.[1]

This view of philosophy should not be presented without the limitations with which Bucer hedged it about. By philosophy he does not mean all philosophy, but what is true (that is, what agrees with the Bible). This it is which is a gift of God, though it is mixed with error.[2] The faith of the philosopher is bound up with opinion, whereas the faith of the Christian is 'from the words of God by the inspiration of the Holy Spirit'.[3] He allows that Gentile prophets were inspired by the Spirit, and that they predicted the coming of Christ, but they were not without error.[4] He does not regard philosophy as having any independent authority; rather it is always to be tested by scripture.[5] (It is, moreover, the Christian who sees that it has all that is necessary to salvation.[6]) Philosophy, he says later in the commentary, cannot 'obtain the favour of God or kindle true zeal for righteousness'.[7]

Salvation is by faith in Christ.[8] This faith is not some undefined faith but is linked to the future death and resurrection of Christ.[9]

---

[1] R 27.52–28.27 (Preface).

[2] 'Hic vero meminisse debemus, aliud esse quod dono Dei hominum imbecillitas admiscuit, aliud ipsum donum. Philosophia Dei donum est, vitiosa administratio, hominum peccatum et error. Nec Philosophiam ilico assecuti sunt, qui Philosophorum se titulo vel ipsi venditarunt, vel ab aliis celebrati sunt. Philosophiae itaque intelligendum non quicquid scriptum reliquerunt qui Philosophi laudantur, sed quod in horum monumentis verum, quod simplex divinisque literis consentaneum deprehenditur. Philosophia, studium sapientiae, non erroris, non inanium deliramentorum dicitur. Sapientia autem est, ut a veteribus Philosophis definitur, rerum divinarum et humanarum, causarumque, quibus eae res continentur, scientia. Lapsus est Plato, quanvis Philosophorum omnium sanctiss. ac ideo certissimus. Aristoteles dum nimio fertur studio ad rationis trutinam omnia exigendi, in foedos se errores praecipitem dedit. Idem usu venit Ciceroni et Senecae: hos enim arbitror Philosophiae principes extare nobis.' R 28.53–29.1 (Preface).

[3] R 21.44–6 (Preface).

[4] R 12.E.11–18.

[5] R 28.47–8 (Preface).

[6] R 33.52–34.2 (Preface).

[7] R 64.E.14–20.

[8] R 64.E.14–20. Compare R 122.D.17–E.1.

[9] 'Since there is no other name under heaven given unto men whereby we must be saved, God has decreed faith in him for all men, raising him from the dead. Therefore without that faith, that is, without faith in the one mediator between

In a similar way Bucer links heathen sacrifices to the Christ who is to come.[1] This suggests some sensitivity to the most obvious weakness in his discussion of Greek philosophy—his failure to relate it adequately to God's revelation in Christ. This failure seems the more surprising in the commentary, where, it has been held,[2] he first does justice to the relation between faith and the death of Christ.

The reason, therefore, may not lie simply in an inadequate grasp of the person and the work of Christ. It may lie rather in the purpose that Bucer has in mind. If his purpose is, as Strohl suggests, the encouraging of humanist studies, then too severe a critique of philosophy would clearly not achieve his end.[3] Such a purpose would also account for some of the difference in tone between the discussion in the preface and the references to Gentile religion and philosophy in the commentary proper, and indeed in Bucer's earlier writings. It is in keeping with various passing references elsewhere, where he commends Gentile writings,[4] and suggests why at this point (and nowhere else) he examines this particular issue.[5] His treatment need not therefore be explained as the relic of a mystical[6] or humanist[7] influence, though there may be such influences in his theology.

> God and men, the man Christ Jesus—without faith, I say, in his resurrection which God decreed for men, which assuredly without his incarnation and death cannot truly be believed—without faith, therefore, in the incarnation, and death, and resurrection of Christ, Christian truth does not doubt that the righteous of old (granting that they were righteous) could not have been cleansed from their sins and justified by the grace of God. [This holds] both in the case of those righteous men whom scripture commemorates, and in the case of those righteous men whom indeed it does not commemorate. Nevertheless, however, they must be believed to have existed even before the flood, or from then up to the giving of the law, or at the time of the law itself, not only amongst the sons of Israel, as the prophets were, but also outside that people, as Job was.' R 199.C.10–200.D.6.

[1] R 30.19–27 (Preface).　　　　[2] Lang, *op. cit.* p. 324, and Itti, *op. cit.* p. 38.
[3] See p. 121, n. 2.　　　　[4] Compare P 11.B.22–C.14.
[5] Bucer's discussion here is, of course, dependent also on what Paul says in Rom. 1:19–20.
[6] Lang, *op. cit.* pp. 338–9.
[7] Müller, *op. cit.* pp. 70–1, and Strohl, *Bucer, humaniste chrétien*, pp. 17–35.

Whatever the explanation of this section of the preface, it should be seen in the total context of Bucer's understanding of the relation of the Holy Spirit to Christ. There is, it is true, an inadequate grasp of history and a certain lack of theological depth in his discussion of the person and work of Christ. This is certainly not the dominant note in his theology. Nevertheless, it does not lie on the circumference. Christ and the Holy Spirit are not vague and unrelated descriptions of God. Christ is essentially the incarnate Word, who is at the same time the eternal Word and mediator between God and man. The Holy Spirit is the Spirit who proceeds not alone from the Father, but essentially from the Father and the Son.

6

THE BIBLE—THE WRITTEN WORD

It is in his debate with catholic opponents of the reformation that Bucer develops his understanding of the Bible. His view emerges clearly in his early writings (*Summary*, *Dass D. Luthers Lehr*, and *Against Treger*) and is maintained without any fundamental change in his later works.

For Bucer the Bible is alone authoritative in all that concerns salvation. Its authority comes from the Holy Spirit who wrote it and who interprets it. Those who have this Spirit can understand it, and learn from it all that is necessary for salvation. For those who lack the Spirit, however learned they may be, it is a dead book. The Christian in reading it, and the scholar in interpreting it, need to pray for the guidance and understanding of the same Spirit who inspired those who wrote it. If they do this, they will be instructed, and will be able to instruct others, to salvation.

THE HOLY SPIRIT AS THE AUTHOR OF THE BIBLE

In an immense variety of ways the Holy Spirit is described as the author of scripture. 'It is written by the Holy Spirit.'[1] It is written at his command.[2] In it he gives things their proper names.[3] He is the true author, so that Matthew in writing his gospel is really only 'an instrument and, as it were, an amanuensis'.[4] He is said to 'use hyperbole'[5] or to have 'written through Paul'.[6] He is the author of the psalms, 'as of the whole of scripture'.[7] Indeed the psalms are the heavenly melody of the Holy Spirit.[8]

---

[1] BW 1.83.25–84.3.   [2] BW 1.121.27–8, 130.19–20.
[3] BW 1.205.16–21, 210.8–17. The reference is to holy communion.
[4] 3.A.11–16; 2.A.18–21; 3.B.5–10.   [5] J 497.4–8.
[6] OB 15.77.26–7.   [7] P 6.B.48–7.A.2 (Preface).
[8] P 276.C.13–17, not in the 1529 edition (334.A).

The Holy Spirit and the Word

The Holy Spirit is the author of the whole Bible, but this does not mean that there is no variety in his expression. In the fifth book of the psalms he is said to sing 'more sweetly, clearly, and familiarly'.[1] He is also described as showing infinite skill in Paul's writings, but especially in Romans.[2]

The Bible is, however, not directly written by the Holy Spirit. It is written by men whom he uses as his amanuenses.[3] This human side of the writing of the Bible emerges primarily in the commentaries. The authors are inspired by the Holy Spirit. They are like the prophets who wrote and spoke 'out of the secret, but certain revelation of God'.[4] The nature of this inspiration is never discussed, but, as a result of it, the Bible is the only book which teaches the will of God and godliness without being corrupted by human inventions. It alone is preserved without error—whereas what is of men is darkness and not light:

...the saints are nourished and enlivened, they can be equipped from no other source than from the divine books, because no other books exist that, without the inventions of man's mind, teach God's goodness and his will and thereby true godliness. For the dregs of nature still so cling to the saints, that whatever is, as it were, transmitted by their minds cannot but drag in some filth. For, so that he might retain for himself the right to be the only one to teach us outwardly as well as inwardly, although he has granted to many to teach an abundance of excellent things, the Holy Spirit, nevertheless, has reserved for his own canonical writings alone this prerogative—that without any sprinkling of error or any illusion they discourse on the divine works, from which may be learnt both the power and the goodness of God

[1] P 276.A.15–16.
[2] 'For truly the skill of the Holy Spirit is without limit. [This is true] indeed in all the writings of this apostle, but in this epistle it stands out with such great splendour and wonder, as are not equalled in any other. May the same Spirit who dictated these things and who has with such divine reason lifted up his treasure in them, give us a mind to [grasp] this treasure of his and with true religion to turn to these mysteries which have never been sufficiently pondered, so that, at last, rightly informed about the immense goodness and mercy of God towards us, we may dedicate and consecrate ourselves wholly to him.' R 429.C. 12–16.
[3] 3.A.11–16; 2.A.18–21; 3.B.5–10.   [4] Z 2.A.4–9.

which leads to the certain increase of godliness and blessedness. And they depict them so graphically that [by comparison] whatever the minds of men have transmitted on these matters is darkness and not light.[1]

Inspiration by the Holy Spirit certainly does not mean an overriding of the human authors. Thus Bucer allows that in Romans there may be imperfections of style. They are, however, due to the message and Paul's feeling for it.[2] Yet at the same time there cannot be mere tautology in his writing, whatever there may appear to be, for he is an instrument of the Holy Spirit and when he repeats things it is 'because we do not yet rightly comprehend them'.[3] Again, Bucer accepts that in the gospels there are errors in transcription,[4] a keeping to the sense rather than to the exact words of a quotation,[5] differences of order in

[1] Z 2.B.1–16 (Preface).

[2] 'Postremo ad quos, eos scilicet, qui huc essent adducendi, ut in cruce domini nostri Iesu Christi, omnem et salutem et gloriam ponerent, satis liquet, quod decuerit Paulum sermonis humilitas, et ea ratio, qua sicut adflatum spiritus, ita neglectum inanis cultus, quem caro admiratur, praeseferret, tum ostenderet rem quam commendat, maxime popularem, et omnibus qui modo eam cupiant, perceptu facilem, denique artem hic tradi, qua toti immutamur, et divinam quandam vivendi rationem consequimur. Atqui ista tamen dictionis in Paulo humilitas sic habet, ut quicunque potis est divinam hanc doctrinam intelligere, in singulis quoque eius verbis, si modo animum advertat, caelestem effulgere sapientiam cernat. Ex Spiritu sancto Apostolus scripsit, imo haec ipse omnia scripsit Paulo usus tanquam organo, nihil ergo hic frustra dicitur, nihil non suo loco, nihil non rei congruens, eoque apposite. Sunt alicubi, ut videtur carni, Anapodota, sunt Hyperbata, sunt Mioses, Tautologiae, Homoeologiae, Macrologiae, Pleonasmi, Anoeconometa, et alia quae inter vitia orationis numerantur. At si tu probe consideres, ut soleant loqui ii, qui sunt vehementer affecti, maxime qui tractant divina, quid deceat Evangelium Christi, et illo quidem tempore, in quo omnia testari debuerunt, virtute Christi, nullis humanis praesidiis omnia geri tum expendas diligenter, quo in loco, qua ratione admissa illa sunt, quae habentur orationis vitia, procul dubio dices, meras virtutes esse, non vitia quae videbantur, arcanamque in his Dei sapientiam mirari satis haudquaquam poteris.' R 38.34–51 (Preface).

Compare Bucer's comment in *Quomodo*: 'In this epistle (2 Corinthians) he burns and glows with such heat, that he has written hardly anything more disordered and for that reason more difficult to understand.' Q 13.3–4.

[3] R 211.A.4–7.

[4] 11.B.25–12.A.8; 4.D.3–7; 10.C.12–17.

[5] 26.A.2–B.18; 9.C.6–31; 21.B.1–22.C.1.

various narratives,[1] and differences of times and persons in a given story.[2]

These factual or historical differences can be reconciled with each other, so that they do not imply any unreliability in the Bible. Indeed, ultimately all differences need to be reconciled if the Holy Spirit is the author, for clearly he cannot contradict himself.[3] The most notable attempt to reconcile seemingly contradictory passages of scripture is to be found in the great theological *conciliationes* of *Romans*. In them Bucer seeks to hold together paradoxical sentences from different parts of the Bible.[4] He expresses this same underlying conviction, that all parts of the Bible can and should be reconciled with each other, fourteen years later, when he says that James obviously uses 'justification' in the second of the two senses he has adduced, otherwise he would contradict Paul.[5]

The books of the Bible are intended for us, but they are not, therefore, timeless books of the Spirit. They are determined in various ways by the situations in which they were written. Thus Paul uses the Septuagint because it was familiar to the faithful,[6]

---

[1] 165.A.17–23; 53.C.10–14; 133.A.21–5.

[2] 322.B.10–323.B.18; 187.A.16–B.20; 479.A.10–B.22; and 190.B.16–191. A.25; 70.C.5–27; 727.A.15–B.12.

[3] This view is clearly formulated in EE 62.E.2–5, where Bucer says that all words of God have the same authority, and are equally to be believed on account of the authority of the one who speaks. This is Bucer's clear conviction from first to last.

[4] Erasmus also used the method of putting scriptural antitheses together. This became a feature of radical apologetic, as for instance in Sebastian Franck's *Book of the Seven Seals* (1539).

[5] EE 62.F.3–7, 16–63.A.1, 15–16. His reference to James in *St Matthew*, omitted in 1530 and 1536, is uncharacteristic. 'Ad haec Epistola Jacobi, ut apud veteres sanctos nunquam id ponderis habuit, ita neque apud ullos scientia pietatis recte praeditos habebit, ut cum reliquis divinae scripturae libris conferri, debeat, nedum sententias in illis positas infirmare, aut ad alieniorem interpretationem pertrahere.' 205.A.15–20; 67.B.9; 170.D.2.

In theory all parts of scripture have equal weight, for they come from the same author. Although one may be interpreted in terms of another, it is not to be rejected in favour of the other. At the same time Bucer can advise a concentration on the New Testament, as Christ is more clearly discerned there than in the Old Testament. Q 3.1–11.   [6] R 475.B.12–14.

though Bucer has hard things to say about the Septuagint[1] in comparison with the Hebrew text of the Old Testament, which 'the Holy Spirit dictated'.[2] Furthermore, Paul could have stopped writing at Rom. 12, if there had not been, among other things, false views of the state which needed to be dealt with.[3] This sense of the Bible, as bound to a particular time and situation, needs to be borne in mind when considering passages in Bucer, which suggest that the Bible was written primarily for us, to instruct us in faith and love. It was written by the Holy Spirit at different times through different men—men, however, who were children of God and who wrote at the inspiration of the Spirit.[4]

THE AUTHORITY OF THE BIBLE

The authority of the Bible is inseparably bound up with its authorship. In the *Summary* Bucer says that what is not in keeping with the apostolic writings is of the spirit of anti-Christ, for the apostolic writings are from the Spirit of God.[5] In the debate with Treger this point is developed. The Bible is 'nothing but the word of the Spirit of God'.[6] Those who wrote it were especially instruments of the Holy Spirit. For that reason what they have written is 'a certain rule of faith for those who love truth'.[7]

As the Bible is written by the Holy Spirit, we can be certain of the Holy Spirit there, but not elsewhere. We cannot be certain of the Holy Spirit in a council as we can in the Bible, for a council consists of men, even if they happen all to be Peter.[8] 'If our teaching and preaching is against the divine scripture, it is devilish, even if we were to have every council for us. If it is from the scripture, then it is divine, even if every council were against us.'[9] Someone who is sent by God does not preach differently from scripture, for scripture is nothing but the word of the Spirit of

---

1 P 6.A.26–30 (Preface). 2 P 216.D.20–1.
3 R 7.13–30 (Preface). 4 BW 1.86.20–5.
5 BW 1.87.6–8. 6 BW 2.137.3–5.
7 BW 2.80.27–34. 8 BW 2.83.29–37.
9 BW 2.160.26–9.

God.[1] The Bible is the sole outward criterion, and every judgment of the church must accord with it.[2] By it heretics are to be refuted. In this 'the elect will recognise the voice of their shepherd', and the rest will be dumbfounded.[3]

This affirmation of the authority of scripture over against the authority of the church raises the question of the relation of the church to the Bible—the problem, that is, of the canon of scripture, the understanding of scripture, and the interpretation of scripture. In each of these three Bucer asserts the priority of the Holy Spirit over the church. It is not the church that decides the canon of scripture, gives the true understanding of scripture, or authoritatively interprets it, but the Holy Spirit. To these questions we shall return. Here we consider primarily the question of the authority of the scripture.

The Bible is authoritative in all that concerns salvation. By it every doctrine and practice of the church is to be tested, and accordingly accepted or rejected. This idea is first expressed in the *Summary* and is developed with increasing sophistication in the course of the debate with his opponents. To the question, whether we may ask the dead to pray for us, as we ask the living, the answer is simple: to ask prayers of the living is in the Bible, to ask them of the dead is not. What is more, the second is contrary to the Bible, for Christ says that those who abide in him shall ask whatever they will and it shall be done. 'If then', Bucer asks, 'you have all you desire, what more do you want?'[4]

---

[1] BW 2.137.1–6.
[2] 'Every judgment of the church must take place in accordance with scripture, as the only outward criterion. For in scripture everything that is to be believed is amply contained.' BW 2.128.39–41.
[3] BW 2.137.35–138.3.
[4] BW 1.101.13–102.2.

A slightly different emphasis can be discerned when Bucer discusses the intercession of saints in *Romans*. 'Moreover, it is not lawful for us to deny that the saints intercede for us, since this is repugnant to no certain oracle of scripture. But neither can it be obtruded as a certain dogma of the church that the saints intercede for us, since that cannot be deduced from any certain oracle of scripture.' R 414.E.9–12.

It is not, however, simply a question of whether something can be found literally in the Bible. For Bucer, as for Luther, the Bible is about Christ. He is the test. In the epistle of John the readers are told to test the spirits and John gives them a sign which is the sum (*summa summarun*) of all scripture. It is that 'the Spirit who confesses that Jesus Christ has come in the flesh is of God'. By this test any doctrine of works is to be rejected, because it ultimately denies that Christ came in the flesh.[1]

In *Dass D. Luthers Lehr* the grounds for the authority of scripture are developed. Here the implications of 2 Tim. 3:16, a text of central importance for Bucer, are the basis of his argument. As everything good is sufficiently contained in scripture, there is no need of a supplement. Hence, any supplement, whether from the pope or a council, must be of human origin.[2] For Bucer, in any case, the inspiration of the Bible is different from the inspiration of other books. It was in a particular and limited period. Therefore, what is taught by those who lived later, whoever they are, must be tested by the Bible.[3] Moreover, no other book teaches so well trust in God and love of one's neighbour,[4] which he regards as the heart of the Bible and the Christian life.

Nevertheless, the authority of the Bible does not stand alone. It is linked with the Spirit. In *Against Treger* the Bible is indeed the criterion (*Richtschnur*) by which something is judged, but the Holy Spirit is the judge (*Richter*).[5] It is by the word and the Spirit that we can tell if something is to be believed—by the word which is contained in scripture and by the Spirit who gives under-

---

[1] BW 1.84.4-35.

[2] BW 1.313.24-314.2.

[3] 'It is a common saying of the ancients, such as Origen, Jerome, Hilary, Augustine, and in general of all of them, that the holy scripture has its time and appointed end. What was written afterwards, however learned and holy the people were who wrote it, one should not believe simply because they said it. But everything should be evaluated by the holy scripture.' BW 1.312.15-21.

[4] BW 1.315.25-8.

[5] 'Therefore to the scriptures, to the scriptures, to the scriptures! They are the rule and criterion. But the judge is the Holy Spirit (1 Cor. 2). He is the judge on earth. There is then no Christ on earth, for the Spirit of God dwells in all Christians.' BW 2.152.10-14. Compare BW 2.138.39-41.

standing. Moreover, the Spirit is possessed by all those who are Christ's.[1]

In later writings the authority of the Bible is affirmed in new contexts and new situations, but the way it is understood remains largely unchanged. It is invoked in varied questions of church order, worship, and doctrine, generally without any wooden literalism. Thus in *Grund und Ursach* Bucer allows that the elevation of the host in the mass may be kept for a while if it is used in faith. It has been kept in Strasbourg for the weak, as they saw it to stand for the elevation of Christ on the cross. Nevertheless, the ministers have industriously preached God's word, so that the people will eventually see that it is best not to have it.[2] Bucer had a similar attitude to ceremonies, despite his strong opposition to them.[3]

The authority of the Bible is asserted not only against the authority of the church but also against the authority of all men, however godly they may be. In *St Matthew* he attacks those who follow a teacher (Luther presumably is meant) rather than the Holy Spirit and the Bible:

They say, indeed, that they follow God's word, but if you ask how they know it be to God's word, if they reply truly, they say, 'because he, even he (vel ille) has taught in this way'. 'We know', they say, 'that he teaches nothing except the truth of the scripture...' What are they doing now but making God out of a man and relying on the authority of a man in place of the testimony of the Holy Spirit in their hearts? That is undoubtedly the reason why everywhere, in so great a throng of evangelicals, there appears no fruit of true faith and a sincere gospel. For it is human opinion, not the Spirit of God, that makes them evangelicals.[4]

---

[1] BW 2.93.38–94.7.   [2] BW 1.219.3–18.

[3] This attitude reveals his conviction that the abolition of externals does not betoken a victory for the gospel, unless a true worship of the Spirit takes their place. It may also spring from his view that what is not in scripture is not necessarily forbidden. This is in marked contrast to an anabaptist view such as that of Grebel, when he finds that Müntzer has introduced the singing of hymns into his German mass. Grebel writes: 'Whatever we are not taught by clear passages or examples must be regarded as forbidden, just is if it were written: "This do not: sing not."' L.C.C. xxv, p. 75.

[4] 275.A.11–B.6; 171.A.2–15; 440.D.7.

A few months later, in his *Getrewe Warnung*, he attacks those who want to be guided by the Holy Spirit without the Bible.[1] Denck does not want to bind the Holy Spirit to the Bible. But, for Bucer, whoever will not have his teaching judged by the Bible cannot have good teaching.[2] The Bible is always the authority against which every human understanding must be tested. By it, all personal revelations, whether dreams[3] or the inner word,[4] are to be judged.

Bucer can speak appreciatively of pagan philosophers and of what can be learned from their writings.[5] In *Psalms* he says they are not to be despised. We should admire them in what concerns honest living, as well as in the mechanical arts, for 'the voice of Christ is whatever is true'.[6] Whoever totally rejects them 'despises the words of God'.[7] But, in saying this, Bucer does not set up any rival to the Bible, which remains pre-eminent.[8] The view expressed in *Zephaniah* a year earlier remains unchanged. It is that there is no book other than the Bible which teaches goodness and the will of God and godliness without the intrusion of man's ideas. It alone is preserved without error.[9] Only in it can the knowledge of God 'rightly be sought, and fully be perceived'.[10]

The later writings, from the middle of the thirties, show a more positive view of the church and the fathers. The prominence Bucer gives to the fathers in *Romans* indicates how he defers to their judgment. He can even say, in the discussion of election, that he hates novelty, seeks only the true meaning of scripture, and

---

[1] BW 2.235.10–12.
[2] BW 2.238.12–24. Already in *St Matthew* he has described the anabaptists as placing so much confidence in their own spirits that they despise the scriptures. 176.A.1–B.2; 137.B.14–C.2; 350.C.16–D.9.
[3] J 497.18–26.
[4] V E.3.B.21–32.
[5] There is a striking parallel with John Wesley here. Wesley can, at one and the same time, tell his preachers and others that they are to be men of one book, and prescribe for them a course of reading, which covers geography, logic, ethics, natural science, history, metaphysics, poetry, and divinity. *The Works of John Wesley*, XII, pp. 244 ff.
[6] P 11.B.22–C.14.
[7] P 11.C.15–D.4.
[8] P 11.C.15–21.
[9] Z 2.B.1–16 (Preface).
[10] Z 2.B.16–22 (Preface).

defers to the fathers and the authority of the primitive church.[1] But they never have any independent standing alongside the Bible. They are always brought to the judgment of scripture. This is abundantly demonstrated in the *Bestendige Verantwortung*[2] where he is in renewed conflict with catholic opponents. The Bible alone, he asserts, contains all that is necessary to salvation. The fathers must be tested by it, as indeed they themselves tested traditions by scripture.[3] With the fathers there is the added disadvantage, in comparison with the Bible, that one has to draw from all their writings. There is no single book, as with the Bible.[4]

The Bible is the only certain word of the Holy Spirit over against every human word, of theologian or philosopher, of church father or church council. Moreover, in it the Holy Spirit has given all that is necessary to salvation. Here lies its authority—that it is from the Holy Spirit and is sufficient for salvation.

EXTRA-BIBLICAL REVELATION

There is, however, one passage in Bucer where the sufficiency of the Bible seems to be questioned. This example in Bucer's *Gospels* is cited by Lang in his *Der Evangelienkommentar Martin Butzers*.[5]

In a discussion of demons, Bucer seems to imply a knowledge that is to be found outside scripture. He says: 'But to anyone for whom it is of some importance to have more knowledge and more certain knowledge of these matters, either for his own salvation or for that of others to whom he must minister, the Lord will

---

[1] R 528.E.11–F.1. This comes no doubt in part from his more detailed study of the fathers. But it is also a two-edged sword against his catholic and radical opponents. Against the first he needed to show that his views were in keeping with what the ancient church taught, and not simply his private interpretation of the Bible. Against the second he was forced to give some weight to non-biblical (or only indirectly biblical) arguments in his defence of infant baptism.

[2] The full title of the *Bestendige Verantwortung*, with its reference to the fathers, shows how important they were for him.

[3] BV 3.A.8–13, 7.B.12–13.   [4] BV 8.A.11–25.

[5] Lang, *op. cit.* p. 127.

kindly reveal to him as much as he needs.'[1] This quotation, however, can be understood only in its context and in the context of Bucer's writings up to this point. The immediate context imposes strict limits on the interpretation of the passage. There is not only the marginal summary that reads 'There is to be no inquiring about demons beyond what scripture has handed down', but there is also what comes before and after. Before this quotation Bucer says that the Bible has everything necessary for salvation. After it he urges us not to inquire into matters where we shall not be made better, but to meditate rather the commands which are given, and to order our life according to them. About demons, it is enough 'to know that Christ our Lord conquered them, so that they should not destroy us'.

The quotation itself does not say, and is not meant to say, that there can be something not in the Bible, that is necessary for salvation. This is clear from what precedes it, with its reference to 2 Tim. 3. Moreover, the quotation itself does not speak of what is necessary for salvation, but of what is of importance (*momentum*) to it for any particular person.

The wider context also throws light on this passage. In *Against Treger* he says that what we are to know, beyond what the apostles

---

[1] 'This would be the place to discuss the nature, power, and works of demons, if the scriptures had handed down fuller and clearer information about them. But since scripture teaches everything most fully and clearly which can make us acceptable in God's sight and therefore saved—for it makes the man of God perfect and equips him for every good work (2 Tim. 3)—it follows that a more certain knowledge of demons is of no concern to our salvation and the glory of God which is to be brought to light in us. But to anyone for whom it is of some importance to have more knowledge and more certain knowledge of these matters, either for his own salvation or for that of others to whom he must minister, the Lord will kindly reveal to him as much as he needs. First, therefore, it seems that we must be warned not to examine with more curiosity these or similar passages when it is not clear how we may be made better thereby. But let us meditate rather in the commands of the Lord which have been given to us, so that we may order our life according to them. About demons it will be enough to know that Christ our Lord conquered them, so that they should not destroy us, and to know that they lie in wait for us to draw us into sin; but for that reason with vigilant faith we must resist them and fight against them.' 35.B.27–36.A.20; 92.A.31–B.11; 233.A.11–24.

have explained, God will reveal to us, referring to Phil. 3:15.[1]
This would show that the word reveal is used by Bucer in a quite
general sense, with none of the overtones that the phrase extra-
biblical revelation would suggest.[2]

THE CANON

Bucer, like the other reformers, totally rejects setting the authority
of the church beside or above that of the Bible. The church is not
a separate, independent source of authority. The church is also not
the source of the Bible's authority. For the church did not give
authority to the Bible, but simply recognised it as God's word.

The debate about the canon of scripture is focused in 1523 and
1524. It is hinted at in the *Summary*, where he writes that the
apostles were children of God and wrote by the Holy Spirit, a
fact which is clear 'if we compare their writings with the prophets and the books of Moses, which the Lord himself...calls the
holy scripture'.[3] It is, however, in *Dass D. Luthers Lehr* and in
Against Treger that his views are fully expressed. Here the fundamental point is that the early church recognised what was by the
Holy Spirit 'through the indwelling Spirit of God and by comparison with the scripture of the Old Testament'. This Bucer
compares in *Dass D. Luthers Lehr* with receiving a mandate from
the emperor. The prince who receives such a mandate must
discern whether or not it is from the emperor. If it is not, he must
reject it. If it is, he cannot change it, only obey it.[4]

This idea is developed in the debate with Treger. The church
accepts the Bible as one accepts a mandate from the emperor, for

---

[1] BW 2.62.17–18.
[2] It may be noted that the quotation is also used by Capito—see Johann Martin
Usteri, 'Die Stellung der Strassburger Reformatoren Bucer und Capito zur
Tauffrage', p. 464.
[3] BW 1.86.20–5.
[4] '...But when they have recognised that a mandate is indeed from the emperor,
then it is not for them to alter it in any way, but to comply with it obediently.
They are also in no way over it to make it mean what they like...' BW 1.315.
9–24.

example, by testing its seal. When men are sure of it, they must obey it, for they are under the mandate, not over it. They can no longer judge as they will, but only according to what is written in the mandate.[1] A further comparison is that with a goldsmith and a gold coin. Like a goldsmith judging whether something is gold, the church judges whether or not something is God's word. It does not give to it trustworthiness or authority.[2] The ground for rejecting a book from the Bible is not that it is condemned by the church or a council but that it is 'quite out of keeping with the apostolic faith'.[3] The test applied in the beginning was whether something was in keeping with the law and the prophets (and hence truly of God and written by the Spirit of God). This test was applied under the guidance of the indwelling Spirit of God.[4]

This early discussion on the canon is taken up twenty years later in *Bestendige Verantwortung*. The *Bestendige Verantwortung* is, in a way, a continuation of the same debate against catholic opponents of the reformation, this time in Cologne. Here Bucer pushes his position to the logical conclusion, that each generation must recognise the canon afresh. It is to be accepted not on the authority of the early church (for that would be to make the Bible subservient to the church), but by the test of the word and the Spirit.

[1] BW 2.98.2–10.
[2] 'Dann die schrifft das Gotts wort ist. so ist die Kirch ein gemeyn der menschen, die wol das yhen so ir für das wort Gottes fürgeben würt, zuo urteylen hatt, wie dann alle und yede Christen, indem, das sye erkenne und ortere, ob es Gottswort sey oder nit. aber nit dermassen, das sye ym die glaubwürdigkeit und auctoritet gebe, das also sye über die schrifft zuo halten sey. Wie auch ein goldschmidt erkennt, das ein kronen guldin ist, durch sein urteyl aber macht er sye nitt guldin.' BW 2.99.22–9. Compare EE 43.B.3–12.
[3] BW 2.95.26–96.12.
[4] BW 2.98.23–9.
 The question of the canon of scripture is also discussed in the preface of *Romans*. Again the analogy of the mandate is used. R 19.48–53 (Preface). From this it is argued that the church's role is to recognise and to interpret, but not to change, or to add to or subtract from, the scriptures, much less to constitute them, in the sense of giving them authority: 'Ex his pii et religiosi homines satis intelligent, Ecclesiam habere in Scripturas ius agnoscendi eas, et interpretandi, mutandi autem eas, vel adjiciendi illis, detrahendive haudquaquam, multo minus constituendi eas, quod utique est dare eis autoritatem. Verbum Dei hic est, non hominum, etsi per homines administretur.' R 20.14–44 (Preface).

For he who has been endowed with the Holy Spirit can, through the biblical word and the Holy Spirit, recognise something as a book of God. It is thus that the early church judged, and that every succeeding generation of the church has judged.[1]

THE UNDERSTANDING OF THE BIBLE

Bucer's attack on the authority of the church over against the authority of the Bible is not only an attack on the authority of the church to teach what is not in the Bible. It is also an attack on the authority of the church to grant men an understanding of what is in the Bible. The church (whether in council or through her ministers) does not possess the power to give men a true understanding of the Bible. The Holy Spirit alone can give this understanding, for only the Spirit of God can understand the things of God. The Spirit, however, is not the possession of so-called spiritual persons, that is, priests and monks, but belongs to all Christians.

There are two ideas here. The first derives from the opposition of the Spirit and the flesh. Man, as flesh, cannot understand the things of God; only the Spirit of God can do that.[2] The second arises from the opposition of spiritual (in the sense of a priest) and spiritual (in the biblical sense of someone who possesses the Spirit, be he priest or layman).[3] Both these ideas are present in the *Summary*. The Holy Spirit understands the depths of God, the

---

[1] '...Darumb da der Herr Christus den seinen erstlich mitt mundt die H. Schrifften des Alten Testaments fürgegeben/unnd sie sich deren hielten/habenn sie durch dieselbigen unnd den H. Geist leicht koennen auch underscheiden/ under den Schrifften/so under der Apostel namen herfür bracht wurden/welche ware Apostolische schrifften weren oder nit/Welches vorurtheil der ersten Kirchen/bey den Nachkomenden billich ein gross ansehen gehabt hat/Noch so ist der rechte hauptgrundt dieser erkantnüss bey den nachkomenden Kirchen nicht auff dem vorurtheyl und mundtlichem dargeben der ersten Kirchen gestanden/sonder auff dem gewissen Schrifftlichen Wort Gottes/und der innerlichen Lehre dess H. Geystes/Auss welchem Geyst und Wort auch die nachkomenden Kirchen haben erkennet/dass solche Schrifften warlich Apostolische schrifften/und auss dem Heyligen Geyst fürgegeben seindt nit/weniger dann die erste Kirche solches auss dem vorgeschriebenen wort und Geist erkennet hat.' BV 9.A.9-B.2.

[2] 1 Cor. 2:10-11.   [3] 1 Cor. 2:14-15.

flesh does not.[1] The Christian possesses the Holy Spirit, therefore he may read and judge the scriptures.[2] Bucer does not imply that all men, willy-nilly, have the Spirit and so can understand the scriptures, as Köhler wrongly maintains.[3] This is never his view.[4] In speaking of all men, he is speaking of all Christians as opposed to the few who belong to the ordained ministry of the church.

Those not rejected by God (for those rejected by God are without the Spirit) will not doubt that what they read in the apostles, prophets, and Moses, is of the Holy Spirit.[5] The Christian, however, needs not only to recognise what is in the Bible as of the Holy Spirit, but also to understand what he reads or hears. For such, Bucer's advice is simple:

Pray God the Father through Christ our Saviour for his grace and enlightenment. Do so with firm faith, and you will obtain it and learn sufficiently everything which it is necessary and needful for you to know. The Spirit of God rests on the humble and has a gracious regard for the poor who has a broken spirit and who trembles at the word of God. Even if you are not a priest or monk, have no Latin, and must work day and night, Jesus our Saviour was also a layman; in the eyes of those of the world who were worthy and spiritual (*geistlichen*) he was uneducated and a carpenter. Paul also worked day and night, so that he should not be a burden to anyone. The holy patriarchs and some of the prophets were good and humble shepherds; yet the Spirit of God with his highest gifts dwelt in them richly. Without doubt the same will also happen to you, if only you will pray to the Father for such a Spirit with an eager and believing heart.[6]

In *Dass D. Luthers Lehr* and *Against Treger* the same basic point is made and the same much-quoted text (1 Cor. 2:10–15) used.[7]

---

[1] BW 1.97.5–8.   [2] BW 1.83.12–17, 84.14–19.

[3] Köhler, *op. cit.* p. 89. He quotes BW 1.82.20–1, ignoring the context, especially the exposition in the following paragraph.

[4] Indeed he says in *St John* in a discussion of Nicodemus that, where the Spirit of God does not teach, those most learned in the scriptures are stupefied at divine things. 74.A.9–14; 25.B.16–19; 623.B.11–15.

[5] BW 1.88.6–11.   [6] BW 1.85.11–24.

[7] The essential role of the Holy Spirit is underlined when Bucer writes: 'Otherwise, although we may have the scriptures and the church as well, even Christ

In *Dass D. Luthers Lehr*, moreover, he introduces the idea of the clarity of scripture. Some points, it is true, are not clear because we have forgotten how the Bible expresses itself; moreover the Bible has been hidden from people for a long time. But we have so many clear passages that anyone who takes these and has true faith will understand everything else 'as far as is necessary for his salvation, and for that of others whom he must teach'.[1] This idea is developed further in the *Bestendige Verantwortung*. There, in the context of 2 Tim. 3, Bucer argues that, if the Holy Spirit is the best master and writer, how would he make what he has written so dark and confused that his children could not learn his will from it, but only from the universal church. That, he insists, is not how a father writes a letter for his children.[2]

The claim that the Christian can understand the Bible does not mean that he understands everything in the Bible, but rather that he can understand all that concerns his salvation. In this crucial matter Christians do not err.[3] Even among those possessing the Holy Spirit there may be disagreement on inessentials, just as the apostles disagreed on laws and ceremonies.[4] But in the central matter of man's salvation the Holy Spirit gives understanding and can give it to any man. For this reason, the Christian in reading the Bible should first pray for the understanding which the Holy Spirit alone can give, for he is the author of scripture.[5] It is the

---

himself bodily as preacher, if the Spirit does not at the same time (*damit*) teach inwardly, then we remain indeed completely without understanding, as happened to the Pharisees and Sadducees, who heard Christ himself expound the scriptures.' BW 2.83.18–22.

[1] BW 1.312.29–313.8.
[2] BV 15.B.39–16.A.40. Similarly in EE 8.E.16–F.2 he describes the Bible as a letter from God which is not obscure or ambiguous. The obscurity is not in the letter, but in the reader.
[3] BW 2.62.24–31 and 141.21–142.31.
[4] PR A.7.A.12–26. In the *Gospels* he says that there are many things that we shall not understand in this life, but that we are to pray that the Holy Spirit may persuade us of the basic things: that God is Father, Christ the Redeemer, and that there is no other life to be lived than that lived by his Spirit, by whom all things are best administered. 221.A.3; 80.D.27–81.A.17; 752.D.24–753.A.19. This position is also affirmed in BV 16.B.10–25.
[5] P 247.D.12–14.

same Spirit who inspired Paul, who must inspire Bucer as a commentator and those who read his commentary:

> Therefore with me, Christian reader, pray Christ earnestly that he may inspire us who labour in such a great matter by the same Spirit, by whom he made his inspired apostle write these things for us, so that our exposition may serve the saints for the same purpose for which these apostolic writings themselves were given to us.[1]

In this context the task of the commentator is simply to remove the veil for weak eyes (for example, difficulties in language and phraseology). Thus he will show 'a little of those infinite treasures of heavenly wisdom'. But whoever desires this wisdom will need the Holy Spirit, who can show far more than any mortal man.[2] It is not the commentator who is important, but the Holy Spirit. The words of scripture 'are dead and can teach nothing, when the Spirit of Christ is absent, who alone leads into all truth'.[3] What is needed is for Christ by the Holy Spirit to open the minds (or hearts) of those who hear or read, as he did with the disciples on the way to Emmaus.[4]

Valuable as the work of the commentator is, it cannot for Bucer equal that of the translator, though in practice the two are hardly to be separated. The simple unlearned Christian might dispense with commentaries, he cannot dispense with a translation.[5] If he cannot read the Bible in the language of the Holy Spirit, he must read it in his own language. The study of languages is essential, therefore, for a true understanding of the Bible and its preservation from error. This problem is referred to in his first biblical work, the *Psalter*, and Bucer's views develop in the course of his

---

[1] R 221.B.7–11. Compare R 232.F.4–9.
[2] P 7.B.9–14.
[3] P 88.B.22–C.19. This can be seen in the birth of Christ. The Pharisees, who knew where Christ was to be born, ought to have outstripped the Magi in their search for him. For them, however, the Bible was letter, for they lacked the Spirit. 'Where faith is absent, where the Father does not draw, Christ is not known...' and 'whatever is read, spoken, or heard about him is dead.' 25.A.15–25; 9.B.8–14; 20.D.25–21.A.6.   [4] EE 10.D.6–14.
[5] The commentaries of Bucer, written in Latin, were scarcely destined for the simple, uneducated Christian.

controversy with the anabaptists. In the *Psalter* he writes that the apostles were taught by the Holy Spirit, for they had no time to learn from men. We, by contrast, have time and teachers. Therefore, if we do not make use of the biblical languages we will fall into error—indeed God will plague us with error.[1] In *Ephesians* he attacks those who want to learn everything from the Spirit. God, he argues, does not teach us by a miracle any more than feed us by a miracle. We have to prepare food, similarly we have to prepare by study.[2]

Bucer can even express the hope in the *Psalms* (in a passage where realism gives way to enthusiasm) that Hebrew should be taught in every town, so that men could read directly what the Holy Spirit dictated, and enter into its meaning.[3] He does not, however, expect all men to be able to do this, though he does expect those who teach to know Hebrew, so that they can hear the Holy Spirit in his own language.[4] This knowledge of the biblical languages is necessary so that the Bible can keep its sacred authority. Without it human inventions would take the place of the divine oracles.[5]

The necessity of a knowledge of the biblical languages is not a denial of the fact that a true understanding of the Bible can come only from the Holy Spirit.[6] The languages are the tool the Holy

---

[1] BW 2.190.6–16.   [2] E 6.A.26–B.6.
[3] P 216.D.16–24.   [4] P 4.B.42–7 (Preface).
[5] 'I also wish the authority of the scriptures to be safe. I wish the way to be closed, so that no one may obtrude his own inventions in place of the oracles of scripture. But we shall not obtain these things until not only in those cities in which Pope Clement has commanded it, but also in all the sacred colleges Hebrew literature is taught, and for that reason there are many who understand the scripture in its own language—though not if, having tried to express the words of scripture, we obscure both the words and meanings by sticking superstitiously to [their original] cases and figures of speech.' P 5.B.14–20 (Preface).
[6] Bucer has to defend the study of languages against those who neglect them and say that the letter kills, that knowledge puffs up, that the Spirit will be given, and that the apostles were but the simplest of men. He argues that God will not let his own perish, but that at the same time he wishes them to work and not to live by another person's bread. Thus Bucer holds that God will teach the elect all things, but that they are also to apply themselves with all their strength. 100.A.23–B.21; 33.B.8–24; 80.D.14–81.A.7.

Spirit has used, and he it is who gives a knowledge of them, sometimes indeed by a miracle. They are not necessary for a person to be a Christian. They are necessary, however, in a Christian teacher, and form, therefore, a kind of bridge between the understanding of the Bible and its interpretation.

THE INTERPRETATION OF THE BIBLE

In *Das ym selbs* the Bible is mentioned with the assumption that it would be understood.[1] There is no mention of the Holy Spirit in interpreting or understanding it. In the *Summary* and the other early works, however, Bucer discusses the problem of understanding and interpreting the Bible. The word understanding is used here in the sense of recognising that the Bible is the word of God and grasping in it what is necessary for salvation. This is open to all men by the gift of the Holy Spirit. There is, beyond this simple understanding of the Bible available through the Holy Spirit to every Christian, a further understanding which is not necessarily available to all. For this further understanding the word interpretation is used. It stands for the whole science of biblical exposition. It is the concern of the Christian teacher, rather than of the Christian layman.[2]

In his debate with Treger Bucer first wrestles with this problem, though already in the *Summary* he has enunciated the principle that the sum of all scripture is Christ come in the flesh, with the implication that this is itself a denial of any doctrine of works.[3] Now he insists on what is for him a fundamental element in his interpretation of scripture, that is, that scripture is to be interpreted by scripture, for 'no prophecy in scripture is a matter of one's own interpretation'.[4] When men prophesied it was by the impulse of the Holy Spirit. The Holy Spirit, therefore, as the author of scripture, is himself the interpreter of what he has

[1] BW 1.67.4–11.
[2] Bucer does not distinguish the words understanding and interpretation. They are, however, used here to distinguish two elements in his theology.
[3] BW 1.84.4–35.   [4] BW 2.59.4–10.

written. Together with this principle, there is what amounts to Bucer's summary of the Bible in terms of faith and love. He says that the church cannot err in interpreting the chief matter, that we are saved by Christ alone,[1] and that the sum of the law is love from a pure heart.[2] He also makes the distinction between commands as bound to a particular time and those given for all time.[3] All these principles are developed by Bucer in his commentaries, as he seeks to interpret the Bible.[4]

The controversy with catholic opponents of the reformation at Strasbourg found expression in *Grund und Ursach*, and there a further principle emerges, which illuminates the relation between the Old Testament and the New Testament. The Old Testament is the shadow of the New Testament and is to be interpreted from the New Testament.[5] The tearing down of altars in the Old Testament is understood in the light of the New Testament command to preach to the heathen. Thus Paul does the second of these, but not the first, in Athens.[6] Similarly, Moses is to be interpreted in terms of Christ and the command of love.[7]

It is in the commentaries, however, that Bucer's working out and application of his principles of interpretation is most clearly seen. In *St Matthew* comes the distinction of the sense of a passage from the mere words that make it up—a distinction used to defend

---

[1] BW 2.141.37–142.6.   [2] BW 2.59.4–10.

[3] BW 2.158.16–24.

[4] The summary of the law in the command of love throws light on all the commands of the Bible. It is the principle that guides Bucer in distinguishing what is temporary and what is permanent in a command. What is permanent is what concerns faith and love. This applies to everyone in every situation. What is temporary is what belongs peculiarly to the historical situation in which the command was spoken. 73.A.1–74.A.25, 81.A.15–23; 103.D.27–104.B.14, 27.C.14–20; 262.D.10–263.B.19, 629.A.13–18. Compare Z 8.A.11–22 and R 249.A.16–B.16.

[5] BW 1.253.5–12. The Old Testament can also throw light on the New Testament. In the discussion of divorce in *De Regno Christi* he argues that what is allowed in the Old Testament is clearly not regarded as adultery in the New Testament. OB 15.177.10–13. What was permitted then remains valid today, as we experience the same infirmity now under the gospel of grace, as they did then. OB 15.185.5–23.

[6] BW 1.224.3–23.   [7] BW 1.224.3–6.

Matthew's not using the exact words of a quotation.[1] Another especially important principle is that all scripture applies to Christ, including passages that are not historically prophesied of him.[2] This view should not be isolated, however, from Bucer's use of typology and his opposition to allegory.

These various principles are for Bucer not simply his own ideas; they are scriptural principles and, therefore, the Holy Spirit's way of interpreting what he has written. Thus the distinction of the sense of a passage from the mere words that make it up is a distinction the biblical authors make. Paul, in Eph. 4:8, says that Christ gave gifts to men, whereas Ps. 68 says that he received gifts from men. Bucer defends this liberty of interpretation as keeping to the sense of the Bible, that Christ must give before he can receive gifts from men.[3] In *Zephaniah* there is a lengthy development of this principle. It is linked with the idea of interpreting scripture by scripture. This time it is a case of interpreting a passage by the whole purpose of the Bible—love of one's neighbour from a pure heart. The person who is a son of God and not just a servant can understand what is said and why it is said. Therefore he does not stick to the letter of a text, as a slave of the letter does. The important thing is not the sense which the given words may seem to show, but the sense which the person who

---

[1] 26.A.2–B.18; 9.C.6–31; 21.B.1–22.C.1.
   This principle is one that Bucer uses in debate with the anabaptists. On the basis of a saying like 'Resist not him that is evil' they deny that the magistrate who exercises the power of the sword is a Christian. Bucer, in replying to this, refers to the use made of scriptural quotations in Christ's temptation to jump from the pinnacle of the temple. On the basis of that example he states that 'they act impiously who, neglecting the analogy of faith and not considering at the same time other passages of scripture, stick to the letters alone'. 100.B.22–101. A.15; 33.B.25–C.10; 81.A.8–22. In a discussion of divorce Bucer argues that, like Christ, we should not stick to the words (*elementis*) of a text, but consider various passages, to find out what corresponds to God's institution. 228.A.12–18; 154.A.1–5; 399.A.9–13. The importance of the analogy of faith is also stressed in P 6.B.12–17 (Preface).

[2] 34.A.10–35.B.12; 11.D.19–12.B.13; 27.A.15–28.D.1.

[3] E 84.A.14–19. This example occurs elsewhere, notably in EE 105.C.10–12 where Bucer says that Paul keeps the sense or purpose of the passage, which is more important than mere words.

spoke or wrote wished. The discovering of this is possible only for someone who is guided by the Spirit:

Now an oath can also be demanded from those of whose faith there is no doubt, so that a law that is useful to many may not be weakened on account of the few who have no need of it. Those who cling to these things do not consider the whole doctrine of God and the analogy of faith, but cling absurdly to the letter, in one or two places neglecting the phrasing and use of words. But where the Spirit is, there is freedom, and something is not done or avoided for the sole reason that it is read in the divine word, but because it is pleasing or displeasing to God, and is recognised for certain as of advantage or disadvantage to one's neighbour—and that by the testimony of the Holy Spirit's persuading the heart. Nor does it befit us now, under Christ, to be moved by the Spirit of fear into slavery, but we should be led by the Spirit of sons into freely-given love, seeing that there is always agreement with this not only in the precept, but also in the reason for the precept. Yet I do not mean that I recognise as the good Spirit, one who departs from the letter of scripture in such a way that he affirms things that are contradictory. But I wish the man who does not allow himself to be taken into captivity by one or two places, rather to turn his mind with care to the whole of scripture, and especially to its purpose and aim, which is love from a pure heart. And since it is universally acknowledged that nothing else is required of us except that a man serve his neighbour to the glory of God, let him always be able to give a reason for what he thinks must be done or avoided, other than 'Scripture says so'. We are not slaves, but sons and friends, whom it befits to do everything from certain knowledge of the good of our neighbours and thence also of the glorification of God. Those who study this, and sincerely seek the glory of God, will devise nothing contrary to the scriptures, even though sometimes to the more unlearned they may seem to depart from the words of scripture. Christ forbade us to call someone father on earth, and this slave of the letter will not suffer himself to be called father by his children, and will thus condemn scripture which in many places deems him worthy of that name. But the freedom of the Spirit will consider that Christ was not at all troubled about that title, but rather that he taught that we should seek our true Father and inheritance in heaven...But what reason could a man give for making it a sin to call his earthly parent father? None indeed except this: 'the Lord says so'. Now this is the answer of [one who is] a slave to the letter, and not a son of God and a friend of Christ, who understands both what he said and why he said it. I pray that those who are more spiritual may ponder such things well. For from this all errors and schisms arise, because some men consider the letter rather than the sense, that is to say, not what the letter seems to declare, but what the man who either said it or wrote it wished. Though here also Satan must be carefully watched, lest there creep in the licence of a false spirit which brings contrary meanings to the scriptures, instead of the freedom of the Holy Spirit, which always agrees excellently with the letter of scripture, but [only when] truly understood. And since it is very difficult, indeed impossible, for man to keep this middle course of spiritual freedom between the slavery of the letter and the licence of a perverse spirit, the divine word must be examined with fear and trembling, and, above all, prayer must be made to the Spirit of Christ, who alone teaches all things aright.[1]

The applying of the whole of the Bible to Christ,[2] and the interpreting of it in terms of Christ, is equally an example of following the Holy Spirit as interpreter. This, Bucer says, is how Christ taught, for there is no other way in which he could have taught his death and resurrection from the Old Testament. Therefore, besides their historical reference, passages in the Old Testament have a christological reference. They find fulfilment in Christ and the church.[3] This christological reference is demonstrated later in *Judges* with a striking eight-point typological interpretation of Samson.[4]

[1] Z 8.B.6–9.A.12, 17–B.8.

[2] Compare R 210.E.9–16. In *Psalms* he asserts that those more richly endowed with the Spirit see that the passage in Ps. 22 refers to Christ. P 101.A.24–6. Thus this method of interpretation is effectively open only to Christians.

[3] E 102.A.19–28. Compare E 101.B–102.A. Some passages have, in fact, a christological rather than a historical reference. This is affirmed in Ps. 45, where much of the psalm is said to refer not to Solomon, but to Christ. For no king had children as in the place of fathers, who succeeded to the kingdom by perpetual order, and who exercised authority through the whole world. There is, Bucer says, nothing that does not announce Christ to us. P 169.A.12–170.A.7.

[4] J 514.47–515.7. Bucer sees Samson as representing Christ not only in general, as saviour of the people, but also in several particular ways—in the annunciation by an angel of his conception, in the miraculous nature of his birth, in his being a Nazirite (in the sense of being separated) all his life, in his being stirred up by God's Spirit to accomplish great miracles, in his oppressing the enemies of God, and in his beginning rather than completing the liberation of God's people

Allegory, by contrast, is resisted, because it is not the Spirit's way of interpreting and imports human ideas into the words of the Spirit.[1] With allegories any ideas can be read into a passage and the clear straightforward meaning of the passage is lost:[2]

It is necessary for the deaf-mute to signify the sinner, Christ indeed to signify the priest, the healing to signify absolution—only then does it appear that we know something. Yet I, despite the antiquity of this abuse, despite its giving nowadays a far too considerable pleasure to some of the learned and good, do not doubt that it is a most serious affront to the Holy Spirit, a cunning imposture of Satan, calling [us] away from the true and efficacious warnings and examples of Christ to the worthless fabrications of men.[3]

His total rejection of allegory distinguishes Bucer from a great many of his contemporaries, not least from Erasmus, for whom it was the natural way of interpreting large tracts of the Bible, especially in the Old Testament.[4] For Erasmus it is in the allegorical interpretation that the distinction between spirit and letter rests (that is, between the husk and the kernel of a passage, the

from the power of the enemy. This last point is developed more than the others, reference being made to the resurrection of the dead and the ministry of the apostles and their successors. The most surprising parallel is between Samson's love of foreign women and Christ's love for the Gentiles.

In *St John*, however, Bucer warns against transferring everything to Christ, urging that one should not transfer to Christ and the church what does not square with them. 82.A.27–B.8, 16–19; 27.D.10–15, 20–2; 629.B.16–21, 630.C.1–3.

[1] 64.A.1–11; 21.C.15–21; 613.B.9–16.

[2] 'But ears that are only inquisitive are stroked by an empty pleasure, when the allegoriser does not allow the loaves to be loaves, nor the fish to be fish. But he makes the latter the two testaments, or the two swords, or something [even] more absurd, and the five loaves indeed he makes the five books of Moses, or the five senses of man, or some such old wives' tale.' Q 6.12–17.

[3] Q 6.29–36.

[4] Nevertheless, examples are to be found in the commentaries. See also Müller's discussion (*op. cit.* pp. 100–14). Bucer allows that a limited use of allegory is scriptural, but it is a case of sure and certain allegories, without obscurities and without variety of meanings. 5.A–7.A. (Preface to *St Matthew* 1527); 10.A–10.B.18 (Preface 1530). There is also the spiritualising, for example, of Gideon's sacrifice in terms of the purifying of the earthly into the heavenly by the Holy Spirit and the service of one's neighbour. J 494.35–40.

outward form and the hidden meaning). For Bucer, by contrast, letter is the Bible as mere letter, something dead, when it is separated from the vivifying power of the Holy Spirit. It is the Holy Spirit who gives the true understanding of the Bible, an understanding which amounts to the response of faith and love.[1] For Bucer it is the historical sense of a passage that is fundamental. It is important to discover the true meaning, however pious and useful another meaning may be.[2] This characterises all his writing and derives from his conviction about the Bible as written by the Holy Spirit, and perhaps also from his concern as a humanist to return to the sources.

It is certainly not enough to stop with the historical sense, for the Bible was written for our instruction. In this context the words of 2 Tim. 3:16–17 orientate his whole approach to the Bible. The purpose of the Bible is practical: 'to know God and Jesus Christ whom he has sent'.[3] It was given that the man of God might be instructed for all good works.[4] Therefore, if zeal for amendment of life does not come from reading or hearing it, we have not read it in the way that is necessary for salvation.[5] Indeed some parts may be said to have happened and to have been written 'for our sake'.[6] It is this practical, pastoral concern that provokes Bucer's commentaries on the Bible. This it is that gives the *Gospels* its strongly hortatory character. If the intention of the Spirit is to lead men to salvation through the scriptures, then the commentator must have the same clearly fixed goal.

There remains a further application of the principle that the Holy Spirit is the interpreter of scripture. It emerges chiefly in the debate with the anabaptists about baptism. They attack infant baptism (and not that alone) on the ground that it is not in scripture. For Bucer there can be no escape into the tradition or

[1] The scriptures are letter for those who read them without Christ. For a discussion of Erasmus, see Kohls, *op. cit.* p. 130 and Spitz, *op. cit.* p. 222.

[2] R 424.D.5–9.

[3] P 5.A.28–31 (Preface).   [4] R 393.B.17–C.3.

[5] R 210.D.13–E.3. Compare P 18.C.18–20 and 88.D.6–10.

[6] 32.B.11–25; 11.B.24–C.8; 26.C.12–21.

teaching of the church to defend infant baptism, though he freely draws on these sources. He must prove from scripture that infant baptism is the will of God. In this he deploys with some subtlety a whole series of arguments which show the influence of Luther's and Zwingli's writings on his thought. In particular, however, he discusses the relation of what is unwritten (*agrapha*) to what is written. Infant baptism is among those things that are unwritten. However, not everything that is unwritten is to be accepted, which is what the papists do, but only those things that are agreeable with what is written or are not disagreeable with it.[1] This idea is expressed again in the *Bericht*, where Bucer argues that there is no need for an express command, if something is contained in what is expressed.[2] A somewhat similar point is made in the *Dialogi*, where he affirms that the commands about how we are to worship imply the command that we are to worship.[3]

It is, therefore, as he wrestles with the biblical text and as he debates with radical and catholic opponents, that Bucer formulates with increasing sophistication his fundamental conviction that the

[1] QD A.3.A.13–B.14, A.4.B.24–A.5.B.17.
There is a further argument that Bucer uses against the charge that he is guilty of breaking the biblical command not to add to, or subtract from, scripture. It is that the Bible is about faith and love, and that this command is to be interpreted according to an understanding of the Bible, as being about faith and love. To add nothing, therefore, means to have faith in no one except God, through Jesus Christ, and to love one's neighbour only in God. H K.4.A.7–12. Bucer has already argued that we are not under the written law, but under grace and the Spirit of liberty. Therefore, we have only one command from God—to believe in the name of his Son and to have love for another. H K.3.B.21–6.
This pre-eminence of faith and love, as an interpretative principle, can be seen in the *Bericht*, where he affirms that in the Acts the apostles instituted what Christ had not specifically commanded. They did this because of the situation of the church. Later, however, acting by the same Spirit, the church relaxed this ordinance, and ordered what would serve the upbuilding of faith and love in a new situation. BH U.3.B.12–4.A.3.
[2] BH U.3.B.6–11.
[3] D C.3.A.29–B.18. Here he adds the point that everyone has always known that assemblies belonged to the worship of God, so that there was no need to tell people to assemble for worship. D D.2.A.7–14. This whole debate is concerned to prove the point against someone who seeks an express biblical command of God for all his actions.

Holy Spirit is alone the interpreter of scripture. Out of the Bible itself he reveals his methods of interpretation. The man who is equipped with the Holy Spirit and with the biblical languages can grapple with the biblical text and find its true meaning. He will eschew methods like allegory, that import human ideas into the writings of the Spirit. He will seek the plain historical sense. He will compare scripture with scripture. Aided by his understanding that the scripture is about Christ and that its sum is faith in God and love of God and of one's neighbour (principles derived from scripture itself), he will discover the mind of the Spirit in any given passage, even though obscurities may remain.

In Bucer's understanding of the Bible the word and the Spirit are essentially joined. The Bible is from the Spirit and, therefore, its words are the words of the Spirit. There lies its authority. It is recognised as of the Spirit by the power of the indwelling Spirit and by comparison with the word (in this case the Old Testament). It is understood by the Spirit and without him it is dead, mere letter. It is interpreted by the Spirit, that is, it is interpreted by men, guided by the Spirit. As they compare scripture with scripture, so they let the Holy Spirit himself interpret what he has written. In this way the authority of scripture remains supreme, as it is not dependent on man for its true interpretation but on the Holy Spirit himself.

7

THE CHURCH—THE PEOPLE
OF THE WORD

Bucer's view of the church is strongly influenced by the historical situation in which he worked and wrote. This does not mean that his understanding of the church is simply a response to that situation. But it does mean that his presentation is coloured by the events and people with whom he had to deal, and that the pressures, to which he was forced to respond, left their own mark on his thought and action.

This presentation of his doctrine of the church does not seek to be all-embracing. It concerns what he wrote, rather than what he did. It treats only the relation of the Holy Spirit to the church, considering chiefly three aspects of this relationship—the church as purposed by God and brought into being by his Spirit, the church as the community of the Spirit, and the church as instrumental in the gift of the Spirit.[1]

Bucer's sense of the Christian life as corporate is evident in his first work, *Das ym selbs*, but it is not until his debate with Treger that a clearly formulated view of the church is presented. Then it is done in a controversy where Bucer's primary purpose is to show the authority of the Lord and the Spirit over against the church. Despite this negative context a positive, if limited, understanding of the church emerges.

The church is seen as part of God's purpose for man. For, in rejecting the idea that one believes in the gospel because of the

---

[1] A detailed historical and theological discussion of the church may be found in Courvoisier, *La notion d'Eglise*, Wendel, *L'Eglise*, and Heitz, Etude.

A discussion of the *Gemeinschaften* is not germane to our study. The subject is treated by Werner Bellardi, *Die Geschichte der 'Christlichen Gemeinschaften' in Strassburg*. They are also referred to by Itti, who distinguishes them from Spener's *Gemeinschaften* (*op. cit.* p. 6).

church, he affirms that one believes in the church because of the gospel. For the gospel teaches us that 'Christ has received us poor sinners and has made therewith a beloved community for himself which he daily sanctifies'.[1] 'The church is born through the word, not through the word of the outward sermon or scripture alone, but through the living word that God speaks in the heart.'[2] This church, that is born through the word and the Spirit, is the true church. It does not consist of all who have been outwardly baptised. It is 'those who have received the Spirit of God'.[3] It can be recognised by the word (1 Cor. 14:24–5) and to some extent by works, though in people's works hypocrisy is always possible.[4] However, the word, like a net, collects good and bad. Therefore, we cannot be said to see the true church but only to believe it to be, wherever the word is purely preached and willingly heard, and wherever people are subject to Christ. The basis for this is the certain word of God that his word will not return to him void (Isa. 55:11) and that a bad tree cannot bear good fruit (Matt. 7:18). Moreover, we can judge where the church of Christ is by the evidence of the fruits of the Spirit.[5]

Bucer rejects Treger's idea of the church as all those outwardly baptised. He also rejects his idea that scripture is given by the church and that the church illumined by the Holy Spirit gives it its true meaning. The church does not dispose of the Holy Spirit in this way, and the true Christian, illumined himself by the Holy Spirit, does not need the church in this role.[6] For Bucer, Treger speaks mistakenly of the church as though it were a person. The church is not like a mother giving birth to children. It does not first receive the Holy Spirit and then pass the Spirit on to its children.[7]

---

[1] BW 2.100.14–19. Stupperich comments at this point 'Zunächst die Schrift, dann als Folge, aber auch als notwendige Folge, die Kirche.' Robert Stupperich, 'Die Kirche in M. Bucers theologischer Entwicklung', A.R.G. 35 (1938), p. 88.

[2] BW 2.87.34–6.   [3] BW 2.147.10–11.

[4] BW 2.112.12–29.   [5] BW 2.112.30–4, 113.17–114.3, 115.21–3.

[6] BW 2.140.29–141.11.

[7] 'Du redest eben von der Kirchen oder Gemeyn, als ob sye ein sondere person were, die alle Christen als ein muoter gepür und den zuoerst den heyligen geist entpfieng und geb darnach iren kindern auch darvon.' BW 2.146.33–147.12.

In each of the three aspects, in which the church is being considered, there is a development in Bucer's thought, above all in the third where he increasingly recognises the role of the church in the bestowal of the Spirit.

Although Bucer regards the church as the community of those who share in the Spirit, he does not, unlike the anabaptists, reject the existing church. In *St Matthew* he emphasises the mixed character of the church over against the anabaptist view of the pure church.[1] The church is also seen in some measure as the instrument of the Spirit, in the authority given to it to proclaim the gospel, including the power of binding and loosing.[2]

Ephesians not unexpectedly produces a stronger emphasis on the church.[3] Christ is depicted as the head, we as the body. Without the body he would not enjoy his happiness.[4] But without him we should be a body without a head, a body empty of life and movement.[5] Within this body gifts are given to us individually for the upbuilding of the church.[6] This idea is somewhat differently accented, when Bucer speaks of the gifts as given to the church, so that in it individuals may grow and receive an increase in knowledge.[7]

This same idea is taken up in *St John*,[8] where a similar concern for the close bonds that God has willed among members of his church is found. This closeness is suggested by the analogy of one body.[9] Indeed 'the Spirit of the Lord will at length gather the elect into one body'.[10] The church has no independence of the Spirit in what it does. Thus in remitting sins its only power is that of the Holy Spirit. He, moreover, absolves and pronounces free

---

[1] 147.B.23–148.A.3; 48.A.6–8; 118.D.3–5.
[2] 214.B.5–6; 149.A.18–19; 386.D.2–4.
[3] The fact that Bucer produced a commentary on Ephesians in the twenties and a course of lectures on it in the fifties, may be a token of the greater weight he laid on the church than did Luther.
[4] E 45.B.5–15.   [5] E 45.B.24–7.
[6] E 82.B.19–23.   [7] E 86.B.7–13.
[8] 41.A.25–8; 13.D.18–22; 595.A.2–7.
[9] 40.A.3–6; 13.B.26–8; 593.B.25–594.C.2.
[10] 188.B.1–9; 69.A.14–18; 724.D.7–11.

from sin only those who believe in Christ. It follows, therefore, that these are the only people whose sins the church is able to remit.[1]

To this picture the *Psalms* adds nothing essentially new. There is, however, simplicity and strength in the picture of the church as the city of God 'where God will rule by his word and Spirit more than anywhere else in the world, and from whence he will spread his saving doctrine into all the earth'.[2] In the third edition of 1532 the church is further described as formed by the Holy Spirit and as 'the fountain of salvation from which all nations drink'.[3]

In all these early writings Bucer's concern is with the church as a community brought into being by the Spirit and made up of those who share in the Spirit. Important as the church is for him, it is not presented in the twenties primarily as a community which bestows the Spirit, although the Spirit is seen as active in the church. The emphasis is rather on the church as having no life apart from the Spirit and as being effective only where he uses the church, whether in word or sacrament.

More than in most aspects of his theology, Bucer's doctrine of the church is developed outside the commentaries. This applies also to those aspects of his doctrine that concern the relation of the Holy Spirit to the church. It is in the confessional, catechetical, and pastoral writings of the thirties that the role of the church emerges.

Tetrapolitana relates the church to our being men who live in, but not after, the flesh. For this reason the Lord has been pleased to teach us with his outward word, and to bind us in an outward fellowship. To aid this, he has given us the sacraments.[4] Bucer accepts that the church is a mixed community, as the parables of

---

[1] 'For neither has the church any other power to remit sins than the Holy Spirit. Moreover, he absolves and pronounces free from their sins only those who believe in Christ. Therefore, there is no other way by which the church also remits sins than by recognising and testifying that they are remitted for those who believe in Christ.' 38.B.13–22; 13.A.9–14; 593.A.6–11.

[2] P 173.A.13–18. [3] P 313.C.17–20.

[4] BW 3.118.16–120.2.

the kingdom of heaven show, but at the same time Bucer claims for the true church the great New Testament descriptions of the church as, for example, the bride of Christ.[1]

To this *Quid de baptismate* and the *Bericht* add an important new dimension. In the context of the debate on baptism, which from the start had forced Bucer to grapple with his understanding of the church, they speak of the church as acting under the leading of the Holy Spirit. It is because the church lives and acts by Christ's Spirit that it baptises infants, even though infant baptism is not explicitly given by Christ in the New Testament.[2] The church, led by the same Spirit who gave the biblical ordinances, later relaxed some of them and appointed what, in their place, would serve to build up faith.[3] This bold assertion of the action of the church in changing or re-interpreting what is given in the Bible is perhaps only possible because the debate is now with the anabaptists and not with Treger. The significance of this new emphasis is not weakened, but only clarified, by the statement that the Holy Spirit in the church never teaches contrary to the Bible. Bucer says this lest the papists ascribe all that is taught in the church to the Holy Spirit.[4]

It is at this point that the positive role of the church as the instrument of God gains strength. He affirms that God wills to give

---

[1] BW 3.112.8–114.5. [2] QD A.3.A.1–12.

[3] 'Do sich der streit erhuob ob den Cerinonien des gesatzes/sahen die Apostel die gelegenheit der kirchen an/und erkanten der zeit zuo Christenlichem friden derselbigen/von noeten sein/wie sy es setzeten. Act. 15. das sich die Heyden des goetzenopffers/des erstickten und bluots zu essen/enthielten. Noch dem aber nun die kirchen her naher vernamen/die selbige notwendigkeit nit meer sein/do haben sy eben auss dem heyligen geist/auss dem sy vorgesetzet was/solche satzung nachgelassen/und yeder zeit das geordenet/das zuo uffbawung des glaubens dienen moechte.' BH U.3.B.12–4.A.3.

This view seems to give the church a role independent of the Bible. Bucer would deny this, for ceremonies are for him only binding in so far as they serve faith and love. Therefore they are always temporary and not permanent commands of the Spirit. The church in this case is acting under the direction of the Holy Spirit and according to the criterion that he himself has given for the interpretation of the Bible. Nevertheless, the role of the church is differently accented by Bucer here, partly because of the new situation that he was facing.

[4] BH X.1.B.6–10.

forgiveness through the ministry of the church.[1] 'Through the ministry of the church he wishes to communicate to us himself and his gifts.'[2] This does not, however, mean that the church is an indispensable or automatic instrument of God. The Lord can help unbaptised infants without the ministry of the church.[3] Moreover, God does not bind his grace and work to the ministry of the church —which means here that the ministry of the church is not automatically effective, rather than that God has other ways of acting.[4]

This new stress on the church as an instrument of God finds expression in the *Catechism*:

The church of Christ where I am, that is, all who call on the name of Christ and gather for his word and sacrament, I ought to esteem and hold as precious, as being that through which the Lord wishes to grant me his word and Spirit, forgiveness of sins and all good. I am to give myself wholly to such a congregation, diligently attend the sermons, hear the gospel, with complete reverence and obedience, and receive the holy sacraments at the [appointed] time. I am to show myself a faithful and obedient member of all those who with me call on my Lord Jesus. I am to let myself be taught, exhorted, punished, and disciplined, and show that even to others in all love and humility.[5]

In the *Shorter Catechism* (1537) the link between the church and the Spirit is even more strongly emphasised. In the discussion of the third article of the creed, there is the following dialogue between the teacher and child:

C. The Holy Spirit regenerates us and furthers us in the new birth.
T. How do you confess that?
C. I believe in one, holy, universal, Christian church.
T. How does that follow from what goes before?
C. The Holy Spirit makes those who believe in Christ our Lord unite and hold to one another as members in one body. It is by using word, sacraments, and discipline in the church that the Spirit builds up Christians in faith.[6]

[1] BH Z.2.B.18–27. [2] BH CC.1.B.16–23.
[3] BH R.1.B.18–22. [4] BH CC.4.B.14–19.
[5] GC C.2.B.26–3.A.11.
[6] Johann Michel Reu, *Quellen zur Geschichte des kirchlichen Unterrichts* 1.1: *Süddeutsche Katechismen*, 76.11–16.

It is later affirmed to be 'a great comfort to all troubled consciences that the Lord has given to his church the keys to the kingdom of heaven, power to bind and loose, to forgive and retain sins'.[1]

This view of the church as the instrument of God can be found in the *Gospels* (1536) and *Romans*. In the *Gospels* the power of the keys is no longer primarily the preaching of the word in the power of the Spirit, but a system of church discipline. It is, however, a power that can be exercised in the church only as it is rightly led by the Holy Spirit.[2] Similarly, Bucer can say that the Lord has chosen 'by the ministry of the church in baptism to offer and bestow on his people this Spirit' who transforms men's lives to the image of God.[3] The church's administration of the sacraments is seen in the same light. 'The Lord wishes to offer (reading *exhibere* for *ex libere*) his gifts and all salvation by the ministry of the church, so that men's sins are fully and really remitted only when the church in the name and word of the Lord remits them.'[4]

By 1536 the broad lines of Bucer's theology of the Spirit and the church are clearly formulated and developed. What follows is at most a filling in of these points in given situations. Thus *Von der waren Seelsorge* does this in terms of the church's total pastoral ministry, stressing the essential place of the church in God's intention for men:

The goal and end of this seeking and leading to Christ of lost sheep... is to bring them into the fold of Christ, so that they give themselves wholly to Christ...hear his voice in all things, and use all those things which the Lord has appointed for furthering the salvation of his sheep ...In a word, in the community of Christ alone the salvation of Christ is to be received...[5]

---

[1] Reu 1.I.78.17–20.
[2] 181.A; 138.D; 354.C.24–6.
[3] 72.A.10–22; 24.D.3–10; 621.A.24–B.11.
[4] 72.B.8–13; 24.D.19–22; 621.B.21–5 and 622.C.9–D.3. Compare R 8.E.6–12 and 161.A.   [5] BW 7.146.14–25.

Bucer regards church discipline, which he seeks to re-introduce, as among those things which further salvation and as itself none other than the work of the Holy Spirit in the church.[1]

If we leave aside the *Acta colloquii*, where Bucer's own thinking cannot be discerned with any certainty, the next most revealing situation is the reformation in Cologne and the *Bestendige Verantwortung* which Bucer wrote for it. Here, where the situation is not unlike that twenty years earlier with Treger in Strasbourg, many of the earlier arguments, particularly concerning the church and scripture, are reproduced. Now, however, they are deployed with greater subtlety. The true church, for example, is identified with the actual church and at the same time distinguished from it by analogy with the *collegium canonicorum* in Cologne.[2] The signs of the church, whether the simple description of the church (teaching, sacraments, discipline), or the more detailed working out of these, mark Bucer's newer appreciation of the total life of the church.[3]

A further variation in Bucer's position can be seen in his treatment of the church as God's instrument. This is now expressed less strongly, partly, no doubt, because the context is one of catholic rather than of anabaptist or spiritualist opposition. Forgiveness is said to be offered often before the ministry of the church in baptism, though it has pleased God to appear to offer this first through the ministry of the church.[4] Moreover, the Lord

---

[1] 'The Holy Spirit strictly and earnestly maintained and practised this his work of discipline and penance in his churches, [even] when the people in them were greater in number than they are now, and also when there were no fewer evil goats among Christ's sheep and likewise no fewer weak and sickly sheep than now.' BW 7.194.23–8.

[2] BV 55.A.38–B.23.

[3] Compare VD 5–7.

[4] 'Wie dan auch an den lebendigen der dienst dess gebets/und der mittheilung Christlicher gemeinschafft/den gaben und dem werck Christi etwan folget/ unnd nit vor/oder mit gehet/ob wol die wort und die handlung also gestalt seind/als ob sie dem werck des Herren vor/oder damit giengen/Dan man ja offt auch den lebendigen bettet umb verzeihung der sünden/unnd absolvieret sie von sünden/teüffet unnd weschet sie von sünden/welchen doch Gott schon zuo vor die sünd verzigen/unnd abgeweschen hat...Nit desto weniger hat es dem Herren also gefallen/die Gemeinschafft/das ansehen und den dienst der Kirch in mehrere achtung unnd würde zuobringen/unnd zuohalten/das die Kirch solche

is not limited to what the church does. Jesus does not say that
what the church does not bind or loose, is not bound or loosed, but
that what the church binds or looses, is bound or loosed.[1] Of
course, Bucer never limits God to what the church does; the point
of interest, in this case, is where and how he places the accent.[2]

A final presentation of Bucer's view of the church is to be found
in *Ephesians* (1550).[3] Here the three main lines, we have considered, can be clearly discerned. First, the church is seen as purposed by God and brought into being by his Spirit. The church
is described as the body of Christ, that is, the congregation of men,
ruled by Christ's word and Spirit. It is made up of the elect in
heaven and on earth, who are united divinely by the Holy Spirit
and not by some natural or political affection.[4]

This church is, further, the community of the Spirit, and bears
in its life the signs of his presence. Only as it has these marks,
which include not only the word and sacraments but also righteousness of life, can it be said to be the body of Christ gathered
by the Holy Spirit.[5] Here Bucer's understanding of the true
church is worked out in further detail. It is distinguished from the
catholic identification of it with all those baptised who accept the
doctrine and discipline of Rome, but whose faith may be dead.[6] It is

rewende und bittende erst mit irem gemeinen ernsten gebet unnd absolution hat
troesten und dem Volck Christi befehlen sollen/gleich als ob die erst durch den
dienst der Kirchen der sünden entledigt würden.' BV 177.A.3–28.

[1] BV 223.A.29–B.18.

[2] The relation of the church to scripture has been discussed in ch. 6.

[3] There is no new development in *De vi et usu* or *De Regno Christi*, though in
both the church has an important place. Compare TA 556.33–8, 557.5–9,
558.40–6, 603.42–6, and OB 15.9.34–10.15, 26.38–27.1.

[4] 'Thus the church is the body of Christ, that is, the assembly of men which is
ruled only by Christ's Spirit and word, just as the whole body is ruled by the
head. In this way it consists only of those who are elect and reborn, and rightly includes all who are united in Christ, both in heaven and on earth.' EE 36.D.12–15.

'But since there is the greatest possible union and unity between the members
of Christ—since indeed they are divinely gathered into one by the Spirit of God,
and not by natural or political affection—assuredly much more properly is their
coming together called a body, in which Christ lives and which lives in Christ.'
EE 37.A.8–11.

[5] EE 37.C.3–12, 38.D.1–14, 39.C.10–13.   [6] EE 41.C.6–14.

rather the elect, indeed, the elect who are living in faith. The elect who live without faith are true members in the presence of God, but are not held as such on earth until they are reconciled to God and the church. Therefore lapsed saints are not of the church until they are reconciled to the church and restored.[1] A true member of the church is marked by 'the Spirit of regeneration'.[2]

The church as the instrument of the Spirit is a little less strongly emphasised than fourteen years earlier but remains a central feature of Bucer's understanding of the church. Through preaching and sacraments it restores and perfects man's redemption and communicates to men the body and blood of Christ.[3] 'The church is to be listened to because God uses its ministry in calling us...'[4] Those who do not heed it are to be regarded as heathen and not as members of Christ.[5]

The church is never considered by Bucer as having some existence independent of the Spirit, who by the word calls it into being and sustains its life. These two aspects of the church (both its being called into being by the Spirit and its being a community of the Spirit) are present through all the periods in which Bucer wrote, though they appear more faintly in some places than in others. The identification of the true church (those led by the Spirit) with the actual church (those baptised) and the distinction between the two are more gradually developed and differently emphasised according to the context of the debate (whether it was with catholic or radical opponents). The character of the actual church as a mixed church is recognised from the start and is affirmed against the anabaptists.

---

[1] 'They are not of God, nor are they members of Christ, in whom every branch that remains in him bears fruit. This indeed they adduce about the elect, that they sometimes live without faith, in unbelief, and yet are true members. I reply: In the presence of God they are true members, but they are not to be held as such by us until they are reconciled to God and the church. We make a like reply to what they say about saints who have fallen. To the extent that they fall from faith, they are not of the church. But afterwards they are reconciled and restored to the church, as happened to Peter.' EE 42.D.7–13.

[2] EE 113.A.10–14.   [3] EE 28.E.11–14.

[4] EE 38.F.10–11.   [5] EE 111.B.14–19.

In the thirties the third dimension of the church in relation to the Spirit (the church not simply as created by the Spirit and sharing in the Spirit, but also as instrumental in bestowing the Spirit) emerges. The earlier debate with Treger had produced a largely negative reaction in this field—Bucer asserting that the church does not receive the Spirit and then hand him on, as a mother to her children. When the debate had moved from this point, where the authority of the church was held to imperil the authority of scripture, a development in Bucer's thought became possible. This happened chiefly through the encounter with the anabaptists (in his defence of infant baptism) and the spiritualists (with their scant regard for church, ministry, word, and sacraments).[1] It is out of this debate that the accent is placed on the church as the instrument of the Spirit,[2] a doctrine that found expression in deed (for example, in church order and discipline) as well as in word.[3]

---

[1] Schwenckfeld's refusal to identify himself with a particular church was characteristic of the problems posed by the spiritualists. See G. H. Williams, *Radical Reformation*, pp. 257–8.

[2] Compare Wendel, *Martin Bucer*, p. 32 and *L'Eglise*, p. 129.

[3] See the discussion in Wendel, *L'Eglise*, pp. 25–125 and Heitz, Etude, pp. 114–215.

8

THE MAGISTRATE—THE SERVANT
OF THE WORD[1]

The description of the reformation as the magisterial reformation[2] indicates how closely it was bound up with the work of the magistrates. As Luther's work cannot be separated from that of his elector, neither can Bucer's be separated from that of the council of Strasbourg.[3]

It was not that the magistrates played their part in the reformation against the better judgment of the reformers; rather, what they did was seen by the reformers as the exercising of a God-given task. This does not mean that theory and practice exactly corresponded. Bucer's running battle with the council is evidence that they did not. But they did not radically diverge, except in a limited number of situations. In Strasbourg as elsewhere the divergence was most notable in the question of church discipline.

The magistrate's concern with church affairs was not something new. It had a long history stretching back to Constantine and beyond him into the Old Testament. It was this tradition that the reformers inherited and from which they benefited.[4] At the same time they reformulated it, though in this, more than in

[1] The magistrate is a servant of the word, not by preaching it, but by ruling according to God's word and furthering its success. 'For although the service which the civil authority owes to the community does not consist in preaching God's word and law, yet it befits it to govern according to God's law and to do what it is able, to help in furthering God's word.' BW 1.55.22–5.

[2] See, for example, the discussion in G. H. Williams, *Radical Reformation*, p. xxiv.

[3] For a discussion of the council, its relation to Bucer, and its part in the reformation in Strasbourg, see Eells, *op. cit.* pp. 19–32 and *passim*, and Wendel, *L'Eglise*. For a comparison of Luther and Bucer, see Heitz, *op. cit.* pp. 185–96.

[4] In the Middle Ages the power of a ruler might include such matters as the appointment of bishops, which provided an obvious precedent for what happened in the reformation.

many matters, the divergences of Luther, Zwingli, and Bucer are clear-cut. Our interest, however, does not lie there, but rather in the way Bucer, in his encounters with the anabaptists and spiritualists, formulated his understanding of the magistrate as the servant of the word (and of the Spirit).

In the *Articles* it is said that God 'who has made us all from nothing, wishes to use the ministry of the word and also of the authorities, to draw his own from themselves and from all evil to himself, through our Lord Jesus Christ'.[1] As the authorities have the task of extending God's kingdom and of seeing that men live according to his will, and as the Spirit of Christ alone teaches what is good, 'no one is more fitted for such a divine office than true Christians whom this Spirit of Christ leads in all things...'[2] The ascribing of this role to the authorities sharply distinguishes Bucer's understanding of the church from that of the anabaptists. It arises in part from the difference in their evaluation of the Old Testament.

The summary form of the *Articles* is filled out in the *Dialogi* where a clear and bold presentation of the role of the authorities is given. Their purpose is again said to be the furtherance of the kingdom of God, for which Christian rulers are the most fitted. Bucer affirms this despite the fact that others often 'appear to be more fitted'.[3] This view is based on the assertion that non-Christian rulers who do not recognise the kingdom of Christ will not be able to direct everything towards it. Moreover, they cannot be expected to have the gifts of the Spirit.[4] By contrast, all who are Christ's have the Holy Spirit, and among the particular gifts of the Holy Spirit is the gift of ruling. The example is given of Israel in Egypt. The people of Israel were a simple people, but as God's

---

[1] KR 2.29.21–4. Wendel comments 'Ce n'est pas forcer le sens de ce texte que d'y voir l'affirmation que le pouvoir civil est, au même titre que le ministère de la prédication, quoique sur un plan légèrement inférieur et avec une qualification spéciale, un instrument de salut.' *L'Eglise*, p. 168.

[2] KR 2.29.33–30.7.

[3] D T.3.B.34–6.

[4] At the same time Bucer does not regard the gifts of the Spirit as dependent on one's being a Christian.

people, they were endowed with wisdom and skill for ruling and fighting.[1]

The task of the authorities is presented in some detail—a detail whose particular relevance to Bucer's needs in Strasbourg it is not hard to see. They are to see that the word is truly preached and the sacraments administered. They are to see that the people give themselves to God, that they hear his gospel, and that no one opposes it. They are to forbid idolatry, though the guilty are not to be completely cut off from human society.[2] With a telling (though, for modern ears, naïve) simplicity Bucer asks: 'When someone does wrong to God our creator, blasphemes and insults him, steals from him his precious creatures and dear children, for whom he gave his Son to die, and leads them to the devil, to their eternal destruction, are the authorities to stand aside?'[3] In all this they act by the word and Spirit of God. For it is the same word and Spirit, by whom Christians receive instruction, that 'drive the authorities to put away false teaching and worship, where necessary with the sword'.[4]

The linking of the task of the authorities with the Spirit is precisely with the Spirit as the Spirit of Christ. This is argued in a strongly biblical dialogue, in which step by step Friedlieb forces Sinnprecht to admit what we may regard as Bucer's view:

F. Dear Sinnprecht, is it not a proper work of the Spirit of Christ that he punishes the world for sins?
S. Yes; but through the word.
F. Through the word? Is then the use of the sword not also a work of the Holy Spirit?
S. Yes, when the sword is used according to God's will.[5]
F. Did the Levites when they killed their sons and brothers because of the golden calf, Elijah when he slaughtered the priests of Baal, and others when they have exercised God's wrath against the idolatrous, do what is righteous or unrighteous?
S. What is righteous.

[1] D T.3.B.36–4.A.33.
[2] D S.2.B.33–3.B.7.
[3] D N.3.B.33–4.A.2.
[4] D Q.4.A.12–15.
[5] D M.4.A.22–7.

F. Is not what is righteous a work of the Holy Spirit?...Is not the Holy Spirit the Spirit of Christ?

S. Yes, but he does not act in the same way in the New Testament and in the Old Testament...In the New Testament he does not punish so quickly as in the Old.

F. The work of whose Spirit was it when Saint Peter killed Ananias and his wife Sapphira...and when Paul made Elymas the sorcerer blind?

S. But that was with words.

F. What difference do the means make? Or can the gentle Spirit of Christ not use the means of the sword? Indeed, if the Spirit of Christ cannot use the sword as well, then the authorities cannot be Christian. For a Christian must do everything out of the Spirit of Christ. Anything he cannot do out of the Spirit of Christ he should leave undone...When you are healed by means of medicine, do you not recognise that it is God alone who has made you well?...When the authorities by means of the sword punish wrong according to God's command and order, then the Spirit of Christ works no less there than through the word of Peter, when he killed Ananias and Sapphira.[1]

In this we see Bucer's sense of the fundamental unity of Old Testament and New Testament. It is the same God who gives his people commands whether before or after Christ, and therefore the commands are valid.[2] In the New Testament period there were no authorities who were Christian and therefore God used other means of carrying out his commands. Now however he desires to use them:

At the time of the apostles and martyrs the Lord wanted to accomplish everything miraculously by the power of his Spirit, so that the whole world might see that the crucified was Lord, to show that he rules in heaven over all. Therefore, he allowed kings and all those who were powerful, to act in complete defiance against him and his people. But when he had converted the authorities, he wished them truly to serve him with their office and power, which is from him and is committed to them only for the good of Christ's flock.[3]

Bucer goes so far as to say: 'when the authorities appoint as preachers men of integrity, see that the ceremonies of the church

---

[1] D M.4.A.36–B.35.　　[2] D N.1.A.32–B.19.　　[3] D P.1.B.6–15.

(*Kirchenübungen*) are observed in a Christian way and that everyone is kept to them, when they exhort, attract, and provoke them in every other way to godliness, and God gives the increase, then do not the authorities in this way come into the heart in [the exercise of] their office?'[1]

The authorities, however, have no independence in their office. It is a God-given office, and only as they are led by the Spirit of God can they accomplish it. Bucer is aware of their abuse of power, but he is not at this point concerned to lay the emphasis there. In the desperate thirties, when he feared that the cause of true reformation would be lost in the turmoil created by anabaptists and spiritualists, he needed to declare unequivocally what God had appointed the authorities to do.

The other works of Bucer do not contribute any important development of this particular issue, though some of them show his attempt to restrict the activity of the civil authorities and to secure an independence for the church to order its own life and discipline. *Von der waren Seelsorge*[2] and *Von der Kirchen mengel und fähl*,[3] while affirming the task of the ruler, as do *Romans*,[4] *Ein Summarischer vergriff*[5] and *De Regno Christi*,[6] show the desire to clarify the extent of his power. His ministry is not to be confused with the ministry of the word.[7] He must not trespass into the sphere of the spiritual realm, except in certain given situations. His positive task, however, remains, as the writing of *De Regno Christi* for the young King Edward testifies.

---

[1] D R.2.A.11–16. [2] BW 7.147.12–25.

[3] VD 1–7.

[4] There is a detailed discussion in Rom. 13, into which we need not enter. Bucer's exposition is directed against radicals and catholics alike. Against the radicals he affirms that the authorities are divinely ordained and have a God-given task. They are in fact ministers of God. R 563.C.15–564.D.7. Against the catholics he argues, for example, that every soul is subject to the authorities, including priests and monks. R 559.B.14–C.4. He holds that the authorities (which means all who have absolute power, whether emperor, prince, or magistrate) have a proper concern for advancing the Christian faith—an argument of importance for Bucer in the introduction of the reformation in Strasbourg as elsewhere.

[5] V D.3.A.24–B.2, E.4.A.25–B.18.

[6] OB 15.99.29–32, 130.8–12. [7] Compare KR 2.30.25–6.

This task belongs to the ruler whether he be king or magistrate. The form of temporal authority is of no importance for Bucer; it could be royal or republican, it could be individual or corporate.[1] It is important rather that those who exercise this authority are men led by the Spirit of God. For only such men can further God's kingdom. To this end when a ruler is chosen, the people should look for 'those whom God wishes to be appointed, to whom he gives the Spirit of wisdom'.[2]

[1] J 500.39–40.   [2] J 498.54–5.

9

THE MINISTRY—THE MINISTER
OF THE WORD

The reformation was not simply a battle for the word of God. It was equally a battle of the word of God. It was the gospel, so freshly rediscovered, that was at stake. But what the gospel needed was not primarily defenders, but heralds—men who would let it sound clearly. This is what the reformers sought to do. They strove to do it by preaching and by writing, that is, by proclamation of the word and exposition of the word. It was this task that determined their understanding of the ministry.

Their view of the ministry was almost certainly coloured by their grasp of what the gospel meant, their experience in proclaiming and expounding it, and their interpretation of scripture. All three influences are to be found in Bucer's understanding of the ministry, and in their way differentiate his understanding from that of Luther. These differences show themselves as his thought develops, but from the start his peculiarly strong emphasis on the role of the Spirit should be pinpointed. This, however, was not what Luther meant when he spoke of Bucer's sermon in 1536 as *im Geischt, Geischt*.[1]

We shall consider four elements in Bucer's view of the ministry:

1. the role of the Spirit in calling, equipping, guiding, and using the minister;
2. the ministry as an instrument of the Holy Spirit;
3. the gifts of the Spirit;
4. the appointment and ordination of the ministry.

Although Bucer's work cannot be divided into neatly separate

[1] Bornkamm's interpretation (*op. cit.* p. 30) of *im Geischt*, as meaning 'in the air, or above one's head', gives the interpretation of this phrase as it is used in the Tischreden.

periods, nor his thought into wholly distinct compartments, yet these four elements correspond in broad measure to his primary concern at different stages in his ministry.

THE ROLE OF THE HOLY SPIRIT IN THE MINISTRY

The role of the Holy Spirit in calling, equipping, guiding, and using the minister is Bucer's primary concern and is clearly formulated with the appearance of *St Matthew* in 1527.

It is first dealt with in *Against Treger*. Here the Holy Spirit is seen, in all senses, as the source of the ministry. The ministry begins with his call. 'Whoever is certain by the Spirit and has scripture for him, should not cease either now or later to preach the certain word of God which he knows. Yet, as Solomon says, he should not pour it out where no one listens, and, as Paul did, so should he give babes milk and not solid food.'[1] The ministry is made effective by the Holy Spirit who speaks through the preacher and makes the preaching bear fruit. The Holy Spirit, however, does not work automatically, once he has called someone, but must every day make the minister a minister of the Holy Spirit:

If you are sent and are Christ's and not the prince of the world's, you have the Spirit of Christ, then indeed it is not you who speak, but the Spirit of the Father speaks in you.[2]

God daily made the apostles ministers of the New Testament, not of letter but of the Spirit. 2 Cor. 3. That is, it was not the intention that the preachers should just convey the letter, merely tell the people the contents of scripture, as though that were all. But they should, with all earnestness, preach the scripture about Christ our Saviour, by the assistance of the Holy Spirit sent from the Father, so that the Father may work with them and make what they plant and water, grow.[3]

St Matthew offers a fuller picture of what it is to be a minister of the Holy Spirit. It does this in a context where the thinking of the anabaptists has already made it necessary to affirm that the

[1] BW 2.129.23-7.   [2] BW 2.136.38-137.3.
[3] BW 2.136.24-30.

ministry is God's will for men, even though he can dispense with it. 'For, even if the teaching and telling of salvation is the Father's own work, nevertheless he has willed to have men as fellow-workers with him in these things.'[1] Normally, the Holy Spirit uses the words of the preacher, even signs, but Bucer can say 'the Holy Spirit will teach the elect all truth (1536 adds: through the gospel) even if they not only see no signs but also hear no preacher...'[2]

The minister must first be called or sent—and this is the work of the Holy Spirit.[3] We can tell who is sent, as such a person will be given 'the mind, the ability, a place, and success in preaching the gospel'.[4] If God means someone to leave his normal work to serve in teaching, the ministry, or government, he shows this by giving him the propensity for it.[5] However, as we are ignorant of the hearts of men, and easily led by hypocrisy, we need to pray the Father to show whom he has chosen.[6]

If a man is called by God he will be equipped by him. Thus the apostles, though they were very simple men, were instructed and equipped by the Holy Spirit to teach the world.[7] This does not mean that God will equip miraculously those to whom he has given the mind and ability to learn from the Bible, if, having the ability, they neglect to learn from the scriptures.[8] But this does

[1] 125.B.22–4; 41.B.13–14; 101.A.19–21.
[2] 120.A.10–18; 38.D.26–39.A.2; 95.A.17–21.
[3] 65.B.4–24; 101.A.21–B.2; 255.A.23–B.11.
[4] 65.B.24–66.A.20; 101.B.2–15; 255.B.12–256.C.3.
[5] 114.B.19–115.A.14; 37.A.30–B.12; 90.D.15–91.A.4.
[6] 126.A.24–B.1; 41.C.5–8; 101.B.14–16.
[7] 87.A.4–13; 28.D.1–7; 68.D.24–69.A.9.
[8] 'He certainly called the most untaught and dull fishermen, by whom he might afterwards teach the world by heavenly wisdom. But he did not leave them dull and untaught. Before he would appoint them ministers of the church, he taught them all the truth by his Spirit. Thus today he will indeed call those who are dull and untaught, but, by having bestowed his Spirit, he will make them learned and instructed unto salvation. He taught the former by a miracle, because that was what the situation demanded. He will give the latter the mind and ability to learn from his writings. And if there is need, he will likewise teach them once for all by a miracle, as much as is required—but not those who, although they are able to, nevertheless do not trouble to acquire for themselves knowledge

not alter the fact that the true knowledge that is needed is given by God, and that God has no need of our wisdom, but can himself give all that we require.[1] The insistence on the learning of languages is a sign that there is no opposition between what the Holy Spirit gives directly without man's doing anything, and what he gives indirectly through man's study. Both are gifts of the Spirit in so far as they lead to an insight into the things of God.

The Holy Spirit sustains his ministers so that they testify of Christ and convince the world. This is difficult and leads to persecution:

> ...thus for all to whom this task is assigned, as to the apostles, it is most necessary that they be clothed with power from on high...that is that they have the Paraclete. He adds not only consolation to the afflicted, but also courage to the timid and to those by nature terrified of death...so that intrepidly they announce to all Christ as king...[2]

The Holy Spirit also helps in preaching and in doing what is pleasing to God.[3]

Supremely, however, the task of the Spirit is to persuade those who hear the word, that is, to make the ministers, ministers not of the letter but of the Spirit. Without his persuasion the word is dead. For this reason we are to pray for the gift of the Holy Spirit 'so that our words and deeds...may have the energy and force of the Spirit...'[4] Certainly God has chosen 'to have men as fellow-workers with him', but that does not alter the fact that 'the teaching and telling of salvation is the Father's own work'.[5] 'It is the Holy Spirit's work, not ours, to persuade men's hearts of the truth.'[6] This essential work of the Holy Spirit is not seen as

---

of the scriptures. For the Lord wills to give to those who ask, but wisdom does not come except to those who watch at its door.' 113.A.14–26; 36.D.8–15; 89.B.6–14. Compare 153.B.16–25; 55.B.1–7; 691.A.11–18.

[1] 113.A.27–B.5; 36.D.16–19; 89.B.15–18.
[2] 79.A.16–25; 26.B.21–C.2; 63.A.10–16.
[3] 8.A.25–B.5; 84.B.11–14; 212.D.3–7.
[4] 251.B.10–16; 81.C.16–19; 206.C.10–14.
[5] 125.B.22–4; 41.B.13–14; 101.A.19–21.
[6] 277.B.9–15; 171.C.24–D.1; 441.B.23–442.C.3.

excluding co-operation. Rather is this presupposed in God's wishing to have men as his fellow-workers. It may be the Holy Spirit's work to persuade, but the minister, for his part, must speak simply and sincerely.[1] As the minister should pray for the Spirit 'so it is not a sin (1536 says: it is his duty) by pious pre-meditation to form the mind through the same Spirit to be an instrument of the Spirit'.[2] The minister's life itself may help or hinder the preaching. 'Thus where the most holy word of God is taught coldly, and when the preacher's whole life cries out that he does not sufficiently believe it, what wonder if it draws very few or none at all?'[3]

The ministry is, therefore, primarily a divine activity. God the Holy Spirit raises up men, gives them insight into the gospel, equips them to preach, guides and uses them in their preaching, so that they may be ministers of the Holy Spirit.

THE MINISTRY AS AN INSTRUMENT OF THE HOLY SPIRIT

The phrase 'minister of the Spirit' is ambiguous. It may mean a minister possessed and used by the Holy Spirit, or it may mean a minister possessing or conveying the Holy Spirit. It is the second aspect that is intended here by the words 'instrument of the Holy Spirit'. The two conceptions are not mutually exclusive, but they may conveniently be distinguished. In Bucer it would be true to say that the accent up to the early thirties lies on the first, and that thereafter it lies on the second. It is not that the second replaces the first, rather it complements it.

There is no period in which Bucer regards the ministry as unnecessary, though in the twenties there is perhaps a greater insistence on the fact that men can be taught without it. In the *Summary* he assures the readers that, even if they are without

[1] 277.B.9–15; 171.C.24–D.1; 441.B.23–442.C.3.
[2] 81.A.12–15; 106.B.4–6; 268.D.19–25.
[3] 2.B.20–3; 82.D.7–8; 208.D.1–3.

true preachers and have to put up with wolves, 'the gracious anointing of God's Spirit, which God has given to you and to all the faithful, will teach you all truth'.[1] In *St Matthew* it is stated that 'the Holy Spirit will teach the elect all truth even if they not only see no signs but also hear no preacher'.[2] With this goes an insistence that the Holy Spirit is not automatically joined to our ministry. In the *Gospels* (1530) he writes:

our ministry is concerned with the outward man, nor does it always have joined with it the operation of the Spirit. Truly, therefore, we derogate from the glory of Christ, and we exalt ourselves far too much, if we make any ministry of ours worth so much that we say the Spirit of Christ is always joined with it.[3]

The force of these passages should not be overestimated, for in *St Matthew* and the *Gospels* (1530) he attacks those who would do away with the public ministry. 'Take it away,' he says, 'and you have taken away piety and every bond of virtue. Wherefore as long as God has had a people on earth, he has taken care to teach and exhort them publicly through his interpreters.'[4] He notes that Paul can ascribe everything to God, and at the same time prize his ministry, and say that 'he had himself regenerated the Corinthians'. He adds, of course, 'when Paul speaks of his ministry in itself, he rightly confesses it to be of no effect'.[5]

There can be no doubt that it was the undervaluing of the ministry by the anabaptists and more especially the spiritualists that led to the stronger accents in Bucer's teaching.[6] It is in the years 1533 and 1534 that these are sounded. In *Contra Bernhard Wacker* he says 'ordinarily he (God) does not impart to any adult

[1] BW 1.96.36–97.5.
[2] 120.A.10–18; 38.D.26–39.A.2; 95.A.17–21.
[3] 57.A.5; 19.C.3–8; 42.D.19. Compare 57.A.5; 19.B.18–20; 42.D.19.
[4] 5.B.48–50 (Preface 1530).
[5] 7.B.36–43 (Preface 1530).
[6] Other influences are not thereby discounted, but whereas, for example, the Bible and the fathers provided the theological material for his doctrine, the conflict with the spiritualists and anabaptists provided the historical stimulus, which led to its formulation. The discussion of the ministry at this point is bound up closely with the discussion of Preaching in the following chapter.

the inward teaching of the Spirit without the outward teaching that comes through ministers'.[1] Here he expounds together 1 Cor. 3, with its assertion that those who plant and water are nothing, and 2 Cor. 3, which speaks of God's fitting men to be ministers of the New Testament and the Spirit.[2] Both texts, but with a varying emphasis, speak of the essential part God plays in preaching, but the second text is more characteristic of the more positive standpoint of this later period.

The *Bericht* presents this view of the ministry in greater detail, and its conclusions are summarised in the *Catechism*. The reason for the ministry, that is, that God acts through men, is to be found in the fact that our life is a bodily one, and therefore needs an outward ministry.[3] It has pleased God to give growth in this way.[4] It is through this ministry that God wishes to give forgiveness[5] and to impart salvation.[6] This does not make the minister independent of God. In the sacraments, for example, the gifts of God and our redemption are given through the Lord and are his doing. They are given through the ministers only as ministers and instruments of the Lord.[7] Indeed, Christ and the minister may be sharply distinguished so that it is said 'one thing happens inwardly through the power of Christ, another... outwardly in the ministry of the church'.[8]

---

[1] KR 2.195.32–4.   [2] Compare Pollet 1.131.3–11.

[3] BH K.1.A.1–9.

Compare 'Therefore while the church of Christ lives here in the flesh, although not after the flesh, it has pleased the Lord to teach, instruct, and exhort it also with the outward word. So that this may happen the more fittingly he has chosen that his own should come together in an outward fellowship. For this reason, therefore, he has appointed for them the holy sacraments as well, but especially baptism and holy communion.' BW 118.16–120.2.

[4] BH H.4.B.26–I.1.A.9.

[5] BH Z.2.B.18–27. Compare SC (1544) D.4.B.15–D.5.A.2.

[6] GC C.4.B.27–5.A.1.

[7] 'From this everyone sees that in the sacraments the gifts of God and our redemption are presented and delivered to us. [This is] chiefly through the Lord and of his doing, [it is also] through the minister, in his role as minister (*dienlicher weiss*) and as an instrument of the Lord. Everything is in accordance with what the Lord said: "Whose sins you forgive, they shall be forgiven" (John 20).' BH H.1.B.20–5. Compare BH AA.3.B.6–11.   [8] GC C.4.A.22–5.

In all this God remains free. He does not bind his grace and work to the ministry of the church, so that it is automatically effective.[1] Rather the work of the ministry is nothing without God who gives the increase,[2] and he gives the increase through preaching 'when and to whom he will'.[3] Nevertheless, Bucer can affirm that the word is not sent out in vain,[4] and that God will make those whom he sends heard and accepted.[5]

A token of this change of emphasis is evident in the *Dialogi*. There Bucer takes up the objection that God can teach now, as he taught Noah and Abraham, without using men—an idea he had himself used eleven years earlier in *Against Treger*.[6] His reply now is:

What can God not do? He could also create trees and other things already full of fruit as at the beginning, without [using] seed and without the efforts of men. His order now is to let them grow from their seed and by the work of men. As once God spoke with the people of Israel without human means and let his voice be heard in another way, so he made it that the people themselves desired henceforth to hear his word through Moses and no longer in this particular way. God then appointed Moses for this, and wished him to be his messenger and servant to his people. Finally, in like manner, he talked with the apostles through his Son, our Lord Jesus himself. But after he had accomplished the work of our redemption and had ascended into heaven he gave some to be apostles, some prophets, some evangelists, some shepherds and teachers... (Eph. 4:11–13.) See, my brother, the Lord gives his ministers of the word and sacraments so that through them the saints may be held together and be built as one body, and so that they may grow in the unity of the faith and knowledge of Christ, and become evermore like Christ.[7]

---

[1] 'God indeed does not bind his grace and work to the ministry of the church, so that whoever simply hears his word outwardly and without faith and receives the sacraments, at the same time has Christ with his redemption.' BH CC.4.B. 14–17.

[2] BH H.4.B.26–I.1.A.9.   [3] BH I.2.B.3–15.

[4] BH K.3.A.10–11.

[5] 'But the Lord will also see to it, that those whom he gives are heard and received.' BH D.1.B.1–3.

[6] BW 2.82.27–38.

[7] D E.1.A.12–36.

The ministry is thus seen to be more than simply valuable and important. It is in some way essential, simply because God has ordered things in this way. This, however, does not make the ministry the automatic bearer of the Spirit of God, nor does it necessarily mean that God cannot act apart from the ministry. In *Romans* he says no more than that 'without it God is not accustomed to bestow his Spirit, his inward teaching'.[1]

In this context Lang overdoes the stress on the necessity of the ministry for salvation in Bucer's comment on 'How shall they hear without a preacher?' The description has more light and shade than Lang's brief quotation suggests.[2] But, at the same time, it does include an insistence on the essential character of the ministry:

It is impossible to come to faith and eternal life unless you hear the gospel and that administered by a man...Yet the apostle knew, since he wrote such things, that God could call people without the ministry of men. He knew all teaching administered by men to be ineffective for salvation without God's giving all the increase.

Faith comes from hearing the word, which God has chosen to administer through men who share our flesh and blood:

Therefore, let us drive far from the church of Christ the assertions that it is not God's word that man speaks, and that the mind is able to be taught by the Spirit, and not by the outward voice, the things which are of God, and such like. These things divert the mind from faith and from a worthy esteeming of the gospel, which is proclaimed in the church, and they break up the society of the church.[3]

Preaching may indeed be described as the cause of man's salvation, though God alone is the total cause of all things.[4]

---

[1] R 42.F.15-43.A.2.   [2] Lang, *op. cit.* pp. 300-1.
[3] R 488.F.11-489.A.13.
[4] 'The fact that the Gentiles cannot come to Christ except by true faith is no objection, for Paul does not here set forth the whole cause of the salvation of the Gentiles. Who would deny that the cause of man's salvation is the preaching of the gospel? But unless men believe in the gospel, the preaching of the gospel brings them judgment and not salvation. God alone is the sole cause of all

Whatever the change in emphasis, so that here the essential role of the ministry stands in the foreground, the fundamental standpoint is unchanged. The ministry is effective only as and when God makes it effective. This depends on the work of the Spirit in the heart of those who hear the word and receive the sacrament, and this in its turn may be said to depend on whether or not they are elect:

The ministry of the church is effective in presenting the gifts of God, which are offered by the sacraments, only when God inspires those who hear the word and receive the sacraments, at the same time as the ministers speak and administer the sacred signs, and effects that they rightly understand what is offered to them and embrace it with firm faith. The ministers are, in this, instruments of God. Hence they can effect nothing more than what the Lord works in them. He has appointed his gifts to be offered, to some to condemnation, to some to salvation.[1]

God does it, yet the ministers may be said to do it. This paradox is, however, to be understood according to Augustine's words, 'I introduce the noise of words to your ears. But unless he who is within reveals, what do I say or why do I speak?', or according to the analogy of the gardener who tends the tree from without and the creator who works from within and gives the growth. In this sense all men have to be taught by God.[2]

The growing emphasis on the ministry is most evident in the exercise of discipline. When the minister pre-eminently has the authority to admit men to the fellowship of Christ or to exclude them from it, as in the *Gospels* (1536), then his essential part in the salvation of men is clear. When the role of the church is stressed, then the role of the minister, especially as the one who administers the sacraments and discipline, is stressed. The two hang together.[3]

things, and a given thing is the cause of something else only in so far as the Lord thinks fit to use it to effect something. As God, therefore, used the rejection of the Jews to gather the Gentiles to himself, so also in its own way the rejection of the Jews was truly the cause by which the Gentiles came to Christ.' R 505.A.7–15.
[1] R 164.E.1–7.   [2] R 164.E.9–20.
[3] 180.B.5–181.B.8; 138.C.16–D.24; 353.B.10–355.A.8.

Von der waren Seelsorge does not offer any further development of Bucer's thinking on the ministry, but gives it a significantly pastoral orientation. It is this that particularly marks off Bucer's understanding of preaching from Luther's. In the context of preaching he states:

the Spirit of Christ cannot leave it at that [for the hearer to accept the word or not]. He is a faithful teacher, who does not stop until he has led his pupils into all truth. Therefore, he goes from house to house, from person to person, to see how his message in the public sermon for the church was received, to see how each one responded. He examines his pupils and sees what they have and have not grasped. He has always acted in this way in his church.[1]

The true Christian will resist the error of those who despise the ministry. To such he will retort:

I wish to hold myself to the ordinance of my Lord, who has appointed his regular ministers for his church through whom he wishes to gather me to his kingdom, forgive me my sin, regenerate me, hold, teach, and lead me into everlasting life. I will hear them as [I hear] him himself. I will hear and receive their word and work in this ministry, when they administer the same according to the Lord's institution, not as their word and work, but as the word and work of my Lord Jesus Christ, as indeed they truly are...[2]

Christ uses the ministry 'to give not only the letter, but also the Spirit'.[3] In this, however, the minister does not act from his own strength. It is the Lord who speaks through him and who gives the increase.[4]

In the last year of his life, Bucer gives final form to his thinking about the ministry in *Ephesians* (1550) and *De vi et usu*.[5] He still

---

[1] BW 7.218.29–35.   [2] BW 7.111.31–112.3.

[3] BW 7.109.8–16 (margin).

[4] 'But they do not do this, however, in their own strength, but in the power and energy of the Lord. Of themselves they could not think of doing this, but God equips them for it. For that reason the Lord gives them his Spirit and understanding of scripture. His Spirit speaks in them. It is his power, his Spirit, and his work. He gives the increase.' BW 7.110.14–19.

[5] His thought is expressed in them in almost identical form.

seeks the middle way between those who despise the ministry, and the papists, who bind salvation to it and so destroy faith.[1] The ministry is God's instrument. 'Today', says Bucer, as in the Bible, 'God speaks and acts with us through his sacred ministries in the church'.[2] Ministers do not simply announce remission of sins, they themselves remit.[3] What they do, is to be compared with someone, who, in the name of his prince, leads a prisoner out of prison, rather than with someone who tells him that he has been set free.[4]

The minister has no power of his own in this. Christ breathes the Holy Spirit on the apostles to show that those who are about to minister salvation to men, do not do so by their own powers, but by the power of the Holy Spirit, of whom the breath is a symbol.[5] The ministry is, in fact, the work of the whole Trinity, which is the reason why it is ascribed at different times to the Father, the Son, and the Holy Spirit.[6] It is always God's work and not man's, however much God uses men as his instruments. 'God has certainly not bound the power of saving his elect to any human works or functions, or to any words or signs administered by men.'[7]

Through all the shifts of emphasis the main lines of Bucer's view of the ministry are clear and fundamentally consistent. Earlier the accent lies on the work of the Holy Spirit who alone makes the ministry effective. This conviction is never given up, but in the

[1] EE 96.E.10–15.   [2] TA 590.24–31.
[3] TA 592.25–35 and EE 141.C.9–13.
[4] 'Finally he brings wonderful consolation to those with bruised consciences, when the remission of sins and eternal salvation is not only announced but also offered to them. When a steward takes a man to court and cancels the debt or gives the bond for the debt back, he gives new life to the debtor, much more than if he only says to him that his master has remitted the debt. And a prince's servant renders a prisoner more sure of the favour his prince has done to him, if he leads him out of prison with his own hand, than if he merely announces it to him.' TA 593.27–33.
[5] 'Indeed he breathed upon them, so that he might teach that they, even they, would minister salvation to men, yet not in their own strength, but by the power of the Spirit, of whom that breath, perceived by the senses, was the symbol.' TA 592.25–7. Compare EE 141.B.6–10.
[6] EE 108.E.11–15.   [7] EE 136.E.11–12 and TA 586.42–50.

thirties increasing weight is placed on the divinely appointed role of the minister, as the one through whom salvation is imparted in word and sacrament. The ministry, however, is never in itself an instrument of the Spirit, but only as the Holy Spirit makes it so. This idea is variously expressed, with the accent sometimes on the minister,[1] sometimes on the hearer.[2] The Holy Spirit is also not bound to the ministry, in the sense that he cannot act apart from the ministry, though this note is more characteristic of Bucer's earlier writings than his later ones.[3]

THE GIFTS OF THE SPIRIT

The most detailed consideration of the gifts of the Spirit comes not unexpectedly in the commentaries, particularly in *St Matthew* and *Romans*. This discussion reveals two closely linked elements in Bucer's thinking—the variety of the ministry and the ministry as the gift of the Holy Spirit.

The gifts of the Spirit are not for Bucer limited to godly men, as the fruit of the Spirit is. The fruit of the Spirit comes from the Spirit of sonship, whom only the elect have. The gifts of the Spirit may, however, be enjoyed by the reprobate. If they are given to ungodly men, then these men serve the glory of God. This argument is based on the example of men like Saul in the Old Testament and Judas and Demas in the New Testament:

In the early church clearly some hypocrites taught the mysteries of the kingdom of God and cast out demons...many devoid of firm faith were given the Spirit of the Lord...so that they might desire and be able to preach the gospel...[4]

---

[1] See the prayer before baptism: 'Wilt thou together with thy dear Son and the Holy Spirit be in our midst, and let us here be thy true ministers, ministers of the Spirit and the New Testament, that we may serve thee with these children to their blessed rebirth...' BW 7.298.30–3.

[2] The hearer is spoken of as being elect, or having faith, or being persuaded by the Holy Spirit. Compare R 164.E.1–5.

[3] Yet, see R 488.F.14–17.

[4] 245.B.15–246.A.15; 79.D.27–80.A.14; 202.C.6–22.

For the Spirit is also frequently given to evil men that they may serve to the glory of God in those things which are beyond the capacity of nature.[1]

The two gifts of the Spirit especially dealt with are prophecy and teaching. A prophet is a man whom the Spirit of God inspires and makes pre-eminent in his knowledge of divine things.[2] Telling hidden and future things is part of his task, but a more important task is to speak of God and religion more skilfully than others. What the prophet has learnt by the inspiration of the Holy Spirit, he uses for the growth of the church.[3] Whereas the prophet is instructed through revelation, the doctor or teacher is instructed through knowledge. The way the gift of teaching is given does not make it any less a gift of the Spirit than prophecy. In his understanding of all these gifts Bucer's characteristic concern for the church is shown. The gifts are for the upbuilding of the church. Moreover, a gift, like tongues, that could not by itself serve the upbuilding of the church, should be exercised only when there is someone to interpret, so that this end may be served. Throughout, Bucer's exposition follows closely Paul's exhortation in I Cor. 14, even to the necessity for one to sit down when another gets up.

In *Romans*[4] there is a more developed explanation and critique of the gifts of the Spirit. They are said to be given according to the measure of faith.[5] Moreover, the Holy Spirit is necessary for them to be exercised fruitfully.[6] This can be seen with the gift of prophecy, which must be exercised in keeping with the analogy of faith. 'For whatever is taught by [inspiration of] the Holy Spirit, it must be in complete agreement with the faith, that is, it

[1] 65.B.26–66.A.1; 101.B.3–4; 255.B.13–14. Compare E 18.A.20–B.26.

[2] 107.B.23–108.A.13; 114.C.1–11; 289.A.17–B.3.

[3] 108.A.14–20, B.14–19; 114.C.12–16, C.28–D.1; 289.B.4–8, 22–5.

[4] The reference in *Ephesians* does not develop Bucer's thought. E 84.B.3–86.A.2.

[5] R 538.E.12–F.2. Bucer generally holds that the reprobate can also receive the gifts of the Spirit, and he refers to this fact in his exposition. R 538.F.5–10. His concern here, however, is with Christians, the exercise of whose gifts for the good of the church depends on the measure of their faith.

[6] R 541.A.10–15.

must preach Christ as our only Saviour, and subject all things to his word.'[1]

In the early church, the gifts of the Spirit were given to excite an admiration for the gospel:

Christ chose men of no ability or position. . . but gave them the secret power of his Spirit, so that nothing was lacking of all those things which are required for the best ordering of a good republic and for its happiness. Indeed, from fishermen and other simple people the Lord appointed the first senate and leaders of the city, and he made them at once to excel in wisdom and understanding, so that no one in the world has ever administered more justly and happily.[2]

Some gifts were conferred by the laying on of hands.[3]

Again, Bucer emphasises that they are given for the benefit of the church.[4] Therefore, when anyone disturbed the tranquillity of the church, he was warned and, if need be, destroyed.[5] The reference here is to the gift of power (*dunameis*) which Bucer saw exercised in the case of Ananias and Sapphira, as well as with Elymas.[6] This gift corresponded to the exercise of discipline in the church. Significantly, it is in the thirties, when Bucer sees the exercise of the power of the keys not simply in terms of preaching the word in the power of the Spirit, but in terms of a discipline that includes excommunication, that he expounds the word *dunameis* in this way.[7] He continues to hold this view and affirms it again in *De Regno Christi*[8] fourteen years later.

---

[1] R 540.D.1–3, E.4–16.   [2] R 539.A.8–18.

[3] R 539.B.3–4. Compare BW 3.270.32–271.2 and 272.14–18.

[4] R 538.E.19–F.15.

[5] 'Si quis tranquillitatem rectamque vitam turbaret, in eum animadvertebant verbo, et si res poscebat, tollebant etiam illum. Morbi si inciderent, quos praestabat depellere, erant qui eos pellerent in nomine Domini.' R 539.B.5–8.

[6] Compare D N.1.A.32–B.19.

[7] In this context it should be noted that a characteristic example of the power of the keys in the 1527 and 1530 editions of the *Gospels* is Peter preaching salvation to those who were penitent, and damnation to those who were not (180.B.5–181.B.8; 138.C.16–D.24). For the 1536 edition, however, it is Peter's exercising pastoral discipline with Ananias and Sapphira (353.B.10–355.A.8). This change corresponds with the new understanding of the keys in terms of church discipline.   [8] OB 15.9.19–26.

Romans also argues that many of the gifts of the Spirit were given directly (or, indeed, given at all) only in the early church. They were given then because of the peculiar need of the church in her mission or internal life, not least to excite men's 'admiration for the gospel'.[1] Now they are not needed in their miraculous form, but are given indirectly, as in the exercise of discipline. Yet nothing that can help towards the godly life is lacking. It is simply given through our works and not by a miracle.[2]

In the later works of Bucer there are few new elements or fresh accents in his treatment of the gifts of the Spirit. But two should be noted. First, Bucer's characteristically corporate understanding of the church and the Christian life can be seen in his discussion of the variety of the gifts. In *Von der waren Seelsorge* he writes: 'The Lord gives indeed to each his own gifts and work. He does not give all the gifts to one or two, but he wishes that one should always have need of and use the other's help.'[3] Bucer values God's ordering of life so as to make us need each other. The gift of the ministry itself is to be understood in this light, even more, the diversity of the ministry. The ministry is diverse because no one has all the necessary gifts. One man is a pastor, another a preacher, another a teacher.[4] All of them are needed in the ministry of the church.[5] This same note is sounded when Bucer is in England in his *De vi et usu*[6] and *Ephesians* (1550).[7]

The second new element is the distinction between two different gifts of the Spirit in the commentary on Judges.[8] There is the gift of the Holy Spirit by which men believe and do good. This is a gift shared by Samson and the apostles, but also one that is common to all Christians. There is as well the gift by which, for example, men do miracles or explain the scriptures. These are 'immense and unaccustomed actions'. This gift he identifies with

---

[1] R 539.A.2–8, B.13–16. Compare D P.1.B.6–15.
[2] R 539.B.16–C.5.   [3] BW 7.117.23–6.
[4] BW 7.117.27–36.
[5] The present-day emphasis on group or team ministry is not an insight, new in the twentieth century.   [6] TA 567.27–31.
[7] EE 119.B.1–C.2.   [8] J 505.29–41.

being baptised in the Holy Spirit, and in this context compares Pentecost and Samson's invasion by the Holy Spirit. Out of these experiences Samson and the apostles became different men. The distinction in *Judges* corresponds to, but is not identical with, the more usual distinction between the Spirit of sonship and the gifts of the Spirit.[1]

The isolation of this particular point, the gifts of the Spirit,[2] reveals the consistency of Bucer's theological position. What is true of his doctrine of the ministry as a whole, is true here. The ministry is the gift of the Spirit and needs the Spirit for its exercise. The Spirit can act miraculously to impart his gifts where that is necessary, but that is not his intention now. The present situation is not that of the first apostles, therefore God's way of acting now is different, though his ultimate purpose remains the same.[3]

---

[1] The phrase 'baptism in the Holy Spirit' is here distinguished from 'baptism with the Holy Spirit'.

[2] The gifts of the Spirit are normally spoken of in the context of the ministry, though the *Bericht* sees the gift of governing as given more often to laymen than to the learned. BH E.2.A.2–5.

[3] It has not been the purpose of this chapter to show the variety of the ministry, except in relation to the gifts of the Spirit. Bucer seems to preserve a fairly fluid understanding of the forms of the ministry. He mentions a fourfold ministry in the *Gospels* (1536) (354.C.11–14), but does not treat it as an invariable norm. He appears more concerned to see that certain things are done by the total ministry of the church, than with the form the church's ministry takes. In England, therefore, he can quite happily accept a threefold form of the ministry, in which the bishop is a chief minister. OB 15.118.22–7. Yet he can speak of a variety of ministers. EE 117.A–120.D. At one time (TA 238.24–32) he distinguishes two kinds of ministry, that of word, sacraments, and discipline (exercised by bishops and presbyters) and that of the care of the needy (exercised by deacons), and at another time (EE 115.B.17–C.2) he mentions three kinds (doctrine, sacraments, and discipline), or even two (temporary and permanent).

In Bucer's theology and practice the importance of the pastoral ministry and the care of the needy should be stressed. They are particularly distinctive of him. It should perhaps be noted that the tasks assigned to the ministry could also in some cases, like teaching (TA 566.49–52 and EE 118.E.15–16) and absolution (TA 578.29–30), be exercised by laymen, where they are judged to be equipped by the Holy Spirit (EE 118.E.15–16).

See also the study by Strohl, *La Théorie et la pratique des quatre ministères de Strasbourg avant l'arrivée de Calvin.*

THE APPOINTMENT AND ORDINATION
OF THE MINISTRY

The wide area covered by Bucer's theory and practice of the appointment of ministers in the church goes far beyond our concern with the role of the Holy Spirit in his theology. It is necessary to limit the discussion to two issues—the signs of a minister who is chosen and endowed by the Spirit, and the role of the Holy Spirit in the laying on of hands at ordination.

THE APPOINTMENT OF A MINISTER

Bucer does not regard the sense of call to the ministry as sufficient authority to exercise one's ministry. The appointment of the minister is distinguished from self-appointment or some kind of immediate appointment by the Holy Spirit. It involves the action of the authorities and the congregation.

In this, the congregation is most suitably represented by a few of its members, the elders, rather than by all of them, for the elders will know the minister and the situation better.[1] The authorities also act as a kind of committee of the church, and their part is important, especially in the towns. That they may abuse this power, Bucer does not doubt, but he affirms that God will not desert his flock though the authorities be wolves.[2] In practice, the whole congregation has an essentially more passive role. From various biblical examples Bucer argues that they are to accept someone who is appointed, provided he preaches Christ.[3]

A detailed treatment of the role of the authorities and congregations would take us too far. It is sufficient to note that it was in the thirties, when the church in Strasbourg was threatened with disruption, that Bucer and the Strasbourg reformers developed their understanding of the appointment of a minister. Danger signals had sounded years earlier when, for example, Hans Wolff

[1] BH E.4.B.1–30. [2] BH F.1.B.14–16.
[3] BH F.3.A.11–27.

had interrupted Matthew Zell in the cathedral for not speaking the truth, whereas he, Hans Wolff, had the Spirit of God, and there-fore could speak the truth.[1] Then, however, the danger of dis-ruption was small and Bucer could allow that in prophecy, following St Paul's admonition, one should give way to another.[2] Now to allow such liberty, or too great a liberty for a congrega-tion to choose its minister, would be to hand over certain parishes to the radical reformers. This is the historical context of the whole movement towards ordinances and discipline in the church.

Von der waren Seelsorge especially deals with this question. It affirms that 'in the choice one ought diligently to regard the choice of the Holy Spirit. He will also reveal this to us, when we are careful about it and pray diligently.'[3] Prayer to discover God's choice and the ability to discern the signs he gives are inseparably joined. Christians are, therefore, to pray the Lord to send equipped, faithful, and able servants into the harvest, and also to enable the church to realise whom he has chosen. The church is to watch with diligence for the indication of the Holy Spirit—to see who are endowed with ability to build up the churches of Christ. The usual sign of the Holy Spirit that someone should be chosen is precisely this will and ability to help to build up the church. Bucer here distinguishes those in scripture who had some special sign of the Spirit (as Paul, Barnabas, and Timothy) from those who had a general sign of the Spirit, that is, those who were learned, eloquent, and zealous in the affairs of Christ (as Aquila and Pris-cilla). He says that they are not to wait for miraculous signs, but to give heed to the general sign of the Holy Spirit.[4]

---

[1] KR 1.56.15–19.

[2] 66.B.24–67.A.12; 101.C.7–16; 256.D.1–10.

[3] BW 7.124.24–8 (margin).

[4] 'Secondly, that the churches should also with the greatest possible diligence give heed to the indication of the Holy Spirit and see who they are who are endowed with fitness and ability rightly to improve the churches of Christ—and this without paying regard to any other person or circumstance. For where the Lord gives the will and ability to people to help to build up his churches, that is the general indication of the Spirit that such people should be chosen for this

The agreement of the congregation is important in the appointment of the minister, for he must not only be without reproach, but also be trusted and loved. However, as the whole congregation, especially when it is large, lacks the necessary experience of a minister's aptitude, a few, who are more understanding, are to act for them. The other ministers, the people, and the authorities, all have their part, but the accent now lies less on the part of the authorities than a few years earlier.

The various signs of the Spirit are later formalised in terms of an examination of ministers.[1] *De ordinatione*, following what it regards as the clear biblical precept of the Holy Spirit, insists on an examination of life, education, and doctrine.[2] The doctrinal test with its thirty-two questions is a sieve through which the theological lightweight and the theologically suspect would alike be sifted.[3] In addition *De Regno Christi* warns against the appointment of neophytes, unless the power of the Holy Spirit is manifested in them in a quite unusual way, as in the case of Paul.[4]

The question of the appointment of ministers was essentially a question of the second decade of the reformation in Strasbourg rather than the first. As the church sought to secure itself against the threat of the radical reformers and, to some extent, that of the magistrates, its theologians wrestled increasingly with questions of church order and discipline. Bucer, therefore, deals with this problem primarily in his writings in the thirties and then in his writings in England, where questions of church order again faced him.

It is characteristic that he applies in detail the precepts of the

---

ministry...Thus indeed we must not wait for miraculous signs, but give good heed to the general indication of the Holy Spirit.' BW 7.134.32–135.17. Compare BW 7.124.30–125.7.

[1] This leaves less place in the ministry for 'godfearing and truly zealous Christians' who are not learned and educated. Yet this lack Bucer, following Ambrose, deplores. BW 7.133.2–5.

[2] TA 242.12–15. Compared V C.2.A.1–10 and OB 15.103.10–12. The nature of the minister's life and its difference from that of the layman is treated in detail in TA 578–86.

[3] TA 245–52.   [4] OB 15.126.17–24.

New Testament, so that his *Von der waren Seelsorge* is almost a running exegesis of scriptural quotations. What he is concerned to do is to discover the scriptural tests of a ministry that is of the Holy Spirit and not of men, and then the scriptural way of appointing such a minister. The first he finds in a combination of the guidance of the Holy Spirit in prayer and the recognition of signs of the Holy Spirit in a person's fitness for the ministry (in life, learning, and doctrine). The second he finds in variations on the combination of the authorities, the other ministers, and the people.

THE ORDINATION OF THE MINISTRY

Here one issue alone demands our attention—the relation of the Holy Spirit to the laying on of hands.[1]

The imposition of hands in Bucer is discussed primarily in the context of confirmation and ordination.[2] In this he quotes the example of the apostles, where the Holy Spirit is spoken of as given after baptism by the laying on of hands and prayer[3] or as given by the laying on of hands for a certain function.[4] The *Bericht* also refers to the ancient practice whereby, at 'confirmation', the bishop laid on hands and bestowed the Holy Spirit.[5]

In the *Kasseler Kirchenordnung* the prayer with the laying on of hands is 'increase them in thy Holy Spirit...Grant them also, as we now lay hands on them in thy name and commit them thereby to thy gracious hand and thy Holy Spirit, the Spirit of all strength and help, for truly Christian living...'[6] The *Shorter Catechism* (1544) shows something of the ambiguity that appears later in the imposition of hands at ordination. It interprets the imposition as

---

[1] It has been argued that Bucer does not link the gift of the Spirit with the laying on of hands. See Hopf, *op. cit.* pp. 91–3. The laying on of hands is also discussed by G. J. van de Poll in *Martin Bucer's Liturgical Ideas*, pp. 71–2 and 104–5.

[2] There are also references to the absolution or reconciliation of penitent sinners by the laying on of hands. BV 64.B.20–6.

[3] Bucer limits this, as anointing, to apostolic times. BW 3.270.32–271.2, 272.14–18.

[4] QD A.7.A.18–B.20. Here it is referred to as a gospel sacrament.

[5] BH L.2.A.2–8. Compare GC E.5.A.23–B.3.

[6] BW 7.313.8–9, 21–7.

meaning that the children are received under the gracious hand of almighty God and are promised his protection and guidance. Bucer adds, however, that the Lord will also be present with his Spirit, and work.[1] The one interpretation of the laying on of hands (being received under God's gracious hand) does not, therefore, exclude the other (receiving the Holy Spirit), but rather would seem to require it in some form.

The references to the imposition of hands in ordination are also normally linked with the gift of the Spirit, by analogy with the New Testament practice of ordination. The gift of the Holy Spirit to exercise the church's ministry is spoken of as given to the elders by the laying on of hands.[2] *De ordinatione* also refers to the gift of the Holy Spirit in the laying on of hands and links it with the word of God and the pious prayer of the church.[3] The fact that *De ordinatione* views the laying on of hands as 'signifying and representing the direction, corroboration, and protection of the hand of God almighty, by whom he who is ordained is able to accomplish and perform his ministry to the glory of God's name and the salvation of the church',[4] does not invalidate this interpretation any more than does the absence of the phrase 'receive the Holy Spirit' from the words of ordination.[5] The act has an unequivocal meaning for Bucer, and the words at ordination are to be understood in terms of this.[6]

[1] SC (1544) E.3.B.10–16.
[2] '...das die gabe des heiligen geists den Kirchendienst wol zuo verrichten mit dem hendtufflegen der Eltisten gegeben würdt.' BW 7.124.17–18 (margin).
[3] 'Or rather, in those who are ordained to the ministries of the church, whenever they are lawfully called to them and tested, and hands are laid upon them, together with the word of the Lord and the pious prayer of the church, one feels that the request is granted by these means and the gift of the Holy Spirit is offered, so that they may more properly discharge the duty that is laid upon them and do so more fitly in the building up of the church. Just as we read that this gift was granted and conferred by the imposition of hands administered with the word of the Lord and the prayer of the church by Stephen and his colleagues, Barnabas and Paul...' TA 249.7–13.
[4] TA 255.18–21. Hopf (*op. cit.* p. 92) uses this passage in his dissociation of the gift of the Spirit from the laying on of hands.
[5] TA 259.20–3.
[6] Compare EE 120.E.2–9.

This does not mean that the Holy Spirit is conveyed by a human act in itself. 'Thus the Lord is in the midst of his people and performs those things which are prayed for and represented.'[1] The association of the act with prayer and the word of God has a similar significance. It would be out of keeping with Bucer's whole view of sacramental action in the church to make it in any way automatic. It is, however, equally out of keeping with his theology to separate the sacramental action from God's action.

[1] TA 255.17–18.

10

PREACHING—THE SPOKEN WORD

The relationship of word and Spirit was one of the major issues dividing the reformers from each other and from the catholics and radicals. The debate concerned not only the incarnate and written word, but also the outward word of preaching. Opinions ranged from the rejection by the spiritualists of the outward word in favour of the inward word of the Spirit, to the insistence by Luther on the outward word as the means by which God gives the Holy Spirit. Within this debate Bucer's position emerges as he encounters in turn the view of catholic, radical, and Lutheran.

His standpoint becomes evident first in his controversy with Treger. In it he denies that the church can of itself give either faith in the Bible or understanding of it. This is the task of the Holy Spirit alone.[1] The same applies to the spoken word as to the written word, for otherwise man's faith would rest ultimately not on God, but on men. Just as the Bible, though it is written by the Holy Spirit, is dead unless the Holy Spirit gives an understanding of it, so without the Holy Spirit the outward word of preaching is dead.

To demonstrate this powerlessness of the word without the Spirit, Bucer quotes not only the example of Paul and Apollos at Corinth,[2] but also the experience of Christ as a preacher:

Otherwise, even if one had scripture and the church as well, yes, even Christ himself bodily as preacher, where the Spirit does not at the same time (*damit*) teach inwardly, we remain indeed completely without understanding, as happened to the Pharisees and Sadducees, who heard Christ himself expound the scripture.

The natural man cannot understand the words of God (1 Cor. 2:14), and no one, however holy, can give this understanding to another, for they must all be taught of God (John 6:45), who alone makes the word fruitful (1 Cor. 3:7).[3]

[1] BW 2.140.6–12, 161.7–15, 161.30–162.4.   [2] BW 2.82.35–8.
[3] BW 2.83.18–22 and 83.11–15. Compare BW 2.93.5–21 and 161.7–15.

Of central importance in this discussion are the texts: 'They must all be taught of God' (John 6:45), and 'So neither he who plants nor he who waters is anything, but only God who gives the growth' (1 Cor. 3:7). Without God's part in giving the growth, man's part in preaching is nothing. This view does not, however, lead to a despising or disparaging of the outward word of preaching.[1] It is what the preachers 'plant and water that God makes to grow'.[2] The two, the outward word and the inward or living word, are not to be separated, but they are certainly to be distinguished. 'The church, indeed, is born through the word, not through the word of the outward sermon or scripture alone, but through the living word, which God speaks in the heart. This does not sound differently from the outward word, indeed it is one and the same word, except that God has made it live in the heart...'[3]

The outward word of preaching is, moreover, not to be separated from the written word of scripture. Bucer says to Treger:

If you are sent, and are Christ's and not the prince of this world's, you have the Spirit of Christ. Then it is not you who speak, but the Spirit of the Father who speaks in you (Matt. 10:20). Therefore, you will not speak differently from scripture, for that is nothing but the word of the Spirit of God; and such words are powerful to destroy every stronghold and attack set up against the knowledge of God (2 Cor. 10:4ff.).[4]

Yet, while it is the word of the preacher to which the Holy Spirit gives growth, the Holy Spirit is not to be tied to this word. Abel, Noah, and Abraham were without the church or scripture.[5] In this, however, Bucer seems more concerned to insist on the necessity of the inward teaching of God, than on the dispensability of outward teaching. His whole emphasis is positive. It is an

[1] In his use of Isa. 55:11, a text almost as popular with him as with Luther, Bucer implies that where the word is preached, there must be true Christians. BW 2.113.33–5, 134.26–7.

[2] BW 2.136.27–30.   [3] BW 2.87.34–9.

[4] BW 2.136.38–137.6. Compare BW 2.136.18–35.

[5] BW 2.82.32–3.

affirmation of the essential role of the Spirit. Therefore he can write: 'If the Holy Spirit teaches inwardly, then we accept it, even if it is only a child who speaks it. If the Holy Spirit does not, then all the councils, even if the whole world agreed, could not convince us of the truth of Christ. For the natural man cannot understand the things of God.'[1]

He does not thereby exclude the role of the preacher. Although he says that the work of the preacher is nothing, it is nothing only in comparison with what God does.[2] His intention is rather to show the total subordination of man's role to that of God. 'Although God has allowed holy men in writing and speech to convey his word to us, yet the word, the preaching, and the efficacy, so that it brings fruit, is God's doing not man's.'[3] To Treger's insistence that Christianity comes through men[4] Bucer replies that all human wisdom is poison. If men teach something good, it must come not from them, but 'from the Spirit of God through them'. 'Therefore, all good teaching is from God and the Spirit of God who speaks in those he sends...'[5]

In the writings of the next twelve years the same underlying emphasis remains. The essential role of the Holy Spirit, teaching inwardly, is distinguished from the role of the preacher, teaching outwardly; but the two are not normally separated. God uses the outward word, though he has on occasion dispensed with it. God is not bound to the outward word, so that he cannot act apart from it, nor does the outward word of itself convey the Spirit—otherwise salvation would be made dependent on man. Within this broad framework there are changes of emphasis (most apparent in the differences between *St John* and the 1536 edition of the *Gospels*) and there are certain new elements that give light and shade to Bucer's position.

In *Grund und Ursach* it is affirmed that 'Christ can convert whom

[1] BW 2.163.25–8. [2] BW 2.85.18–20.
[3] BW 2.165.34–7. [4] BW 2.164.22–5.
[5] BW 2.165.14–22.

he will, without my preaching, but he wishes to use my ministry in doing so, as well with deeds as with words'. Thus the importance of man's part is not denied.[1] Men must preach and be skilful in their preaching; but at the same time everyone must be taught of God.[2]

God's using of preaching is equally affirmed in *St Matthew*. The angel could have taught Cornelius everything concerning Christ, and Christ could have instructed Paul. But it was necessary for Cornelius to submit to Peter as a teacher, and Paul to Ananias.[3] Here the accent lies more heavily than before on the fact that God can dispense with external preaching, and that he has done so. For Bucer, however, this is not so much a general theological principle, as a simple lesson to be drawn from scripture. The Magi provide him with an example of this. They were not taught by a preacher. Yet they knew that Jesus was king of the Jews and that salvation was not to be for the Jews alone.[4] It is, therefore, clear to Bucer that God knows his own, in other words, those who are elect, and 'can teach them about himself, even without outward preaching'.[5]

It is notable that there is now a clearer association of the inward teaching of the Holy Spirit with the doctrine of election.[6] This has a growing importance, and is used to explain both why God dispenses with the outward word, and how the outward word can be effective. The linking of the word with faith is another way of denying that the word is automatically effective, and at the same time of affirming that it is effective. After quoting 'Already you

---

[1] BW 1.223.13–15.   [2] BW 1.223.35–224.2.

[3] 'No doubt the same angel who bade Cornelius send for Peter could have taught him everything about Christ. Equally, Christ could himself have instructed Paul about each of his mysteries. But the former had to be subject to Peter, the latter to Ananias, as teacher. And although each was full of the Holy Spirit and divinely declared to be a member of Christ's flock, yet still the Lord willed that each should be initiated by his teacher, by means of baptism.' 50.B.25–51.A.5; 17.B.2–6; 40.C.11–16.

[4] 22.B.17–23; 8.C.17–20; 19.B.5–8.

[5] 23.A.1–5; 8.C.23–5; 19.B.11–14.

[6] 22.B.17–23; 8.C.17–20; 19.B.5–8. See also 23.A.1–5; 8.C.23–5; 19.B.11–14; and 51.B.16–20; 17.C.3–5; 41.A.25–B.3.

are clean because of the word which I have spoken to you', Bucer adds 'However, it is certain enough that the outward word of the Lord did not make them clean, but faith in the word, for hearts are purified by faith...'[1]

The Holy Spirit is still seen as working alongside the word, or simultaneously with it. With the apostles, who were endowed with the Spirit, the Spirit is spoken of as 'persuading in their words'.[2] Indeed, outward things can be nothing, 'while the Spirit does not teach inwardly'.[3] At times, moreover, the work of the Holy Spirit may seem to follow the word, rather than to be simultaneous with it. 'For to adults it is necessary first that the gospel be preached, after which, if they are among the sheep, they are given the Spirit, so that they have faith in the gospel, then next, when they have professed their faith, they are received into the church by baptism.'[4] There is, however, one reference that suggests a prior operation of the Holy Spirit. In the parable of the sower the stony ground, where the seed is not fruitful, is described as being 'hearts, which are not transformed to piety by the Holy Spirit'.[5]

Bucer describes the word that is preached, as having three elements: (*a*) the exposing of sin ('since only to those knowing themselves to be sinners will Christ come'); (*b*) the testifying to Christ as Saviour ('who will baptise them with fire and the Holy Spirit, that is, who will renew them to salvation by inspiring a new and divine mind'); and (*c*) the announcement of judgment (so that those who hear are eager 'to consecrate themselves to him').[6]

In *Getrewe Warnung* there is no new development, though, in the context of a debate with the anabaptists, there is renewed emphasis on the fact that God uses the spoken word. Bucer argues that if Denck means to reject God's word, then he is acting against

[1] 51.B.24–52.A.6; 17.C.8–13; 41.B.4–13.
[2] 26.B.15–18; 9.C.30–1; 21.B.24–22.C.1.
[3] 173.A.20–1; 136.A.19–20; 347.A.7–9. Compare 17.B.10–18.A.5; 6.C.9–23; 15.B.1–16; and also 267.B.3–12; 168.A.27–B.2; 443.B.16–22.
[4] 51.B.16–20; 17.C.3–5; 41.A.25–B.3.
[5] 296.A.15–19; 177.C.19–21; 456.D.20–3.
[6] 81.A.25–B.12; 27.A.13–21; 64.D.18–65.A.2.

God's Spirit. To prove this, he adduces a variety of biblical examples, where the saints make use of the spoken word.[1] But Bucer
emphatically rejects the idea that the outward word is like 'a
vehicle, by which the Spirit of God is led into the heart'. The
planting and watering (which is what preaching the word is) are
nothing, if God does not give the growth. Once more he affirms
that 'everyone must be taught of God'.[2]

With *Ephesians* there is a greater emphasis on his view that the
word is not an automatic vehicle of the Holy Spirit.[3] He explicitly
rejects the dogma that God does not give faith and the Holy
Spirit, unless the word and sacrament go before. Such a view he
regards as contrary to scripture and the analogy of faith.[4] However, Bucer still insists that God uses the word. Those who attack
the public preaching of the word, he regards as led by an evil
spirit, for it is by the preaching of the word that the elect are led
to faith in Christ. The increase, however, is always from God's
Spirit.[5] Indeed, God may be said to penetrate the hearts of the
elect through his word, of which he persuades them by his Spirit.[6]
There is also the implication in one passage that the word is
preached and evokes a response in those to whom God has *already*
given his Spirit.[7] It is this last note that is sounded clearly and
controversially in 1528 in *St John* and, to some extent, in the
Berner Predigt.

The *Berner Predigt* has, as is to be expected in a sermon, a more
practical slant. Bucer preaches from the text 'Come unto me...'

---

[1] BW 2.240.16–17.   [2] BW 2.238.30–239.15.

[3] E 6.A.6–18. In this context Bucer commends Schwenckfeld. However, as
Schwenckfeld's position becomes clearer, Bucer more and more dissociates
himself from it. We may note that Bucer is throughout sceptical of the inward
voice, which is the impulse of the human mind rather than the voice of God.
For him faith comes from hearing God's word, and from it, moreover, as 'not
departing a hair's breadth from the outward word of scripture', from which it
is nourished. E 39.A.23–B.5.

[4] E 99.A.15–B.14. Bucer's attack is now directed not against traditional catholic
theology, but against the theology of Luther.

[5] E 37.A.15–27. Compare E 20.B.4–25.

[6] E 20.B.20–5.   [7] E 26.B.16–20.

(Matt. 11:28–30). He denies that merely hearing the word is coming to Christ, for the planting and watering are nothing. Rather, Christ must speak in the heart. He reminds his hearers that Judas received the sacrament, which should serve them as a warning against putting their trust in word or sacrament, that is, in a human work.[1] He urges that true knowledge of God is the work of the Holy Spirit, without whom the things of God are foolishness,[2] illustrating this with the example of two people hearing a sermon, but responding differently.[3] The work of the Spirit can be seen already, before the word is preached, in making the elect heavy laden.[4] Without this burden, a man who is called will not know what the gospel is.[5]

It is in *St John* that the distinction of word and Spirit is almost a temporal distinction as well as a logical, or theological one. It is not surprising, therefore, that the more extreme passages were omitted in the 1536 revision of the commentary. Their importance, however, should not be exaggerated. They are intended to refute the Lutheran position that the Holy Spirit can be given only where the outward gifts (word and sacrament) go before. This position Bucer regards as unscriptural, and he argues with scriptural examples against it.[6]

---

[1] BW 2.290.8–291.2.   [2] BW 2.284.5–8, 14–17.
[3] BW 2.283.25–32.
[4] 'Alle zwar hoerend das Evangelium, aber die armen am geist, die iren sünd empfindend, nemmens allein mit froeuden an und bringent frucht. Secht ir, die Gott erwelt hat, denen verlyhet er synen geyst, das sy in foerchten, und wenn sy schon noch on besonderen verstand gottes sind und in aller yppigkeit laeben, doch so trybt sy ein forcht gottes, es ist inen imer angst vor dem gericht gottes, etliche heben denn ouch an inen selbs hilff zebuwen, daher hat mancher im Bapstum nit gnuog koenden bichten, fasten und doch nichs dester besser worden, und hat doch ouch kein ruow kinden haben, denn ye die verworffnen eintweders verruochend gar oder machend in sollich questen von iren wercken, das sy sicher und on forcht werdend, oder aber, so sy schon in forcht blibend, ist es keyn Gottes forcht, sonder nun der straffen Gottes...' BW 2.285.16–286.7.
[5] BW 2.286.18–22.
[6] 'For thus writes their chief: God has determined to give no man what is inward, that is, the Spirit, faith, and other gifts, without what is outward, that is, the preached word and the sacraments. He has done this on this principle and law, that what is outward must and should come first, and that afterwards follows

It is in this context that Bucer affirms that the Holy Spirit must be there already if the word is to be grasped and understood. Without the Spirit of sonship:

man is natural man, unable to receive the things of God. Certainly, if the Spirit is not present, the word which is preached is never understood, and the sacraments are received without fruit. The Spirit, therefore, is not offered with the word, but is poured from heaven, so that the word may be understood. Thus, in fact, 'faith is from hearing' proves nothing else than that, if something is to be believed about God, it is necessary for it first to be heard. Gladly, therefore, we confess that God normally uses his outward word to teach his own, but that it is therefore a means and instrument, by which the Spirit and other gifts of God are given, will never be proved either from these passages [Gal. 3:2 and Rom. 10:17] or from others.[1]

So far the Spirit might seem to be poured simultaneously from heaven to lead to understanding and faith. But in what follows it appears that the Holy Spirit is there beforehand. Again, the primary concern of the passage is to affirm that the word does not automatically bring the Holy Spirit. Bucer relates the possession of the Spirit to election, for he is given only to the elect. If the word were an instrument of the Spirit, it would have to be an

what is inward, that is, the Spirit and faith, and that this is by means of what is outward, namely, word and sacrament. This is what he says—*verbatim*... [By contrast Bucer states:] Thus Peter baptised the household of Cornelius after he had heard them speak with tongues and magnify God—and that by the Holy Spirit. Moreover Ananias baptised Paul also when he had already long since been granted the Spirit and endowed with faith. How then do such men dare to write that the Spirit and faith are not given to anybody, except through what is outward, namely, word and sacraments?' 140.A.5–11, 24–B.3; 50.B.3–7, 16–19; 682.C.3.

The similarity to and contrast with Luther's view should be noted. Bucer does not oppose the outward means as a way appointed by God, by which he gives his Spirit. However, he affirms God's sovereign freedom both in deciding (in election) who shall receive the Spirit and (in vocation) when they shall receive the Spirit. Again, he recognises that faith is related normally to the preaching of the word, but he holds that man can believe the word only when God gives the Spirit, which he does either before or simultaneously with the word. The Spirit is never given automatically with the word, which for Bucer would be tantamount to putting the Spirit at man's disposal.

[1] 139.A.17–B.2; 50.A.4–11; 682.C.3.

instrument of the Spirit for the reprobate as well. But that for Bucer is impossible:

In Acts 13 it reads: And they believed, as many as were ordained to eternal life. Hence indeed the Spirit is given, because whom God has foreordained he also calls. This Spirit is the seed of God, of whom the elect are never destitute, since indeed they are separated from their mother's womb, as Paul also was. This Spirit, this power of the favour of God, does not offer himself at all times equally, but when the time comes, which God has appointed. Nor is he hidden in the flesh, as fire in limestone, but is impressed (*imprimitur*) from on high to those who are elect to life. Indeed, he offers himself a little in every life, more fully and clearly, however, at one time before, at one time after the gospel has been received. For from this same Spirit Cornelius, before he was taught about the gospel, did his alms and uttered his prayers. The same Spirit also compelled the Ethiopian eunuch to seek Jerusalem to pray. It was out of the same Spirit that Paul was zealous for the law before [all] his contemporaries. The infant John was also full of the same Spirit. What [shall I say]? None of the orthodox, either normally or exceptionally, assigned this Spirit to the word, so making it an instrument and means, by which he is given to the saints. The word is preached to the reprobate also, but rather so that they may be blinded. As for Isaiah 6, of which spirit will they make the word an instrument there? That philosophy concerning the instrument and means, by which the Spirit and the grace of God are given, belongs to sophists not to Christians. It is their invention that the sacraments are instrumental causes of grace. No such thing is to be had from scripture concerning the word, much less concerning the sacraments.[1]

There is a certain lack of clarity in Bucer's position here. He does not say explicitly that the elect have the Spirit of sonship before they believe; but he seems to imply it.[2] There are, in any case, various degrees and kinds of possession of the Spirit. In some

---

[1] 139.B.3–27; 50.A.12–27; 682.C.3. This point, that the Holy Spirit must be there before the word and sacraments, is also argued with New Testament examples of baptism and holy communion. They were given only to those who had the Spirit, or who professed faith, which itself implies having the Spirit. See p. 202, n. 6.

[2] Their faith is linked to the proclamation of the gospel. 227.B.21–228.A.7; 84.C.4–11; 761.A.15–23.

measure, however, the Spirit is active in the elect before the preaching of the word, by virtue of their election. The most obvious example is that of John the Baptist, who was full of the Holy Spirit from birth. But Cornelius and Paul are also examples of those who were impelled by the Spirit before they heard the gospel.[1] The idea that there is some (at least preparatory) work of the Spirit, which makes the elect responsive to the gospel, is an abiding feature of Bucer's theology. It is to be found in the case of Nicodemus,[2] and is expressed more generally in the view that 'the minds of men are prepared for the gospel', so that many receive it when it is first announced.[3] The idea that the Spirit is there independently of, and prior to, the word, is normally expressed in the most guarded terms. It is significant that both the comments in the sixth chapter of *St John* are dropped in the 1536 edition.[4]

Despite this change of accent in *St John* there remains an insistence on the outward word. It is still a case of the Lord adding everywhere increase to the planting and watering, lest the word be empty and dead.[5]

This double emphasis is clear in the *Gutachten*. Here Bucer asserts that God can teach his own without our help, and that we

[1] This point is discussed in the Conclusion in the section on the Holy Spirit and the Word.

[2] 'But the seed of God which was in Nicodemus conquered all these hindrances and delays, and had caused him, as a result of the signs which the Lord did, to be already persuaded that the Lord had come from God as a teacher and master for all to listen to.' 70.A.4–8; 24.A.19–21; 619.B.18–21.

[3] 105.B.5–10; 35.C.13–16; 649.B.25–650.C.3.

[4] 139.A.17–B.17; 50.A.4–27; 682.C.3.

[5] 12.A.12–15; 4.A.11–12; 570.C.17–19. *Psalms* shows a stronger emphasis on the preaching of the word. In commenting on Ps. 22 Bucer says that the perpetuity of the church depends on the proclamation of the gospel. P 103.A.12–20. In Ps. 26 he says that the chief thing in the assemblies for worship is the proclamation (or praise) of God's goodness. P 115.A.8–12 and D.5–20. Bucer affirms that the Spirit of God can lead the elect into all truth without any outward teaching. But, when he has said this, he immediately adds that God has given us the scriptures. P 11.A.5–B.1. Commenting on Ps. 23 he says that the elect will be brought to God by the preaching of the gospel. P 104.B.24–C.2.

should not speak, as though God were bound to the outward word. He sees the danger of ascribing faith to the word, and thus of relying on what we do. By contrast, when Paul ascribes something to his ministry, he goes on to ascribe it to God. In fact, everything is of God, though we are his fellow-workers. For Bucer the word is God's usual way of leading to faith, and whoever despises it lacks the Spirit of God.[1]

The 1530 edition of the *Gospels* again insists on the role of the Spirit. Bucer says in the beginning that Luther's writings outside the controversy that has arisen do not bind God's word to our ministry, and do not deny that God could send the Holy Spirit to the elect without men to give the word and the sacraments, nor do they deny that the field of the heart must be prepared by the Holy Spirit before the seed can be received, since the natural man cannot grasp the things of God. Bucer, for his part, regards as an enemy of man's salvation and a destroyer of God's work, anyone who wishes to do away with the ministry of word and sacrament. His concern is to distinguish what God does in giving growth, from what man does in planting.[2] He affirms that it is the Holy Spirit who effects faith through the outward word, and that he does this where and in whom he will.[3]

There are, however, two passages which urge the necessity for the Holy Spirit to be there already, if the word is to be understood and believed:

Faith, indeed, comes from hearing, that is, it is necessary for what the mind believes to be announced to it beforehand; and unless, before the word is heard, the Spirit of God is in the mind, it will understand nothing of what is said (1 Cor. 2). It is thus necessary for the goodness and the Spirit of God to come before all that is outward. Adults, unless they believe beforehand and live in the Lord, when the sacraments are given to them, receive death, and not signs of God's goodwill.[4]

---

[1] BW 3.456.17–458.29.   [2] 7.B.11–48 (Preface 1530).
[3] 'Libenter igitur illa recipimus spiritum sanctum cum externo verbo et per illud operari et efficere fidem, ubi et in quibus ipsi visum fuerit.' 7.B.35–6 (Preface 1530).   [4] 57.A.5; 19.A.29–B.1; 42.D.19 (omitted).

The second passage is more strongly expressed and shows more clearly the motivation of Bucer's argument. He is concerned first with the example of what happens in the Bible, second with our arrogating to ourselves some greater power than Christ and the apostles had, and third with the sovereign freedom of the Spirit:

But when not only the apostles, but the Saviour himself, taught outwardly those whose hearts, since they were empty of the Spirit, never perceived anything of the heavenly teaching, we should be acting most unworthily, if we were to arrogate it to ourselves, that at the same time as we pronounce the word of God, baptise with water, administer the bread and cup of the Lord, the Spirit of Christ accomplishes inwardly what outwardly we say or represent with symbols. The Spirit blows where he wills, and they are not ignorant of his power, whom he truly inspires. In this way it is necessary for our consciences to be strengthened, and not by what is done through men.[1]

The debate with the spiritualists and anabaptists and the closer association with Luther provoked a somewhat different formulation of the relationship of word and Spirit, but not a radically different one. It is primarily a re-formulation of the same underlying position. Typical of this is the change of emphasis in *Quid de baptismate*, where he says 'Through our planting and watering God has decided to raise his plants, but [only] when he adds the growth'.[2] In this formulation of the quotation from 1 Cor. 3, the accent is placed more heavily than sometimes before on the planting and watering. The role of the Spirit, however, is still fundamental in the preacher, as in the hearer.[3]

Two typical examples of Bucer's position in the midst of this controversy are *Contra Bernhard Wacker* and the *Bericht uber dem eusserlichen und innerlichen Wort*. In them he dissociates himself from the spiritualists with their over-emphasis on the inward word (and consequent undervaluing of the outward word) and those who over-emphasise the outward word (with the consequent seeking of salvation from it without faith). He sees himself,

[1] 57.A.5; 19.C.8–14; 42.D.19 (omitted).
[2] QD C.1.B.20–2.   [3] BW 3.226.33–227.15.

as in the debate on the sacraments, steering a middle course.[1] He allows that the word of God may be found in a revelation or an oracle, in the written word of scripture or the spoken word of the minister.[2] Now, however, the emphasis lies on the fact, that, when the word is administered outwardly, God at the same time teaches inwardly in the heart, though this is not without exceptions.[3]

Bucer insists on the distinction between the outward and inward word. Each may occur without the other, but they are not to be opposed to each other. Moreover, the inward word, or inward teaching of the Holy Spirit, is not to be confused with any and every private revelation. Such revelations are to be tested by the written word of scripture.[4] Normally, however, God uses the outward word and does not give the inward teaching of the Spirit without it:

...there is a fundamental difference between the word administered outwardly and the inward teaching of the unction, the teaching of the Father, by which he draws to the Son, for to many the very word of God is outwardly preached and heard, without that vivifying inward teaching and prompting of the Spirit. On the other hand as well, the Spirit sometimes teaches inwardly without [using] the outward ministry, as is the case with all revelations and intuitions of the mind. No one ought to condemn what some say, that is, that there is an inward and an outward word. In other words, God expounds his intentions to men inwardly through his Spirit who teaches all truth, and outwardly with the help of man's ministry. Sometimes he does both at once, sometimes the first without the second, and sometimes the second without the first. Likewise both are sometimes accompanied by a saving transformation of the mind, sometimes not. Equally, however, it is also to be taught that faith is in no way to be put in inward teaching or revelation, unless they agree with scripture, and thus have analogy with the faith. It must also be added that God makes the church and the ministry of the word in her of such worth, that ordinarily he does not grant to any adult the inward teaching of the Spirit without the outward

---

[1] KR 2.193.28–33. For a treatment of the synod, especially the debate about the outward and inward word, see Wendel, *L'Eglise*, pp. 69–96.

[2] KR 2.193.34–194.6.   [3] KR 2.194.21–39.

[4] KR 2.200.24–7.

teaching through ministers. Wherefore it was also necessary for Paul to hear Ananias, and Cornelius Peter, after the one had had Christ himself, and the other an angel, as teacher. I have said expressly adults, because many infants die before they are able to enjoy the outward ministry of the word. I added also ordinarily, because there is nothing which God is not able to accomplish of himself, even without the ministry of any creature. That, however, he is not accustomed to do, except rarely and privily (*tectius*).[1]

The *Bericht uber dem eusserlichen und innerlichen Wort* adds little to *Contra Bernhard Wacker*. There is the same denial of salvation from the word and sacraments without faith in Christ, and the same insistence on God's giving the increase to the proclamation of the gospel, when, to whom, and as much as he wills. Thus the emphasis is on the work of the Spirit, not on the work of the minister.[2] God can teach us both with and without the outward word.[3] As he describes the variety of response to the word, as revealed in the parable of the sower, Bucer adds that, in some cases, the understanding, which is the work of the Spirit, comes later. Only then does the word bear fruit, as was to happen with the apostles in John 14:26.[4] His position is summed up in the words of Augustine, that the word brings fruit to the heart 'not because it is said, but because it is believed'. To this he adds: 'Whoever says that the outward word of God, without the inward, effects nothing in man to salvation, speaks Christianly and rightly, and no one should contradict it.'[5]

With the 1536 edition of the *Gospels* the debate may be said to be over. The discussion of word and Spirit is less prominent in Bucer's later writing, and there is no further development of it. The only exception to this could be the references in the *Acta colloquii*, but these are not directly from Bucer's hand. There the idea of the word as an instrument is expressed less equivocally than is Bucer's custom. 'God does not use the spoken outward

---

[1] KR 2.195.19–40. The allusion to Augustine that follows this quotation is indicative of Bucer's study and use of the fathers in this period.

[2] KR 2.198.4–15.   [3] KR 2.198.16–21.

[4] KR 2.199.17–33.   [5] KR 2.200.21–4, 31–3.

word other than as an instrument, by which he offers that inward discourse (Latin text *affatum*, German text *seinen Geyst*) by which alone hearts are opened.'[1] In *De Regno Christi* the word and Spirit are frequently bracketed with each other.[2] In *Ephesians* (1550) Bucer insists once more that God does not bind the salvation of the elect to any human works or words.[3] Redemption is applied to us by the Spirit and the word,[4] yet planting and watering effect nothing, unless God gives the increase.[5]

While the relationship of word and Spirit in the *Gospels* (1536) remains fundamentally unchanged, it is presented with a new accent. This can be seen in the preface, where Bucer says that he opposed the idea that words and symbols are:

vehicles of the Spirit or instruments of grace...in so far as they are outwardly administered, when the Spirit of Christ is excluded...Apart from the effective power of Christ the word of the gospel and the sacraments do not of themselves confer the Spirit of salvation and grace...As God has commended them to his church and wishes them to be used, I long ago recognised and affirmed that it can be rightly said of the word and sacraments, when we speak of them simply (*simpliciter*), that they are the administration of salvation, channels, vehicles, and instruments of the Spirit and grace...For of themselves, that is, as instituted by Christ...they always confer the Spirit of Christ and salvation. These no one fails to receive from them, unless he disdains to receive them as the Lord instituted them.[6]

The new accent is striking, and there are other passages that sound the same note.[7] He affirms, for example, that:

[1] AC 11.A.5–7.
[2] Thus the elect are gathered through the preaching of the gospel, the Holy Spirit at the same time inspiring and giving true faith. OB 15.56.1–6. Compare OB 15.5.36–6.5 and 54.31–55.11.
[3] EE 136.E.11–12.   [4] EE 24.E.4–7. Compare EE 28.E.11–14.
[5] EE 25.A.4–8.   [6] 5.A.5–22 (Preface 1536).
[7] There are changes in the 1536 edition. Thus Bucer omits 'The Lord can teach his own about himself even without outward preaching' (23.A.1–5; 8.C.23–5; 19.B.11–14), as well as the phrase 'hear no preacher' in the comment 'He [the Holy Spirit] will teach the elect all truth, even if they not only see no signs, but also hear no preacher...' (120.A.10–18; 38.D.26–39.A.2; 95.A.17–21).

Christ, indeed, alone effects the whole of salvation in us, and he does it not by some other power, but by his Spirit alone. However, for this he uses with us the word, both the visible word in the sacraments and the audible word in the gospel. By them he offers and presents remission of sins, communion in himself, and eternal life.[1]

He admits that he has not everywhere satisfactorily expressed the offering of the Spirit of Christ, the remission of sins, and the regeneration that occurs by the word of the gospel.[2]

The strong positive linking of word and Spirit is expressed with the reservations characteristic of Bucer's theology, and which, in one shape or form, are there from the beginning. The word is effective, but only for those who are elect, or who have faith. The word is effective, but only in accordance with its institution by God, only by the power of Christ, or the Spirit of Christ, working within:

By themselves, without the force and effective power of the Lord, neither words nor symbols profit anything. The Lord said to the disciples 'You are clean because of the word, which I have spoken to you'. John 15. However, it is certain enough that the outward word of the Lord did not make them clean, but the power of Christ, by which the apostles received the word of the Lord with faith.[3]

Without the power of Christ, by which he draws us to himself, the work of ministers, and the outward word and signs themselves, cannot be of salvation to anyone.[4]

To say that Bucer's position is fundamentally the same in 1536 as in 1524 is not to deny the more positive accent of 1536.[5] It is rather

[1] 329.A.1; 188.D.21; 485.B.3–6.   [2] 4.A.38–41 (Preface 1536).

[3] 51.B.24–52.A.1; 17.C.8–10; 41.B.4–8.

[4] 53.B.3; 18.A.14; 44.C.1–3. Compare 5.A.5–22 (Preface 1536).

[5] *Romans* adds nothing new, though in it there is the clearest expression of the idea that the Spirit works alongside the word. With the elect Paul's gospel was not in words only, for the Holy Spirit was there with it. At the same time as Paul preached, the Lord breathed his Spirit, so that there was a response and also a willingness to suffer for the gospel. R 47.C.10–48.E.12. Faith remains the work of God, but he uses outward preaching to implant it in the elect. R 487. C.8–488.D.6. Compare R 162.E.1–163.A.14 and 164.D.14–165.A.12. See also the discussion of the Ministry as an Instrument of the Holy Spirit.

to recognise that the controversy, first with Treger, then with Luther, the anabaptists, and the spiritualists, played its part in the formulation of his view. A different accent is to be expected in the debate with Treger or Luther with their emphasis on the outward word, from that in the debate with the anabaptists and spiritualists with their stress on the inward word. That is not all, however. A more sophisticated association of the word and the Spirit with the doctrine of election helps Bucer to a more clearly positive position. The least satisfactory stage in the development of this doctrine is in *St John* and the 1530 edition of the *Gospels*. There he fails to distinguish the working of the Spirit before the proclamation of the gospel from the Spirit of sonship. This is a point that he seems never to have expressed clearly; perhaps because it ceased to be an issue for him in 1536.

Throughout, however, the primary role of the Spirit is unaltered. Salvation comes from God and is effected by his Spirit. No work or word of men can of itself convey this Spirit, but the Spirit himself can and does use the work of men. Only as the Spirit teaches inwardly does the outward word bear fruit, for the Spirit alone opens the hearts and minds of men. In the last analysis the Spirit can act freely apart from the word to teach the elect; but this is exceptional. Normally it is with the word that Spirit comes to the elect, and evokes faith in them.

11

THE SACRAMENTS—THE
VISIBLE WORDS

The development in Bucer's thinking about the sacraments runs in many ways parallel with his thinking about the word. It takes place in the same context and is influenced by the same factors. In the twenties his concern was to oppose the idea of the sacraments as instruments, bringing the gifts of God automatically to all who receive them. In the thirties the accent was rather on the sacraments as bringing the gifts of God, but not automatically to all who receive them.

Bucer gives a number of related reasons for the Christian's need of sacraments. Fundamentally they are needed because in his present state the Christian cannot do without outward ceremonies. Thus *Grund und Ursach* speaks of our having sacraments, because we are still clothed in our sinful body, and hence in part under the law, and thus in need of outward ceremonies. It holds that 'to the New Testament...belongs nothing but the spiritual, that is, the baptism of Christ through the Spirit and fire, and the spiritual enjoyment of the flesh and blood of Christ'.[1] *St Matthew* also grounds the sacraments in the fact that we live 'in the body'.[2] In *St Matthew*, rather than in *Grund und Ursach*, this reason is given a positive orientation, for already the danger presented by those who oppose the outward word and sacraments is evident. The fact that Christ was baptised is used as an exhortation not to despise outward ceremonies which are 'divinely instituted'.[3]

At this stage the view of the sacraments that Bucer attacks most fiercely and persistently is that which regards them as automatically

[1] BW 1.253.28–34.
[2] 46.A.15–22; 15.D.18–22; 35.B.18–23.
[3] 86.B.21–7; 28.C.24–8; 68.D.18–21.

bringing to men the gifts of God. He does not deny that they can bring God's gifts, but it is not of themselves. It is the Lord who 'accomplishes inwardly by the Spirit what is signified by the signs'.[1] Since they are instituted by God, they will not be without fruit, 'if faith is not absent'.[2] It is not the outward thing, whether water or word, that in itself makes a man clean, but 'faith in the word'. Without the response of faith they do not make the recipient clean.[3]

The *Getrewe Warnung* and the *Berner Predigt* show two of Bucer's fundamental reasons for objecting to the sacraments as automatically effective. To ascribe this power to them, is to repose our confidence in what man can do, rather than in what the Spirit of God does:

> ...he speaks truly...against those who now anew want to give to the sacraments and the outward word, power to strengthen our conscience, which, however, according to the whole of scripture, is the work of the Spirit of God alone. For those who have no part in God, may give and receive sacraments, speak and hear God's word outwardly.[4]

It also ignores the testimony of the Bible, that such as Judas received the sacrament outwardly. Therefore, Bucer warns against a facile confidence in the fact that one has received the sacrament outwardly. '...Christ himself must make us eat and drink. For when you would defy the devil and say "I have received the sacrament, a seal of divine grace, you have no hold on me", how quickly will he say to that "many Judases also receive it".'[5] Nevertheless, Bucer goes on to assert the use of the sacraments.[6]

---

[1] 46.A.15–22; 15.D.18–22; 35.B.18–23.

[2] 86.B.21–7; 28.C.24–8; 68.D.18–21.

[3] 51.B.24–52.A.6; 17.C.8–13; 41.B.4–13.

Ritschl (*op. cit.* p. 131) would appear to misunderstand Bucer's meaning, where he ascribes to the sacraments a passage (120.A.10–18; 38.D.26–39.A.2; 95.A.17–21), which speaks of our having no need of signs (that is, miracles). In an absolute sense Bucer holds that man has no need of the sacraments, for God can always act apart from them. But it is in that limited sense, rather than in a general sense, that Bucer affirms that men have no need of sacraments.

[4] BW 2.240.10–15.   [5] BW 2.290.25–9.

[6] BW 2.290.32–291.2.

Ephesians, which comes between these two works, affirms the same points, though in a different way. It is not the sacraments which are the seal of Christians, but the Holy Spirit; for there are many who receive the sacraments who are reprobate and who therefore lack the Spirit.[1] He attacks those who make the sacraments vehicles of the Holy Spirit and faith; since it is the goodness of God through the death of Christ that gives these.[2]

The insistence on God's part in the sacraments is dominant in *St John*. He alone accomplishes what is done. Without him even a Moses would strike the rock in vain, for no water would flow:

Strike the rock with a rod yourself, if you will, anoint the sick with oil, finally, wounded by a serpent, look up at the bronze likeness of a serpent and see what you have achieved. Therefore, we must learn from this that we depend on the one Lord in everything, recognising that he is all in all, and that he alone does everything and brings it to completion. (1536 continues:) That indeed is what we are to learn— and this as well, that the symbols of the sacraments are the instruments of salvation, and that baptism is a washing of regeneration, and the bread and wine of holy communion are a drawing into one place of the body and blood of the Lord. Certainly in themselves the dipping in water, and the breaking of bread, and the distribution of wine do not possess anything of this, nor yet the minister who administers them. But when it seems good to the Lord to confer on his people these his

---

[1] E 90.A.4–12.

By contrast Bucer writes seven years later: 'The Holy Spirit is indeed the true pledge and seal of divine grace. But where the Holy Spirit speaks and acts in the ministers of the church, why should one not also be able to say that the sacraments are as seals of the divine grace and mercy. One must not divide the Spirit of Christ here, otherwise baptism would not be a washing of rebirth and renewal by the Spirit (Titus 3), and no baptism of Christ, who baptises with the Holy Spirit (Matt. 3). The holy communion would be no communion of the body and blood of Christ, for he who has not the Spirit of Christ, the true seal and pledge of the divine goodwill, is none of his (Rom. 8).' BH I.3.B.17–27. Compare 57.A.5; 19.A.23–8; 42.D.19. It is evident that the difference is essentially one of emphasis. The two passages show, in fact, where the real difference of emphasis in these two periods lies.

[2] 'Vehicula enim illa faciunt, spiritus sancti, et fidei, cum haec donet sola bonitas Dei, impetrata morte Christi.' E 4.A.21–3.

gifts by these symbols of his, then the saints as truly lay hold of these gifts in these signs, as the people [of old] were truly healed from the serpents' bites, when, relying on the word of the Lord, they looked up at the bronze serpent, and as the rock truly gave water, when struck by the rod at the Lord's bidding... [1]

Whatever man does is ineffective 'without the co-operation of the Spirit of Christ'. [2] The Holy Spirit, therefore, must be at work at the same time in the recipient, for, if the recipient lacks the Spirit, 'the sacraments are received without fruit'. [3]

The *Gospels* (1530) is perhaps the most vigorous in its attack on the automatic view of the sacraments. The Holy Spirit does not work willy-nilly in the sacraments. Such a view derogates 'from the free election of God, who has mercy on whom he wills, when he wills, and as much as he wills He gives, strengthens, and increases his Spirit out of his goodwill alone, in no way provoked [to this] by our words or signs'. [4] Such an automatic view of the sacraments also runs contrary to what happened even when the apostles and Christ himself taught those who were without the Spirit. [5] The sacraments are not in themselves effective. But 'to those endowed with the Spirit of God, the words, even though administered by men, are words of God, words of life...' [6] The Holy Spirit is, however, not clearly seen as acting in and through the sacrament, but rather as working in the recipient. [7]

The early thirties sees the shift of emphasis to the idea of the

---

[1] 87.B.13–18; 29.B.22–5; 633.B.13–24.

[2] 141.B.9–14; 50.D.14–17; 682.C.3.

[3] 139.A.17–B.2; 50.A.4–11; 682.C.3. Compare 141.A.6–16; 50.C.9–16; 682.C.3.

[4] 57.A.5; 19.A.23–8; 42.D.19.

[5] 57.A.5; 19.C.8–14; 42.D.19.

[6] 57.A.5; 19.A.14–15; 42.D.19. The context concerns both word and sacraments.

[7] In the *Zürich Interpretation* with its contrast of the visible and outward (that is, breath and water), which is the sign, of which the agent is the minister, and the invisible and inward (that is, the Holy Spirit) given with the sign, of which the agent is Christ, the emphasis lies more on the Holy Spirit as given with the sacrament. Pollet, 1.59.4–21 (BW 3.395.24–396.16).

sacraments as imparting what they signify. The *Handlung* speaks of them as 'offering and presenting the redemption of Christ'.[1] They are God's action towards us, not ours towards God.[2] They are not just a sign among men.[3]

This view is firmly stated and firmly safeguarded from misunderstanding in the *Gospels* (1536) and *Romans*. In the *Gospels* he writes: 'the sacraments, which are as it were visible gospels, instituted by Christ the Lord, so that he may communicate his redemption to us through them. Thus it is quite clear that they are in a certain way instruments and channels of the Spirit and his grace.'[4] They are spoken of as signs, 'by which the redemption of Christ is efficaciously offered'.[5]

They are, nevertheless, not in themselves efficacious 'as magicians wish their words and signs to be'. They depend on 'the power of our Lord Jesus who speaks and does everything in these very words and signs that are his':[6]

Christ alone effects the whole of salvation in us, and he does it not by some other power, but by his Spirit alone. However, for this he uses with us the word, both the visible word in the sacraments and the audible word in the gospel. By them he brings and offers remission of sins…Zwingli recognised that; hence, when he denied that the sacraments dispense grace, he meant that the sacraments, that is the outward action, are not of themselves effective, but that everything belonging to our salvation depends on the inward action of Christ, of whom the sacraments are, in their way, instruments. Thus Zwingli opposed what

---

[1] H L.3.A.5–10.

[2] H K.2.B.13–26.

[3] H K.2.B.10–13. *Ephesians* had stressed rather more their being symbols of 'outward communion among Christians'. E 6.A.11–18.

[4] 53.B.3; 18.A.14; 44.C.21–5. In the preface he defends his past statements, in which he resisted the idea of the sacraments as, in themselves, 'vehicles of the Spirit' and 'instruments of grace'. When, however, they are used and received according to Christ's institution, he allows that they can rightly be said to be 'channels, vehicles, and instruments of the Spirit and grace'. 5.A.5–22 (Preface 1536).

[5] 199.A.16–23; 73.B.12–17; 734.D.3–8. Compare 53.B.3; 18.A.14; 44.D.18–25.

[6] 51.A.11; 17.B.10; 40.D.18–26. Compare 51.B.24–52.A.1; 17.C.8–10; 41.B.4–8.

Luther did not affirm. For Luther was the first of all in this century to deny the opinion of the schoolmen, that the sacraments confer grace without the good response (*motu*) of the heart, without faith.[1]

Thus this positive view of the sacraments is safeguarded from misinterpretation by reference to the Holy Spirit and to faith.[2]

Romans offers an extended discussion of signs in general and of the sacraments in particular. Its distinction between various kinds of signs (for example, according to their being natural or given, according to their concerning one sense or another, and according to their signifying something present or absent) need not detain us.[3] Signs are regarded as making a deeper appeal to the mind, because what is said by words is addressed to the senses by signs.[4] They are important for us, as we are born with senses, and in matters of moment we express ourselves with signs as well as words.[5]

Among the signs, Bucer discusses in particular circumcision. It is a sign of the covenant. It is a given one, not a natural one. It is not only visible, but also tangible. It is a sign of something present, not something absent. It offers what it signifies. In other words, it is not just a sign of the covenant, but it is the covenant. 'Therefore, by this sign God offered what he promised, namely to be God to the circumcised...'[6] It is this close relation between the sign and what it signifies that is important now.[7] Signs 'signify God's favour and benefits by offering them, and offer them by signifying them'. In affirming this he expressly rejects the view of those 'who separate the offering of God's gifts from the sacra-

---

[1] 329.A.1; 188.D.21; 485.B.3–11. The quotation is of interest for its positive reference to Zwingli in 1536, as well as its reference to Luther rather than Erasmus as being the first. See, by contrast, the reference to Erasmus in DV 161.4–17.

[2] Compare 53.B.3; 18.A.14; 44.D.18–25. See also 86.B.21–7; 28.C.24–8; 68.D.18–21.

[3] R 147.C.9–149.B.1.

[4] R 150.E.2–4. Compare 51.A.11; 17.B.10; 40.C.21–5.

[5] R 149.B.2–12.

[6] R 150.E.13–F.5.

[7] Contrast this with the distinction between the two in the *Apologia*. AP 28.B.7–13.

ments', and so repudiate them or in their place 'leave nothing but flesh':[1]

...with the thing itself they offer what they signify...God chose to work in and through these things, not so much to represent his gifts to the senses, and through them to the mind, as to give them at the same time with the thing itself, and as it were to hand them over.[2]

However, there is nothing automatic about this. The sacraments are effective, when they are administered according to God's institution, to those whom he has appointed.[3] They do not of themselves bring righteousness, but require faith:[4]

...for adults, as the sacraments offer God's gifts to them by signifying, so they receive them by discerning with faith. For sacraments administered to adults to effect and be, what they are said to be, it is necessary for God to work in them, and thus to inspire by his Spirit the minds of those who receive the sacraments, so that even with certain faith they embrace what they hear to be signified by the sacraments...Where faith is absent the gospel itself is foolishness, and is the odour of death that kills...Therefore, the sacraments, as visible words, just as the audible word of the gospel, have their saving power from the increase that God gives and by the secret inspiration of the Spirit. This God imparts according to his will...[5]

This argument is then supported by Augustine's view that the word is effective not because it is said, but because it is believed.[6] Thus the sacraments are effective to salvation by the power of the Spirit for those chosen by God, who, having been inspired by the Spirit, receive the things which are offered in the sacraments with faith.[7]

This remains Bucer's understanding of the sacraments. In *Ephesians* (1550) he reaffirms that they 'are not bare signs, but offer what they show' and 'in a certain measure, with these outward signs, we touch and see what we receive'.[8] But he adds that

[1] R 159.C.3–160.D.4. [2] R 160.D.8–10.
[3] R 160.E.7–161.A.1. [4] R 138.E.16–F.10.
[5] R 162.E.4–14. [6] R 162.E.14–20.
[7] R 163.A.3–15.
[8] EE 104.F.11–105.A.2. Compare EE 35.C.6–8, EE 120.E.1–3, and OB 15. 66.25–8.

'God indeed has not bound his power of saving the elect to any human works or functions, to any words or signs, administered by men'.[1] 'He can indeed offer his benefits to whom he wills, without any signs.' However, that is no reason for neglecting the signs God has given us: 'For it is not for us ourselves to prescribe, but for God himself to prescribe to us, by what way we are to receive his gifts.'[2]

This general discussion of the sacraments indicates a movement from the earlier distinction of the sign and the thing signified, with its assertion that the sacraments were not automatically bearers of God's gifts, to the later linking of the sign and the thing signified, with an emphasis on the sacraments as offering God's gifts. In this shift of emphasis the underlying insistence on the essential role of the Holy Spirit in accomplishing what is signified, and on faith in the person receiving, remains. Moreover, at no point is God held to be bound to the sacraments, so that he must act in them and cannot act apart from them.

[1] EE 136.E.11–12.
[2] EE 155.A.18–B.18. Compare TA 608.45–609.4.

12

BAPTISM—THE VISIBLE WORD 1

Baptism focuses more sharply than any other issue the varied positions of the reformers. The spiritualists, with their rejection of outward means, could dispense with it. The anabaptists, with their particular understanding of the Bible and of faith, replaced infant with adult or believers' baptism. The Lutherans, with their understanding of faith and their insistence on outward means of grace, re-interpreted baptism. These varied positions reflect fundamentally different attitudes to the Bible, the use of outward means by the Spirit, and the relation of grace and faith.

The same is true of Bucer's understanding of baptism. Like the other reformers he had to wrestle with the issue theologically and practically. His position, moreover, was expressed primarily in reaction to what he regarded as erroneous views, whether catholic, Lutheran, spiritualist, or anabaptist.[1]

1523–1530

The debate about baptism in Bucer's earlier writings centres in the distinction he makes between baptism with water and baptism with the Spirit. Its immediate context is the controversy with Treger, in which Treger argues on the basis of Gal. 3 that all who are baptised have put on Christ. This position Bucer rejects by referring to Rom. 8. It is significant that Rom. 8:28–30, which plays such an important part in the developing of Bucer's doctrine of election, is first quoted here.

---

[1] Usteri offers a useful general discussion of Bucer's view of baptism in the context of views circulating at the same time and in particular of the influence of Zwingli on Bucer. See J. M. Usteri, 'Die Stellung der Strassburger Reformatoren Bucer und Capito zur Tauffrage', especially pp. 462, 487–90, 517, and 521.

G. H. Williams gives a summary of various anabaptist views of baptism. See *Radical Reformation*, pp. 300–19.

Bucer argues that Gal. 3 applies to those who believe in Christ, and not to those not elected to life:

Paul, therefore, to prove that all believers are children of God, says: 'For as many of you as are baptised, have put on Christ.' He must indeed be speaking of spiritual baptism, by which alone one puts on Christ etc., and becomes a child of God...not all those baptised can be meant, but only those called according to God's purpose, foreknown and foreordained, to be conformed to the image of his Son...For he speaks of the baptism in which one puts on Christ, is Christ's, and abides in him...That is what the baptism of Christ does, for he baptises in Spirit and fire and not in water alone, like John the Baptist. Those who receive only the sacrament of baptism, and yet are foreknown to be damned, are not inwardly baptised in the Spirit by Christ, for they will not be glorified and therefore they are not justified by Christ.[1]

The distinction here between baptism in water and baptism in the Spirit represents primarily a fundamental opposition in Bucer between elect and reprobate, rather than an opposition between outward and inward. There is, therefore, a distinction between baptism in water and baptism in the Spirit, not a separation.

In *Grund und Ursach* the theme is developed and a clear distinction is made between Christ's baptism, which is a baptism in the Spirit, and man's baptism, which is in water. The context is now chiefly the abuse of baptism, which has led to a false confidence in outward baptism. This has already been hinted at in the letter of the Strasbourg preachers to Luther on 23 November 1524. In it they refer to baptism as an outward thing and show some inclination for the practice of the earliest church where baptism was administered to those who had been instructed about Christ. This linking of baptism with a confession of Christ would, they think, take away a false confidence in the baptism of water and doubt about unbaptised infants. They tell Luther, however, that with him and against Carlstadt they hold to infant baptism.[2]

The arguments are given in detail in *Grund und Ursach*. They are presented in answer to the belief that baptism in itself saves a

---

[1] BW 2.119.26–120.4.   [2] W.A.Br. 3.797.95–107.

child, without which he will not see God's face. Baptism in this case, moreover, is taken to include as essential such elements as the chrism and the salt. Such a view, Bucer holds, 'belittles the death of Christ, through which we are sanctified'.[1] In opposition to this view he asserts that forgiveness is through faith and that there are two baptisms, one of water, the other of the Holy Spirit. These he contrasts. 'With the baptism of the Spirit Christ alone baptises; with water baptism John baptised, and the apostles and all others baptise. The baptism of Christ, who baptises with the Holy Spirit and fire, blots out sin and makes [people] children of God. Water baptism is an outward sign of this.'[2]

Baptism with the Spirit is not separated, but only distinguished, from baptism with water. Those who believe in Christ receive the Holy Spirit,[3] likewise those who are elect.[4] (These are not, of course, two separate categories, but ultimately different descriptions of the same people.) That the two baptisms are linked in the New Testament is shown by a series of quotations in which baptism is linked with faith.[5] However, it is not outward baptism that saves. 'The Lord certainly says "He who believes and is baptised will be saved, but he who does not believe will be damned". But he does not say "He who is not baptised will be damned". For God does not bind his grace to water.'[6]

There seems a sense in which baptism with water is disparaged

[1] BW 1.254.22–30.

[2] BW 1.254.31–255.6. Compare BW 1.256.11–21, 256.39–257.6, 32–3 and 258.6–13.

[3] 'For Peter says to the Jews in Acts 2: "Repent and be baptised every one of you in the name of Jesus Christ for the forgiveness of sin, and you will receive the gift of the Holy Spirit". That is, confess that you have need of repentance, and be baptised in the name of Christ, that is, with faith through the name of Christ to attain forgiveness of sin, and you will receive the gift of the Holy Spirit. See, this then is the baptism of Christ, with which he baptises.' BW 1.255.13–20.

[4] 'For forgiveness of sins is the baptism of Christ, which he works in the elect through his Holy Spirit.' BW 1.257.4–6.

[5] BW 1.256.22–257.25. See also BW 1.259.13–38 and p. 226, n. 4.

[6] BW 1.257.25–31. Compare 72.B.22–73.A.9; 25.A.3–11; 622.D.10–22. See also BH Y.2.B.15–29.

when Bucer, in arguing for infant baptism on the basis of God's care for us from our mother's womb, says:

What is there in so much water? If we are to pray to God for all men, should we not wish also to commit to God our children, to whom Christ acted with such kindness? Even if we baptise a few goats, whom Christ does not will to baptise with his Spirit, it is only a matter of so much water and prayer. Likewise the apostles did not always succeed in baptising only believers.[1]

This is not essentially a disparagement of baptism, for Bucer has earlier argued that Christ by his baptism showed us what follows, if we receive baptism in faith: 'the Holy Spirit assuredly comes over us, the Father recognises us as his beloved children'.[2] It is rather an expression of his continuing conviction that the water of baptism is nothing in itself. It is an instrument or vehicle of the Spirit only when the Spirit uses it, which he does only in the elect (that is, with the sheep and not with the goats). Such a positive affirmation of baptism as an instrument or vehicle of the Spirit is not, however, clearly expressed until the thirties.

The arguments that Bucer uses for infant baptism in this debate do not, for the most part, directly concern the relation of the Holy Spirit to baptism, and may be left on one side.[3] It may be noted, nevertheless, that even at this stage the doctrine of election is used as an argument for infant baptism, as is the assertion that the New Testament does not necessarily link baptism and the confession of faith,[4] though these arguments are in a rudimentary form.

The *Apologia* and the *Preface* do not take the discussion further. The *Apologia* seeks to safeguard the fact that our salvation is by faith alone and therefore ascribes it to Christ and the Holy Spirit, not to water.[5] It rejects the idea that baptism is an instrument of

---

[1] BW 1.260.34–9.
[2] BW 1.255.39–256.3.
[3] In the writings between *Grund und Ursach* and *Romans* more than twenty specific grounds for the baptism of infants are advanced.
[4] BW 1.259.13–38. See also BW 1.256.22–257.25 and p. 226, n. 4.
[5] AP 12.A.18–B.1.

salvation, like herbs for the body,[1] and affirms that faith is engendered by the work of the Spirit.[2] The *Preface* underlines the fact that our salvation is from God, by asserting that our works have no power to justify and that to baptise or to be baptised is our work.[3] For Bucer 'the work of man in itself is nothing except a sign'. This does not mean that baptism with water and baptism with the Spirit are mutually exclusive. On the contrary, 'where baptism is undertaken with faith', then burial with Christ, the putting on of Christ, the washing of regeneration, and the washing away of sins, are not only signified by baptism, 'they are indeed really present through the Holy Spirit'.[4]

St Matthew equally attacks the view of the sacraments as automatically effective. It rejects the idea that 'the word of the person baptising is a vehicle of the Holy Spirit, by which he is conveyed into the water, which is then not water, but is really the Holy Spirit, which at once purges the baptised infant of all sin, giving faith and everything'.[5] This view, in effect, ascribes to the water, what is the work of the Holy Spirit.[6] 'Nevertheless, baptism is no more than planting and watering, of which Paul writes as follows in 1 Cor. 3: "Thus neither he who plants nor he who waters is anything, but God who gives the increase".'[7] As baptism is 'a work of man', the ascription to it of saving power is a denial of justification by faith.[8] Nevertheless, within the situations for

---

[1] *De vi et usu* offers a contrasting emphasis, characteristic of the later Bucer, when it calls the sacraments instruments of salvation and compares them with effective remedies for sickness. TA 597.26–30, 38–42; 598.11–25.

[2] AP 12.B.7–14.

[3] PR A.8.A.10–13.

[4] PR A.8.B.5–18.

[5] 236.A.20–B.7; 156.B.8–16; 405.A.3–5.

[6] 'But none of these things is present by the power of the baptism or the ministry. They are all the work of the Spirit of Christ. They are only represented by baptism, but are truly represented, when those who are baptised are of those elect to the kingdom of Christ.' 56.A.11–15; 18.D.6–8; 42.D.19.

Bucer views the relation of the Holy Spirit and the water differently from Luther. See Köhler, *op. cit.* p. 289 and Hopf, *op. cit.* pp. 68 and 96.

[7] 57.A.2–5; 19.A.9–10; 42.D.19.

[8] 51.A.15–26; 17.B.13–19; 41.A.3–14.

which God has appointed baptism he baptises with the Spirit—
that is, with those who are elect[1] and who have faith.[2]

It is, however, characteristic of this period that the definitions
of baptism speak of it frequently as a sacrament of initiation and
incorporation into the church. Baptism was instituted 'so that,
by this sign, those who are Christ's might openly be inscribed into
his flock...'[3] Baptism is at the same time an action of God; but
the accent does not lie there when Bucer is discussing baptism with
water, lest such baptism should be identified without more ado
with baptism with the Spirit.

In discussing infant baptism, Bucer allows, indeed insists, that
infants have no faith, for that would involve hearing the gospel
and being persuaded of it. He holds, however, that faith is not
necessary for baptism.[4] Nevertheless, if infants are elect, they will
have the Holy Spirit, just as John the Baptist did, who was full
of the Holy Spirit from his infancy. At the appointed time they
will be led to faith in the word of God.[5]

[1] 56.A.1–15; 18.C.32–D.8; 42.D.19.   [2] 56.A.16–27; 18.D.8–16; 42.D.19.
[3] 57.A.2–5; 19.A.9–10; 42.D.19. Compare PR A.8.A.1–5. The influence of
Zwingli may be seen here.

[4] 'Those who say that infants are baptised upon their own faith (when, if you
speak in accordance with scripture, faith is from hearing), and who wish those
words "I baptise thee" and so on, to be for infants in the place of the gospel and
to be heard and understood by them, so that they may be able to believe them,
they themselves are recommending something which they have invented. For
that scripture does not teach, nor is it proved from any part of it, that it is
necessary for those who are baptised to believe. Otherwise those who baptise
infants would be committing a sin, because, as I said, if you speak in accordance
with scripture, faith is to be persuaded of the gospel when one hears it—but
infants cannot, except by a miracle, be persuaded of it. For if, as they say,
contrary to the use of reason, infants could nevertheless hear the words of the
one who baptises and have faith in them, it would be better, indeed it would be
necessary for charity, to preach the gospel to them at the same time.' 46.A.24–
B.10; 95.D.23–96.A.4; 242.C.13.

This passage shows that Bucer does not agree with Luther about the presence
of faith in infants. The apparent contradiction here with Bucer's earlier position
(BW 1.256.22–257.25, but see also BW 1.259.13–38) is due to the difference
between adult and infant baptism. In adults faith is necessary. In them faith
depends on their being elect and having the Spirit. In children faith is not possible, but equally they must be elect, and if they are elect they will have the
Spirit.   [5] 235.B.8–12; 156.A.13–16; 404.C.26–D.3.

There is no significant change of emphasis in Bucer's writings until after the 1530 edition of the *Gospels*. We may, therefore, treat *Getreue Warnung, Ephesians, St John*, the *Gutachten*, and the *Gospels* (1530) as one, and as, in some measure, a summary of his position in the twenties. They are directed against the automatic view of baptism, 'that it cleanses children from all sins...that, as soon as one baptises them, Christ imparts to them his Spirit...or that by virtue of the word "I baptise thee etc.", the Holy Spirit comes into the water and is communicated to the baptised children...'[1]

The grounds for rejecting this doctrine are varied. It ignores the doctrine of election:

God calls and makes holy whom he has foreordained...when he pleases, and has not hung his Spirit and faith on any sacrament...It is certain many reprobate are baptised; so it is totally mistaken to say that everyone who is baptised has the Holy Spirit and faith, for he who is born of God, cannot ever sin, so that he will be damned (1 John 3:6). Whoever believes is born of God (John 1:12–13).[2]

It ignores the necessity of faith.[3] Moreover, it places confidence in the water, in what men can do, rather than in the Spirit and grace of God.[4] What happens in baptism is that 'from the Lord we ask for them the Spirit of God, and do not presume to impart (*infundere*) the Spirit with the water'.[5] Bucer likewise rejects the idea that God has ordered things so that he does not give faith and the Holy Spirit unless his word and sacraments come first. Such a view he regards as contrary to the Bible and the analogy of faith.[6]

Rather, for Bucer, must the Holy Spirit be there before the word and sacraments, so that the word is understood and the

[1] BW 2.241.6–12.
[2] BW 2.241.14–24. Compare E 98.B.1–5, 98.B.16–99.A.10. See also 57.A.5; 19.B.22–C.3; 42.D.19.   [3] 7.B.49–8.A.19 (Preface 1530).
[4] BW 2.241.30–242.4. Compare E 99.A.15–B.14. See also 71.B.22–72.A.22; 24.C.27–D.10; 621.A.15–B.11.   [5] E 99.B.7–9.
[6] E 99.B.9–14. This argument, as many of the arguments of this period, is directed against Luther.

sacraments are received for salvation and not damnation.[1] This view is pushed even farther when Bucer asserts: 'Faith and the Spirit are the gift of God, which he imparts when it pleases him—not at our words. Certainly those whom the apostles baptised who already believed, were indeed sealed beforehand with the Holy Spirit. What therefore did baptism or the word of the baptiser bring to them?'[2]

Bucer not only rejects the automatic character of baptism, he also rejects the necessity of baptism for salvation. 'Baptism with water is not in itself necessary for salvation, so that no one can be saved without it.'[3] In this context he argues that Christ did not say that he who is not baptised will be condemned, but 'he who does not believe will be condemned'.[4] 'Regeneration comes totally from the Spirit. If one has the Spirit, even if he has not received baptism with water, he is nevertheless a new creature in the Lord.'[5] It is, in other words, the baptism of the Spirit that is all important.[6]

His insistence on the baptism of the Spirit does not lead to indifference to outward baptism. 'No one who is godly will heedlessly neglect baptism with water and outward reception into the church.'[7] Such baptism 'while God's word is there, and it is founded on God's word, is a blessed, living, and powerful thing'.[8]

1530–1539

This positive note is sounded more clearly in the thirties. The conflict with the spiritualists and anabaptists, the reconciliation with

[1] BW 3.460.7–12. Compare 57.A.5; 19.A.29–B.3; 42.D.19.
[2] E 99.A.21–6.
[3] 72.B.22–6; 25.A.3–5; 622.D.10–13.
[4] In the *Bericht* Bucer interprets this differently. He argues that it is used in the context of preaching to the heathen, where he who does not believe is also clearly not baptised, and he who does believe is baptised. BH Y.2.B.15–29. This, in its way, betokens the later shift of accent.
[5] 73.A.3–5; 25.A.8–9; 622.D.16–18. This passage is kept in the 1536 edition of the *Gospels*.
[6] Compare 70.A.24–B.1; 24.B.2–5; 620.C.8–11.
[7] 73.A.7–9; 25.A.10–11; 622.D.19–22.
[8] BW 3.460.23–5.

Luther, the closer study of the fathers all contribute to this. They provoke a different orientation of his theology of baptism. If the dominant error attacked in the twenties is the catholic (and, according to Bucer's understanding of it, the Lutheran) one of making the sacrament an automatic instrument of the Spirit, that of the thirties is the viewing of baptism as a human rather than as a divine action. In both periods Bucer seeks the middle way between what he regards as two errors, but in steering his course he inclines more towards the side from which he directs his assault.

The *Apology*[1] already shows a change of emphasis which is taken further in the *Articles*. Thus, whereas Article 6 is aimed against the automatic view of the sacraments, Article 8 presents a more positive evaluation, of which the use of *anbieten* (offer) is a token. 'In baptism the washing of sins is offered (*anbotten*)... Baptism is, therefore, not just a mere sign for us to recognise each other, but much more that which God wishes to be to us through our Lord Jesus Christ, and to give to us according to his divine ordinance.'[2]

This position is strengthened in *Quid de baptismate*. Our regeneration through the Holy Spirit is now said to be 'offered and presented to us... by words and baptism in water'.[3] '...in baptism we see the chief thing to be what God promises, gives, and presents through his church.'[4] Precisely because the fathers held this view and held that it was equally true of infants, they could say that infants who were unbaptised, were not partakers of salvation. In this Bucer argues that they were not ascribing the power to the water rather than to Christ, nor were they limiting God to the sacraments. In his judgment they, like him, expressly attributed

---

[1] Bucer quotes Augustine with approval, that the water has its power from the word, not in that the word is spoken, but in that it is believed. He accepts Augustine's definition of the sacrament as a visible word. 'Where one holds the sacraments rightly, one proclaims the gospel of Christ, and what is conveyed in that in words, the very same is also represented to the eyes and in like manner visibly offered through the holy signs.' BW 3.272.38–273.3. See ZP 207–8.

[2] KR 2.27.5–10.

[3] QD A.7.B.24–A.8.A.1. Compare D D.2.A.23–7.

[4] QD A.8.B.4–7.

the power to the Holy Spirit 'acting in the church through his words and sacraments'.[1] It is striking that the accent at this stage does not lie, as in the late twenties, on the recipient's already having the Spirit. Not only does Bucer reject the idea, that baptism is given as a sign that a person is already dead to sins and renewed by the Spirit,[2] but he also insists that one cannot be certain that those who are baptised, already participate in the Spirit.[3]

In the *Bericht* the close relationship of sign and thing signified is unquestioned. As the sceptre and the giving of kingly power go together, so do baptism and the washing of sins, 'for it is communicated to us in baptism'.[4] This linking of the two, however, presupposes the activity of the Spirit, without whom the sign is dead. 'The sacraments are outward signs and thus representations of the grace of God; and so, without God's blessing, they are nothing and do nothing (1 Cor. 4). The Spirit of the Lord must always be there, and accomplish the matter inwardly.'[5] The conditions are, therefore, the activity of the Spirit on the one side, and the grasping of the sacrament with faith on the other.[6] Given the presence of the Spirit, baptism can be spoken of as a seal of God's grace.[7]

The linking of the sign and what it signifies is taken up in the *Catechism* in the dialogue between teacher and child:

T. Why are they called sacraments?

C. Because in and with these visible signs, God gives and delivers his invisible and hidden grace and the redemption of Christ.[8]

T. How can water and the outward word, with which baptism is given, regenerate people, renew them with the Holy Spirit, incorporate them in Christ, clothe them with him, and make them participators in his death?

C. Our Lord Jesus, our high priest and saviour, acts and accomplishes all this through his Holy Spirit. He uses for it the ministry of the

[1] QD B.4.B.14–B.5.A.24.   [2] QD B.8.B.9–20, C.5.A.14–B.11.
[3] QD C.6.A.14–B.12.
[4] BH AA.3.B.18–4.A.5 and BH K.1.A.26–8.
[5] BH I.1.A.30–B.4.   [6] BH I.1.B.16–19.
[7] BH I.3.B.17–27. See p. 215, n. 1.
[8] GC C.3.B.26–9. Bucer now says 'in' as well as 'with'.

church, in outward words and signs. Therefore they are called sacraments and *mysteria*, that is holy secrets—that while one thing happens inwardly through the power of Christ, one sees another outwardly in the ministry of the church...

T. He acts in the sacraments. Therefore they are called sacraments of Christ, not of his minister.[1]

The close linking of the sign and what it signifies is always safeguarded, however, by an affirmation of God's accomplishing what is signified, by his Spirit.[2]

Perhaps most surprising is the new confidence in the fact of baptism itself. This is not, as might at first sight appear, an accepting of the position he had remorselessly attacked in his earlier writings.[3] It is not a case of placing one's trust in baptism, but rather of having confidence in God. It is to be understood not only in the narrower context of the newer, more positive evaluation of baptism, but also in the wider context of the doctrine of election. This is, moreover, no sudden conversion quickly repented of, but is re-affirmed in 1537 and 1539, though it does not appear in the *Shorter Catechism* of 1543:

Whatever happens to me all my days, I do not doubt, since I am baptised in the name of God the Father, the Son, and the Holy Spirit, that I am called, and am a child and heir of God, and am under the protection of the divine name, who will forgive me all my sins, and let everything serve me to eternal salvation.[4]

T. Are you a Christian?

C. Yes sir.

T. How do you know?

C. Because I have been baptised in the name of God the Father, the Son, and the Holy Spirit.

T. Good, for through baptism you were incorporated into Christ our Lord, and became a member of Christ and his disciple.[5]

---

[1] GC C.4.A.13–29.
[2] See also GC O.3.A.2–4.
[3] In terms of holy communion in BW 2.290.8–291.2.
[4] GC D.2.A.25–B.4.
[5] Reu 1.I.68.18–21. Compare BW 7.310.17–21.

Bucer, aware of the change of emphasis that his thought has undergone, says in the preface of the *Gospels* (1536) that he has 'not everywhere satisfactorily expressed...the offering of the Spirit of Christ, of the remission of sins, and of the regeneration that happens...with holy baptism'.[1] Certainly he does not surrender his previous position. But he presents it differently. Baptism is still not automatically effective, but is dependent on the action of the Spirit and on its being rightly used and received. It is not baptism in itself that has power to purge sins. 'It is the Lord who sanctifies in renewing men by his Spirit...'[2] The washing of regeneration is not merely a matter of baptism outwardly administered, but one in which, at the same time, Christ inwardly gives us his Spirit.[3] While true baptism is marked on the godward side by the power of the Spirit, it is marked on the manward side by being rightly received, by being used as instituted by God. When it is rightly received, God is accustomed to join the inward with the outward, the sign with the thing signified.[4] 'These things they receive by it who use it according to the Lord's institution.'[5]

The problem of what baptism does for those who already have the Spirit, which was treated negatively in *Ephesians*,[6] is now dealt with more positively. In baptism 'they receive remission of sins fully through the sacred ministry of the church'[7] and are also given eternal life.[8] This new answer does not seem to have been worked out satisfactorily, and this may in part account for the

---

[1] 4.A.38–41 (Preface 1536).
[2] 51.B.5–10; 17.B.23–5; 41.A.17–21. Compare 52.B.6–8; 17.C.30–D.1; 41.B.24–42.C.3.
[3] 52.B.23–5; 17.D.11–12; 42.C.10–12.
[4] 'Sunt enim signa exhibitiva, cunque de signis in veritate perceptis loquatur, quo pacto simul adest, quod significant, solet interna simul cum externis, hoc est, signum et signatum coniungere, atque ita iunctim ea praedicare.' 53.A.20–7; 17.D.26–18.A.3; 42.D.5–7.
[5] 73.A.7–9; 25.A.10–11; 622.D.19–22.
[6] E 99.A.21–6.
[7] 51.B.16–18; 17.C.3–5; 41.A.25–B.3. Compare 72.B.8–13; 24.D.19–22; 621.B.21–5; and 72.B.13; 24.D.22; 622.C.21–D.3.
[8] 50.B.7–13; 17.A.23–6; 40.C.1–4.

continued, though differently accented, emphasis on baptism as the sign by which the baptised are received into the church.[1]

The distinction of baptism with water and baptism with the Spirit remains, and with it the possibility that the first may happen without the second, and the second without the first. Here Bucer's theology, for all its difference in accent, is unchanged. 'The baptism of Christ, which he performs by himself, with or without outward baptism, is through the Spirit and fire...wherefore he did not confer baptism in water...'[2]

Romans presents a more detailed and systematic treatment of baptism, in particular relating it to Gentile and Jewish baptisms. All baptisms are regarded as 'symbols by which remission of sins through the gospel of divine grace is announced and the renewal of the Spirit is offered'. There is, however, a contrast:

the baptisms used by the early fathers [of Israel] and pious Gentiles were symbols of a more general gospel and a more infantile Spirit...

the baptism of the church of the glorified Christ by the light of the gospel, by the fulness of redemption, which Christ brought us, by the power of the Spirit which he gives, so excels those that went before, that there is none that surpasses it.[3]

He regards all baptisms as instituted by God; their effectiveness, however, depends on the degree to which God has revealed himself and given his Spirit. This revelation and gift of the Spirit is fuller with the glorification of Christ[4] than in his life or before his incarnation; and, therefore, Christian baptism gives the Spirit more fully.[5]

In this whole discussion of the various baptisms and the various degrees in which they impart what they signify, it is important to

[1] 50.B.13–16; 17.A.26–9; 40.C.4–6.
[2] 57.A.18–21; 19.C.23–4; 45.A.15–17 (1536 adds 'with or without outward baptism'). Compare Pollet 1.169.25–30.
[3] R 325.B.10–19.
[4] A more detailed treatment of this question is found in the sections discussing the relation of the Old Testament and the New Testament and the relation of Christ to the Gentiles on pp. 109–28.
[5] R 325.B.19–326.D.13.

note Bucer's exegesis of Acts 19 and the reference to the baptism of John.[1] He holds that the reference here is not to John's baptism, because the text says that these men had not heard of the Spirit. As John spoke of the Spirit and indeed baptised with the Spirit,[2] then this baptism could not have been John's. By contrast with other baptisms, Christian baptism cannot be repeated. It is the symbol of the full revelation of Christ, so that there is no more perfect offering of Christ to men.[3]

The defence of infant baptism is now firmly rooted in the election and promise of God:[4]

However, God is not accustomed to reveal publicly those whom he has elected and destined to be his sons. As with adults, the confession of faith, which their life does not falsify...so with children he has commanded that we need have no concern other than for them to have Christian parents or otherwise to be under the authority of Christians, or finally to be brought for the blessing of Christ, that is, if this is sought by those whose power they are in.[5]

The church cannot know the elect, only God can. It acts therefore according to God's promise 'I will be your God and the God of your children'.[6] To those who argue that the sacraments should be given only to those who show communion with Christ, Bucer can reply that John the Baptist had the Spirit as a child.[7]

1540–1551

The following years bring nothing new to the debate on baptism, though it is conducted more with catholic than with radical opponents of the reformation. The *Bestendige Verantwortung*, in its summary of original sin, says that Christ 'has redeemed us from this corruption through the regeneration which he communi-

---

[1] R 322.D.6–E.18.
[2] 59.A.9; 20.A.26; 47.A.21–B.7. Compare BW 1.255.21–256.10; TA 595.39–50; and EE 144.D.10–16.
[3] R 322.E.13–323.A.1.   [4] Compare QD B.5.B.9–B.6.B.17.
[5] R 161.B.7–12. The last phrase may refer to the civil authorities, who are given the right to baptise compulsorily children whose parents refuse to have them baptised. See BH Y.4.A.31–B.31.
[6] R 161.B.17–162.D.1.   [7] R 330.F.2–6.

cates to us and initiates in us in baptism'. 'Thus the Lord washes and purifies us in baptism from all sins, so that he will reckon none of them to us for guilt and damnation.'[1] He also refers to our receiving in baptism justification, that is, forgiveness of sins, sonship, and the right of inheritance to eternal life.[2] It is Bucer's doctrine of election that enables him to take a position that comes close to that of his opponents, though it should be noted that these comments are not in a context where the debate is about baptism, where Bucer would use his characteristic safeguards. Although in one place Bucer can identify justification and baptism, in another he can place the forgiveness of sins before baptism, as with Paul and Ananias.[3]

The safeguards are present in *Ein Summarischer vergriff* where baptism regenerates and renews 'when given and received according to the command of the Lord'. Not only is sin forgiven in baptism, but also evil desires 'are greatly weakened by the grace and the Spirit of Christ, whom we receive in baptism...'[4] In these later writings the strong distinction between the baptism of water and that of the Spirit has receded, and the gift of the Spirit in baptism is often expressed indirectly in terms of what he effects (forgiveness or purification) rather than directly.

De ordinatione also holds the safeguards in close association with its belief in the efficacy of baptism. Baptism must be apprehended with 'the living faith of the gospel',[5] and it must be received as it was instituted.[6] Moreover, God's sovereignty is once more insisted on.[7] 'For although he has not so bound his benefits to the sacraments, that he does not gladly distribute them to his own, when without their blame the sacraments are not present for them; yet our Lord wishes... us by them, as by his instruments, to receive from him his benefits...'[8]

De vi et usu and *Ephesians* (1550) express themselves in almost identical terms. The sacraments are 'visible signs by which the

---

[1] BV 26.B.20–6.
[2] BV 40.B.29–31.
[3] BV 177.A.7–16.
[4] V C.2.B.16–18 and C.1.A.5–7.
[5] TA 246.14–21.
[6] TA 248.5–12.
[7] Compare QD B.4.B.14–B.5.A.24.
[8] TA 248.29–34.

invisible gifts of God are offered'.[1] Baptism in water is not to be separated from baptism in the Spirit, as though in the quotation 'unless you are baptised by water and the Spirit...' water simply stood for the Spirit. That, Bucer says, would be mere tautology.[2] Rather is baptism 'administered by the word and command of Christ an instrument for him, for purging his elect of sins'.[3] This does not mean that God needs it; on the contrary, he judges it useful for us.[4] 'Therefore our salvation, which consists in our regeneration and renewal, which the Holy Spirit effects in us, and to that extent even the Holy Spirit himself, and indeed our regeneration and renewal, are administered to us through baptism.'[5] Baptism is no less efficacious than a remedy for bodily health. Indeed, Bucer can even say 'Nay, much more certainly do the elect receive the benefits of God which have been enumerated, than human bodies their health through those things which are called natural remedies'.[6]

Bucer's doctrine of baptism, in particular in its relation to the Holy Spirit, displays a fundamental consistency. New situations provoke new arguments and new accents, but not a radically different doctrine.[7] The earlier distinction of baptism with water and baptism with the Spirit was developed against a given catholic dogma and the abuses which sprang from it. This distinction remains in Bucer's theology, but it is less often expressed when the debate is with the anabaptists and spiritualists. Against them he urges the association of the two baptisms, although he still maintains a distinction between them by means of various safeguards—the role

[1] TA 568.32–3. Compare EE 160.F.13–161.A.4.
[2] TA 596.20–34.
[3] TA 597.26–8.
[4] '...not what he of himself would need, but what in his eternal wisdom he judged useful for us and caused to be so.' TA 597.29–30. Compare EE 145.B. 11–14.
[5] TA 597.38–42.
[6] TA 598.23–5. Compare E 146.D.1–E.3.
[7] The shift of emphasis in the understanding of infant baptism, and in the arguments for it, lies outside the scope of this study.

of the Spirit, the necessity of faith and election, the use of baptism according to God's institution. The holding of these two emphases in tension can be demonstrated by the fact that almost any quotation from Bucer on baptism from the later period can be paralleled with one from the earlier period. However, within that fundamental unity in his thought, the different accents of the two periods are unmistakable.

13

HOLY COMMUNION—THE
VISIBLE WORD 2

The eucharistic controversies are among the bitterest and most complicated events of the reformation. They produced a vast literature and a succession of formulas in the attempt to defend, explain, and reconcile the opposing positions. An understanding of even one of the positions is difficult without a detailed exposition of the others, and of the changing historical scene with its political, ecclesiastical, and theological pressures. Such an exposition is beyond the scope of this work.[1] Our concern must be to follow in broad outline the unfolding of Bucer's thought, documenting it in general from year to year, rather than from month to month, highlighting the moments of new development, and noting how the Holy Spirit works in this domain. If the detailed treatment of the influences at work on Bucer's thought finds but a small place, this is not because it is without importance, but

[1] A complete historical and theological account of Bucer's position will not be possible until all the manuscript material has been finally collected. The most detailed treatment of his position is in Köhler, *Zwingli und Luther*.

Among the discussions that throw light on the early years of the debate in Strasbourg are the following: Eells, *Martin Bucer*, pp. 20–98, Stupperich, 'Strassburgs Stellung im Beginn des Sakramentsstreits (1524–1525)', A.R.G. 38 (1941), pp. 249–72, Rott, 'Bucer et les débuts de la querelle sacramentaire', R.H.P.R. 34 (1954), pp. 234–54, and Peter, 'Le Maraîcher Clément Ziegler, l'homme et son œuvre', R.H.P.R. 34 (1954), pp. 255–82.

For a discussion of various sacramentarian views both before and in the early years of the reformation, see G. H. Williams, *Radical Reformation*, pp. 27–44.

In our discussion the subject has been divided into certain periods which reflect, in some measure, the changes both of concern and of emphasis in the debate. The section 1523–5 considers chiefly the issues of flesh and Spirit, spiritual enjoyment, and remembrance. The section 1526–30 treats the issue of the presence of Christ and the relation to it of the Holy Spirit. The section 1530–9 discusses Bucer's deepening understanding of this question, with a new emphasis on communion in Christ; and the section 1540–51 presents some later expressions of his eucharistic theology.

because it would hinder the endeavour to let Bucer speak for himself.

Yet, to let him speak for himself is not as straightforward a matter in this field as in many others. His view of his own position is not entirely consistent and is necessarily influenced by the situations in which he was writing. Nevertheless, his own judgment is a safer guide than that of many who have written about him. Two quotations from the period in which at least a change of emphasis is evident in his theology of holy communion provide the clue.

In May 1532, in writing to Bonifacius Wolfhart, he insists that in the *Apologia*, the *Gospels*, and the *Vergleichung* (that is, in 1526–8) he expressed the view that the body and blood were 'truly present and offered' in the holy communion,[1] and that he attacked the view that the body and blood of the Lord were present 'in a physical way' once the words of the Lord had been recited.[2] By contrast, four years later in the preface to the *Gospels* he admits that he has 'not everywhere satisfactorily expressed that offering of the body and blood of Christ by the sacred ministry'.[3] These two statements are ultimately not contradictory but complementary. They record Bucer's judgment that his theology has an inner consistency, even though at any one time it may have been inadequately expressed.

This judgment is close to the truth. There is a development in Bucer's theology. After *Tetrapolitana* he stresses positively what in the twenties he stresses negatively. But there is little in the thirties that is not, in some measure, already present in the twenties, though differently accented. Moreover, most of the characteristic notes of his theology (the words true and with, the emphasis on celebrating holy communion according to the Lord's institution and receiving it in faith, the necessity of the Holy Spirit in those

[1] Pollet 1 94.3–9. Eells comments '. . . there was practically no change in his belief [i.e. 1524–30] and very little alteration in the expression of it. The difference was in his understanding of his doctrine, for it had clarified and deepened.' 'The Genesis of Martin Bucer's Doctrine of the Lord's Supper', p. 251.

[2] Pollet 1.106.12–107.6.

[3] 4.A.38–41 (Preface 1536).

receiving it) are present in his earlier writings. Nevertheless, 1530 marks a turning point in his development and one useful dividing point in our discussion.

1523–1525

The *Summary* seems to mark a stage before the controversy. Here the expressions Bucer uses do not divide him from Luther, but reflect something of the profound influence that Luther had on all his thought. The body of Christ is spoken of as being given 'under the bread, as a pledge and token (*Wahrzeichen*), which is indeed much more than if he had given a ring, a seal, or a letter'.[1] The body and blood of Christ are a token (*Wahrzeichen*) that Christ has left us, 'so that we may be wholly sure of the grace which he has won for us by his death and blood'. He gives them daily to us 'to enjoy in bread and wine, as often as we thirst for this grace'.[2] At the same time, he speaks of their enjoying holy communion spiritually, where they cannot enjoy it sacramentally[3]—a use of the word spiritual that can be paralleled in Luther.[4]

Against Treger, however, shows a divergence between Bucer and Luther that was to last until 1536.[5] It is expressed in the interpretation of flesh and Spirit in John 6. Bucer takes flesh to mean the outward thing in itself (whether bread or wine, water or word). This it is that 'profits nothing', for it is the Spirit who makes alive. The activity of the Spirit is seen primarily in the recipient and expresses itself in faith. Spiritual eating is, therefore, eating in faith in Christ and in his death for us. Where there is such spiritual eating, there is eternal life.[6]

A month later come the *Strasbourg Propositions* (mid-November) and the Strasbourg letter to Luther (23 November). The one

[1] BW 1.118.15–18.   [2] BW 1.119.28–32.
[3] BW 1.124.31–3.   [4] W.A. 6.372.12–373.8.
[5] Compare 147.B.9; 52.C.6; 685.B.3–21.
[6] 'Therefore, although he says "The flesh profits nothing" for of itself it cannot profit anything, yet he also says "He who eats my flesh and drinks my blood has eternal life". Thus the flesh indeed of itself profits nothing, but if one believes that it is given for us, which is then the spiritual eating of which the Lord speaks, one has eternal life; for in him is life.' BW 2.72.30–6.

affirms: 'we are certain that...the bread and cup of the Lord are an outward thing and therefore by themselves can do nothing to salvation, but that the remembering of the death of the Lord is saving and necessary...'[1] The other states that they preach the bread to be the body of Christ, the wine his blood, though mostly they 'exhort people to remembrance of the death of Christ, preaching this one use of the holy communion. Otherwise it does nothing to salvation as the flesh profits nothing, even if Christ be there, as much as when he hung on the cross and in the same form.'[2] Here the remembrance of Christ's death is central and is set over against the bread and wine as mere flesh. This remembrance is a filling out of what is meant by spiritual eating.

The discussion is taken a stage further in *Grund und Ursach*, where the word spiritual is used with further overtones. *Grund und Ursach* offers a more extended treatment of holy communion, set in the immediate context of the reform of worship in Strasbourg. This gives its own particular slant to what Bucer says, especially in the concern he shows to remove the host of secondary and often superstitious practices that had gathered round the mass. Though they are not at the centre of the debate (indeed Bucer can allow some to remain), they occupy an important part, because they obscure the meaning of the sacrament. For Bucer, for whom ceremonies were a mark of the Old Testament not of the New, they are contrary to a worship 'in Spirit and in truth'.[3]

Bucer's opposition, however, is not to the outward in itself, but to the abuse of the outward, for example, the bodily adoration of the elements in place of their bodily reception leading to a spiritual

---

[1] BW 3.407.17–19.

[2] W.A.Br. 3.797.27–30.

[3] Thus he opposes various outward actions in the mass, such as beating one's breast, arguing that love will express itself spontaneously, and that its outward forms cannot be prescribed, any more than one can prescribe how someone will laugh. BW 1.237.21–238.20. This distortion in externals led to further distortions, so that, for instance, what is confessed is not real sin, but the failure to do certain things prescribed in the mass. BW 1.238.36–239.5.

G. H. Williams refers to the spiritualism indigenous to Strasbourg; but his example from Ziegler has few parallels in Bucer. *Radical Reformation*, pp. 337–8.

remembrance.[1] A certain ambiguity in the word spiritual is now apparent. It describes our believing that Christ was offered on the cross for our sins as against his bodily presence in the flesh or in bread and wine.[2] (The context is 'the flesh profits nothing, the Spirit makes alive' and 'my words are Spirit and life'.) In another sense it implies that which is inward and concerns the mind and spirit, as opposed to that which is outward and concerns the body:

The Lord commanded the bread to be eaten and the cup to be drunk, and directed and commanded [to go] at once from the bodily to the spirit, to remember him... The Lord has given nothing bodily in holy communion except eating and drinking, and that for the sake of the spiritual, that is, his remembrance.[3]

(The context is of a 'worship in Spirit and truth', in other words a genuine inward remembrance which is the real point of an outward ceremony.) John 6:63 may be said to view the sacrament rather from the godward side and John 4:23-4 from the human side.[4] There is a further sense of the word spiritual corresponding to a contrast between our flesh and the Holy Spirit—a use more frequent outside Bucer's discussion of the sacraments. Here, however, this sense is encompassed by a 'worship in Spirit and truth', when that is seen, less as an opposition to outward forms of worship in themselves, and more as the affirmation of a worship arising out of faith, that the Spirit alone makes possible.[5]

[1] BW 1.228.39–229.15.
[2] BW 1.228.8–20.
[3] BW 1.228.39–229.1, 230.1–3.
    There are many passages in Bucer where it is not clear whether *Geist* or *spiritus* refers to the Holy Spirit. Unfortunately the English translation cannot preserve this ambiguity.
[4] 'It is the Spirit who gives life, the flesh profits nothing. The words that I have spoken to you are Spirit and life' (John 6:63). '...the true worshippers will worship the Father in Spirit and in truth...' (John 4:23).
[5] Spiritual eating and drinking stand for eating and drinking in faith, and are to be distinguished from an outward eating and drinking in the sacraments. BW 1.261.29–39. Parallel to this is the fact that Bucer keeps vestments until the people are first persuaded of the word of God, as otherwise there would be no profit, for to the unbeliever all things are impure. BW 1.231.22–8.

When Bucer now urges spiritual enjoyment of the sacrament, he does not use spiritual as distinct from a physical reception of the sacrament (as in the *Summary*), but as a physical reception in faith that includes or leads to an inward remembering.[1] This involves accepting as true the words 'This is my body...' and thinking of what Christ adds 'Do this in remembrance of me':[2]

If you could take the flesh as a figure or sign and in true faith remember how he gave and sacrificed his body and blood on the cross for your redemption, then you would also truly enjoy the true body and the true blood of Christ and have eternal life. But if you should not receive and use the cup and bread for that, you would be guilty of the body and blood of Christ, whose memory you dishonour. What is bodily there cannot help you. But if you can grasp the spiritual (*das geistlich*) it brings you eternal life.[3]

Spiritually enjoying the flesh and blood of Christ by faith, means wholly believing 'that through this sacrifice you are rescued from evil and become a child of God'.[4]

The emphasis on the words 'Do this in remembrance of me' continues in the writings that follow. Sometimes it is closely associated with the idea of spiritual eating, sometimes not. In his letter to Johann Ritter Landschad von Steinach he writes:

we say the words 'This is my body' are to be believed, and that one is not to give oneself to disputing whether they are to be understood bodily or spiritually, but to consider what immediately follows 'which was given for you' 'do this in remembrance of me' 'proclaim the death

---

[1] The temporal sequence is not consistent. The eating can either include or lead to the remembrance. BW 1.228.39–229.1, 252.1–18.

[2] BW 1.249.22–250.7.

[3] BW 1.252.1–10.

[4] 'Darumb lass übrig fragen faren, die wort seind war: *diss ist mein leib, diss ist mein bluot*, so redt der geist gottes in Paulo auch recht, das er spricht (diss brot, den kelch), die lass bede recht und wor sein, sihe allein, was du da niessest, das du es dem herren zuo gedechtnüss niessest, auff das du durch den glauben das fleisch und bluot Christi geistlich niessest, das ist, gaentzlich glaubest, das du durch solich opffer von allem übel erloesst und ein kind gottes worden seyest. Was uns weiter zuo wissen nutz sein mag, würt uns gott wol offenbaren.' BW 1.252.11–18.

of the Lord'. If you do that with faith, you will truly enjoy the body and blood of Christ, if not, everything will be to you for death.[1]

He urges that, in eating the bread and drinking the cup with faith, the whole heart and mind should be not on the bread and wine, but on Christ crucified, who is our Saviour.[2] In the *Psalter* the meaning of this 'remembrance' and the hidden depth behind the word find clear expression. The remembrance is essentially of the death of Christ, by which he has saved us and made us children of God, in whom we freely trust as Father.[3]

For Bucer this is what it is to be a Christian, and the holy communion is essentially an expression and renewal of this and therefore of the whole Christian life:

The remembering of this great wonder of God, that he has given his only Son to die for our redemption, brings it about in all believers that they freely entrust themselves to God, since through the blood of Christ they have come to the New Testament, that God will be eternally gracious to them, likewise that they will lead their life with more fear since they are so dearly bought from sin. They will also be inclined to do good to all, as they recognise what God has done for them, and thus wait in all patience until the Lord calls them from hence. In this the whole Christian life consists. This comes truly (*eygentlich*) when one eats the flesh and drinks the blood of Christ, that is believes and daily strengthens this faith, that he has given his body and blood for us. Therefore one ought to remember, preach, and offer praise for this by the table of the Lord, as Paul says 'As often as you eat this bread and drink this cup, you proclaim the death of the Lord till he come.' It all hangs on such preaching and remembering.[4]

This remembering is distinct but not separate from the eating. It is essentially bound up with it, seeming in some instances to precede, in others to follow it. Without it the eating cannot be spiritual. In holy communion we ought to

remember and ever more strongly believe, that our Saviour once gave his body and blood for our sin, so that we enjoy them spiritually and

---

[1] BW 3.439.20–5. In point six of his seven point summary Bucer says that though Luther has not failed in great matters, this does not mean that he will not fail in small ones. [2] BW 3.434.16–31.
[3] Compare BW 1.252.13–17. [4] BW 2.219.36–220.13.

are fed inwardly to our salvation. If we do that, we eat for ever the body of Christ and drink his blood, if not, then were we to eat the bread of the Lord and enjoy the cup of blessing every hour, we should not enjoy anything but our damnation... Fleshly enjoyment does not profit, therefore all disputing and preaching about the fleshly presence of the body and blood of Christ in the bread does not become an evangelical, who should be a servant of the Spirit, and teach only what makes us godly. Receiving the sacrament does not do that, still less adoration of the bread and cup, but only remembering, believing, and giving thanks that Christ died for us.[1]

What emerges so far in Bucer's understanding of the sacrament is that the bread and wine are in themselves flesh, without the Spirit, that they should lead to a remembering of the saving death of Christ which is the source of Christian faith and life, and that this remembrance in faith, together with the physical eating and drinking, is equivalent to a spiritual enjoyment of the body and blood of Christ. This somewhat stark summary of Bucer's position highlights the absence of certain elements that are later to fill out his theology. The presence of Christ (and, in particular, the manner of his presence) in or with the elements, the understanding of the sacraments as a communion between Christ and the Christian, the role of the Spirit in making the death of Christ a present reality, and the relation of the sacrament to Christ's intention in instituting it have yet to be discussed. These gaps reflect in part Bucer's caution and his desire to avoid unnecessary strife and in part a relatively undeveloped stage in his theology of the sacrament.

1526–1530

The *Apologia* takes this development further.[2] In it Bucer rejects a physical presence of Christ,[3] but, after quoting parallels like the

---

[1] BW 2.220.16–31.

[2] Its thought is reflected in the *Preface, St Matthew*, and *Getrewe Warnung*, which appear shortly after each other. Some parallels from them are cited in the footnotes.

[3] He finds no scriptural support for the body of Christ 'adesse in pane realiter ac physico quodam modo' (AP 22.B.6–11), but allows that for the faithful the bread is 'corpus Christi corporale, sed spiritualiter, sed beatifico modo' (AP 27.A.7–10).

handing over of a staff of authority, he says that 'the faithful truly receive the body of Christ with the bread'.¹ This sense of an action taking place at two levels Bucer does not relinquish, though it later has a more positive orientation. At this stage it accompanies a view of signs which stresses that they signify something rather than that they are identified with it.² The *Preface*, in discussing Christ's presence, draws the analogy with the gift of the Holy Spirit in John 20. It argues that 'the Holy Spirit was not transferred bodily into that breath, nor was the breath transubstantiated into the Holy Spirit'. Likewise, 'Christ was able by means of bread and wine to give his body and blood to his own truly and yet spiritually without any real change (*realem immutationem*) of the bread and wine...'³

The work of the Spirit in making alive is identified with his making men believe. He is sent to the elect, and where he is present there men eat and drink to eternal life.⁴ Spiritual eating and eating in faith are therefore the same.⁵ In this eating, while the bread is eaten by the teeth, the body of Christ is eaten by the mind.⁶ The impious cannot eat the body of Christ, for Christ said 'whoever eats my flesh and drinks my blood, abides in me and I

---

¹ '...if I confess that the faithful truly receive the body of Christ with the bread, but do not assert what some would have me confess, that they receive the body of the Lord in the bread.' AP 19.B.26–20.A.1. Compare 334.A.1–5; 190.B.9–11; 483.B.15.

² AP 28.B.7–13. The *Getrewe Warnung* likewise distinguishes the sign and the thing signified, and speaks of the bread and wine as signifying the body and blood of Christ. It explains that signs are common to all people, who use them when they do something great or remarkable, and that the Bible follows the same custom. BW 2.245.33–246.10.

³ PR B.5.A.7–15. The analogy with the gift of the Holy Spirit in John 20 is frequently used by Bucer.

⁴ AP 18.B.17–19.A.3.

⁵ 'I have consulted all the scriptures and we are not taught otherwise than that life and salvation consist only in the spiritual eating of Christ's flesh and drinking of his blood. And each of these means assuredly to believe with certain faith that we have been grafted into eternal life by the sacrifice of his body and blood, and that that covenant has been made and confirmed between us and God, so that he himself is our Father, and we are his sons and heirs.' AP 14.B.10–17. Compare 330.B.24–331.A.5; 189.B.17–22; 483.B.15.

⁶ AP 17.A.5–14. Compare 330.B.4–7; 189.B.4–6; 483.B.15.

in him, and he has eternal life'.[1] This quotation from St John is one of the fundamental elements in Bucer's understanding of the presence of Christ. It argues against a physical presence of Christ's body, for then the impious (that is, the reprobate) would eat Christ's body, which this text implicitly excludes. It argues for some relation of Christ's presence to the faith or election of those who receive the sacrament.

Although the *Apologia* and *Preface* point to a further stage in Bucer's sacramental teaching, they show only a partial step forward. Thus, for example, he still thinks of the sacrament as given 'for confessing faith and for mutual communion'[2] or as a sacrament 'by which we testify our perseverance'.[3]

The relation of the Spirit to the presence of Christ is touched on, though not greatly developed, in this period. *St Matthew* discusses it in opposition to the idea that men somehow, by repeating the words of Christ, make Christ present. This Bucer rejects, saying 'we ascribe all things to the one Christ, working everything that belongs to our salvation through the Spirit'.[4] Here it is not clear whether Bucer sees the work of the Spirit as being in the action of the sacrament or in the heart of the believer, although the immediate context suggests the former.

In the *Getrewe Warnung* and *St John* it is rather that Christ is now present in the Holy Spirit and not present in the flesh:

Christ is invisibly present through his Spirit to the end of the world (Matt. 28:20). But that he is bodily and invisibly present is not supported by any scripture...[5]

In his saving power, that is, in the Paraclete, the Spirit, Christ is present to the end of the world. We preach that he has gone away in the body,

---

[1] AP 20.A.27–B.2. Compare 330.B.24–331.A.5; 189.B.17–22; 483.B.15. *Getrewe Warnung*, after making the same point, says that the eating must be in faith, and that therefore the only way in which the sacraments can be eaten is through the Spirit. BW 2.246.29–41.

[2] AP 21.A.16–22.

[3] PR A.8.A.1–5.

[4] 338.A.24–5; 191.C.13; 438.B.15.

[5] BW 2.244.10–12.

so that he may be present to his own in a better way, that is, through his vivifying Spirit.[1]

His presence in this way is an argument against a local bodily presence in the bread—a point that the 1530 edition of the *Gospels* accentuates when it makes the second half of the quotation read: 'In his place he has promised the Paraclete, not bread or himself in bread. Whatever, therefore, of Christ is had in word or sacraments, it is had because the Paraclete works in the heart what they signify.'[2]

This interpretation of Christ's presence in the Spirit does not rule out a view in which the Spirit works through the elements, but it lays the emphasis on what the Holy Spirit does directly in the heart. This is not simply the same as the spiritual eating of the elements of which Bucer speaks in the earlier works, for then the role of the Spirit was implicit, here it is explicit. There the emphasis lay on the remembering in faith (certainly not viewed as the merely human act of remembering a past event), here it lies on the Spirit making present and effective both what is signified and what is remembered.[3]

In *Zephaniah*, which comes between *St John* and the *Gospels* (1530), the role of the Holy Spirit is explicitly limited to the recipient. Bucer affirms (with the Lutherans, as he says) a unity which is sacramental. He argues that the mode of Christ's presence cannot be known and therefore is not to be inquired into, adding that Christ promised to be present in the Paraclete and that they preach him 'to be present not only in the midst of his own, but also in the hearts of individuals'.[4]

[1] 231.B.6–16; 86.B.1–10; 765.A.7. The opposition is to a localised, bodily presence in the bread. 'Nor can it be in so many corruptible loaves and at the same time in so many different places. We freely confess that all things are possible to God, but God at the same time speaks the truth...' 148.A.2–5; 52.C.19–20; 685.B.3.   [2] 231.B.6–16; 86.B.1–10; 765.A.7.

[3] Compare '...the only eating which is of itself saving is of the Spirit, and it is through faith...For neither [that is, neither Luther nor Zwingli] denies that the eating of Christ in itself does not bring salvation, if the spiritual eating is absent, rather perdition.' 5.A.40–5 (Preface 1530).

[4] Z 5.B.18–6.A.1 (Preface).

The *Gutachten* rejects the idea that the sacrament conveys the Holy Spirit and insists on the need for the Holy Spirit to be already present, unless the sacrament is to lead to death:

To say that God through such [baptism and holy communion] offers, gives, and confirms his Spirit, raises such a work too high. Many are baptised and fed with the bread of Christ without ever having faith or the Spirit of God within. For when an adult comes to baptism and holy communion without already having the Spirit and faith—for no one can believe without the Spirit of God—he receives both sacraments to his death.[1]

The Holy Spirit, therefore, is essentially in the believer, to whom he has given faith before he receives the sacraments, and to whom he makes present what the sacrament signifies. In a sense that is not clear the Holy Spirit is seen as working alongside or through the elements, so that the believer receives with them the body and blood of Christ.

From the role of the Holy Spirit, which is being gradually more sharply defined, we may go on to consider a parallel development in the understanding of the presence of Christ. This is expressed mostly in terms of negative definitions which are themselves hedged round with safeguards. Beside the negative definition that Christ is not bodily present, comes the affirmation that the union of his body with the bread is sacramental.[2] His body is not to be described as 'in the bread', a phrase not in scripture, which says 'This is my body'. This means Christ

gave his body and blood to his disciples and those who would share in forgiveness of sins and the new covenant, and called the same bread and wine. Now, if one has and enjoys these through faith, as John 6 teaches, one has and eats them truly, not as one has one's absent wife present with him through remembering [her], but in such a way that through this the spirit is fed and renewed to eternal life.[3]

[1] BW 3.460.7–12.
[2] Z 4.A.6–B.7 (Preface).
[3] BW 3.462.15–22. Compare Pollet 1.23.9–19.

Christ's spiritual presence and spiritual eating are not, says Bucer, a fiction, for they change the whole man and bring resurrection to eternal life.[1]

1530–1539

The early thirties mark the period in which Bucer's view of the sacrament is sounded with a more positive note. The historical circumstances aided this in some measure. They encouraged renewed attempts at understanding the opposed positions, for the sake of political as well as theological unity. But though the threatening situation on the right and on the left may have helped (like the prospect of one's execution six months hence) wonderfully to concentrate the mind, the source of the change is not to be found there. Bucer's position is not fundamentally different in the thirties; it is simply differently oriented, differently emphasised, and, to some extent, differently expressed. To this Bucer's deeper study of the fathers undoubtedly contributed, along with a better understanding of what Luther was seeking to say.

The meeting at Augsburg was an important moment in this whole process, although Bucer's position there is expressed in formulas which he did not find entirely satisfactory.[2] The *Apology*,

[1] 'Therefore no one should say that this spiritual presence and eating is a fiction, if it changes the whole man and brings resurrection to eternal life.' BW 3.331. 35–8.

[2] Compare Eells, *Martin Bucer*, p. 100.

Bucer was undoubtedly enabled by his encounters in Marburg and Augsburg to understand the Lutheran position better. It is not, however, easy to point to the exact moment from which his new attitude can be dated. The comments of Eells may be noted:

'In later years...he testified that he was first awakened to the fact that they were fundamentally agreed by reading Luther's *Confession*. Consequently his concord work must be dated, not from the Marburg Colloquy, nor from the *Vergleichung*, but from the day he finished reading Luther's *Confession*, April 15, 1528.' 'The Genesis of Martin Bucer's Doctrine of the Lord's Supper', p. 245.

'Bucer's criticism of the Schwabach Articles marked his last stand as a Zwinglian partisan. Still contending that he was right on the Supper and Luther in many things was wrong, he was ready to meet Luther half-way and lay down his weapons.' *Martin Bucer*, p. 98.

'Martin Bucer came to Augsburg a Zwinglian, so hated by the Lutherans that for a time they refused even to talk with him about the Supper. He left the

in answering the question what need there is of the sacrament if Christ is always present and is food for the soul, says:

It is one Christ who is always present to all believers and is their food. But it especially belongs to this sacrament that in it the gospel is really preached, the death of Christ is proclaimed, with the sacraments as seals of the promise of God, the body and blood of Christ are equally visibly presented and thereby faith is awakened...and the whole Christian life powerfully and essentially renewed, inflamed, and strengthened.[1]

He rejects equally the idea that the bread is just baker's bread, as that there is a natural union between it and the body of Christ.[2] Rather, there is a sacramental unity between the bread and the body. 'But because this unity rests on the word of God and the working of Christ, to all for whom Christ ordained this sacrament, that is, his disciples and believers, the true communion and food of the body of Christ is imparted as surely as the bread...'[3]

The presence of Christ is limited effectively to believers, but it is not thought of in a spiritualised way. It has its profound outworkings in the total life of the believer:

...there is such a communion in Christ that we are therefore his flesh and bone, in that we become sharers of immortality. And, as Hilary and Cyril write, he thus dwells in us now bodily and naturally, and brings this destructible nature of our body to indestructibility and to the divine life...and we gladly confess with Saint Irenaeus and Hilary that our bodies are also fed and that the body of Christ in its measure is present in the bread and in our bodies.[4]

Along with this he can affirm 'the true and essential presence of the true body and blood of Christ',[5] and that 'the Lord gives and

---

city on September 19, 1530, a prophet of concord, recommended to Luther by both Melanchthon and the Elector of Saxony' (*op. cit.* p. 109).

Köhler unnecessarily accuses Bucer of mere juggling with words (*Dogmengeschichte*, pp. 322–3). He is certainly concerned to find a formula that will reconcile differing positions, but there is a consistency and integrity in his position that Köhler only partly recognises.

[1] BW 3.282.34–283.4.   [2] Compare Pollet 1.74.25–35.
[3] BW 3.282.14–18.
[4] BW 3.282.22–31. Compare Pollet 1.42–3.   [5] BW 3.276.23–6.

imparts to us also his true, only, and natural body and his true, only, and natural blood'.[1] 'Where one holds the sacraments rightly, one proclaims the gospel of Christ, and what is conveyed in that in words, the very same is also represented to the eyes and in like manner visibly offered (*dargebotten*) through the holy signs.'[2] In all this there is nothing that comes automatically from the words of the minister. On the one hand, it is said that God must give the increase, on the other, following Augustine, that the power comes from the word, not in that it is spoken, but in that it is believed.[3]

The accent on the giving or presenting of Christ's body and blood is found again in the *Schweinfurt Confession*, though, as always, it is only when holy communion is celebrated according to Christ's institution. '... when his believers, assembled in his name, hold holy communion as he has commanded, then he certainly offers and gives to such disciples of his his body and blood, to be received and enjoyed with believing hearts, as the bread and wine are to be taken, eaten, and drunk with the bodily mouth.'[4]

The development in the understanding of the presence of Christ is similar to the development in the understanding of the role of the Spirit. They both stress the godward side of the sacrament. They fill out what Bucer says about 'remembering Christ's death' and 'eating in faith', which lay the accent rather on the human side. They make it clear that the action of the sacrament is essentially God's action through his Holy Spirit, rather than man's action in believing and remembering. It is not that believing and remembering are to be construed either as a merely human action or as giving reality to the sacrament. They are rather the God-

[1] BW 3.279.14–15.
[2] BW 3.272.38–273.3. This new word in Bucer's presentation finds an echo in the letter of mid-November 1530 to Ernst von Lüneberg:
  'Dan wir zu beyden theilen bekennen, das der ware lyb und das war blut Christi im abentmal warlich zugegen seye und mit den worten des herren und sacramenten dargereicht werde.' Pollet 1.55. Compare Pollet 1.60.1–13 (BW 3.396.16–27).
[3] BW 3.273.8–24.
[4] Pollet 1.74.9–22. Compare Pollet 1.70.28–71.9, 73.1–13.

given way by which men respond to the sacrament. But they stress the human side, and easily make the human response the dominant element.

The *Augsburg Summary* underlines an idea that is frequently used in Bucer in his treatment of Christ's presence—the idea of Christ's institution. He argues that the sacrament was instituted by Christ not for unbelievers, but for the disciples and for those who believe. It is to such that he wishes to give it. 'Now if Christ the Lord himself is the true priest and chief actor here (he who does not bind his doing to our work and knows everyone), how are we to say that he does what he has forbidden us to do...?'[1] To the Lutheran rejoinder that God's promises stand by themselves and do not depend on man's faith, with the implication that the body and blood are given to believer and unbeliever alike, Bucer replies: 'We agree. When, however, a promise of the Lord is expressly, in as many words, made for believers, we cannot make it apply to unbelievers.'[2]

This is a point of crucial importance for Bucer. The body of Christ is intended for the elect, the believers, and they alone can enjoy it; for to feed on Christ's body is to have eternal life. Bucer is, however, eager to find a formula that can unite him with Luther, with whom he feels himself in fundamental agreement.[3] He considers that the formula of Augustine and the fathers, 'if the evil have presented to them as much as the good, yet in truth they receive nothing from Christ our Lord', would be a suitable one, 'had the strife not gone so far'.[4] He would be happy if Luther would leave the matter unexplained 'and say no more than that the Lord is there and is enjoyed'.[5] In this context he prefers 'truly' (*wahrhaft*) while Luther wishes to use 'orally' and 'bodily'. Here Bucer would adopt the phrase of Brenz 'the mouth of faith enjoys the body of Christ, the mouth of the body the bread'.[6]

---

[1] Pollet 1.133.3–13.   [2] Pollet 1.134.19–29.

[3] Compare Pollet 1.131.18–132.18, 140.1–141.18.

[4] Pollet 1.140.16–19. A similar distinction was made by Luther between giving and receiving in a letter of 22 January 1531. Pollet 1.146.

[5] Pollet 1.140.24–5.   [6] Pollet 1.140.26–31.

In 1536, with the Wittenberg Concord, peace was established and the two positions were, at least outwardly, reconciled. Bucer's interpretation of the Concord, however, was coloured by his view of Christ's institution of the sacrament. He accepts 'that the truth of this sacrament is not grounded on the merit of the men who receive it or distribute it', yet immediately adds 'but is grounded on the word and institution of the Lord, and therefore all those who receive the sacrament unworthily, receive for themselves judgment'.[1] He accepts the word *substantialiter*, but his use of it is important. He says 'the body and blood of Christ himself are truly present, not just *effective*, powerfully, effectively, spiritually, but *vere*, *substantialiter*, *essentialiter*, essentially, and truly, and are given and received with bread and wine'.[2] The more emphatic position of the words truly and with serve to interpret the word *substantialiter*, which he would not himself have chosen.

The effect of this shift in emphasis and understanding is seen in the *Gospels* (1536). References that might offend are omitted[3] and any idea that the bread and wine are bare signs of an absent Christ is rejected.[4] The interpretation of flesh in John 6 as applying to Christ's flesh (and therefore to the bread) is changed, though not without a subtly self-justifying reference to the different interpretations of the fathers. Chrysostom's view he now accepts, in place of Augustine's and Cyril's which he previously accepted.[5] This change should not be exaggerated. What Bucer accepts (an understanding of flesh as our flesh unable to perceive the things of the Spirit) is not new. What he rejects (the elements as mere flesh) enables him to express more satisfactorily his more positive understanding of the sacrament, without his rejecting the real meaning of his interpretation—that without the work of the Holy Spirit the outward elements are of no value.

---

[1] Pollet 1.165.13–17. Compare Pollet 1.168.19–27, 172.11–25. See Köhler, *Zwingli und Luther*, 2.454.   [2] Pollet 1.166.15–18.

[3] Compare 265.B.20–266.A.2; 167.D.5–11; 432.D.8–11; and also 307.A.26–B.17; 180.D.6–17; 464.D.10.   [4] 6.A.40–7 (Preface 1536).

[5] 147.B.9; 52.C.6; 685.B.3–21. Compare 144.B.16–145.A.1, 146.A.27–B.5; 51.D.14–21, 52.B.1–6; 684.C.4–8, 685.A.3–5.

These changes are safeguarded by a reiteration of what Bucer regards as essential. There is nothing automatic about the sacrament. Its effectiveness comes not from the symbols, but from Christ acting through the Holy Spirit. Not until now does Bucer link the work of the Holy Spirit unequivocally with the elements, without making the primary reference to the work of the Spirit in the heart.[1] The confirmation of faith rests not on the power of the symbols themselves, but on Christ's power which is dispensed 'by his Spirit through word and sacred symbols':[2]

Christ alone by his Spirit effects the whole of salvation in us and he does it not by some other power but by his Spirit alone. However, for this he uses with us the word, both the visible word in the sacraments and the audible word in the gospel. By them he offers and presents remission of sins, communion in himself, and eternal life.[3]

The other characteristic safeguards are references to Christ's institution,[4] faith in the receiver,[5] and the distinction of godly and ungodly.[6] In this last point Bucer and Luther had found eventual agreement by distinguishing the unworthy from the impious. This satisfied Bucer's insistence that only the elect (the pious) may consume the body of Christ; for he accepted that in the elect there were degrees of faith and that some might, for a period, lapse. The elect, therefore, could be unworthy but not impious.

To preserve the sequence of thought, we have followed the debate concerning the presence of Christ through from 1530 to 1536, when it found its solution. Now we return to the *Bericht* to highlight a further feature in Bucer's sacramental thinking, that was almost entirely absent from the earlier Bucer—an under-

---

[1] The two are complementary, not exclusive, for the Spirit does not make the elements real and effective apart from those who receive them. In other words, it is where 'the Spirit of Christ is at work and the words and visible signs of the sacraments are grasped with faith'. BH I.1.B.15–19. Compare BH I.3.B.17–27.

[2] 329.A.1; 188.D.21; 484.C.23–D.1.

[3] 329.A.1; 188.D.21; 485.B.3–6.

[4] 5.A.5–22 (Preface 1536).

[5] 6.A.6–9 (Preface 1536).

[6] 329.A.1; 188.D.21; 485.B.20–486.C.1.

standing of holy communion as communion.[1] In the *Bericht* he
describes the relation of Christ to the believer as an indwelling:
'he lives in us, clothes us with himself, gives us his flesh and blood
to eat, so that it is not we who live but he in us, so that we are his
members, flesh of his flesh and bone of his bone'.[2] This communion with Christ which, at one and the same time, involves a
communion with each other, is necessary for us to enter the kingdom of God, and is God's intention with this sacrament:

It is not enough that he died on the cross for us, he must also himself
live in us and make us sharers of his flesh and blood. For our flesh and
blood cannot inherit the kingdom of God. If he, our Saviour, God, and
Lord, who is love itself, lives in us, then we are also united with all our
fellow members in true divine love, one body, one loaf, sharing in one
loaf. Everything is to be done for the sake of faith in Christ. Therefore
all words and sacraments of the Lord are directed first to this, that he
may not only represent us with the Father, but that he may also live in
us...[3]

That this is a genuine change of emphasis is apparent in his
insistence on the command 'Take, eat: this is my body' over
against 'Do this in remembrance of me', a reversal of the order
in his early writings.[4] He argues that the preachers about whom
he is writing 'do not express well the communion in Christ which
is supremely presented to us in holy communion. It is true we
ought to remember the Lord then, proclaim his death, offer our
praise and thanks for it...' The growth and brotherly love that
result

come, however, alone from this, that Christ lives in us. That is the
highest and supreme thing. Therefore, before everything in Christ's
words comes 'Take, eat: this is my body', 'Take, drink of this, all of

[1] In *Psalms* Bucer writes '...he who eats truly believing that eternal life is obtained
for him by the flesh and blood of Christ, will never be hungry or thirsty, but
will have the Lord dwelling in him and he will dwell in the Lord...' P 102.A.
7-15. But it is the *Apology* that first stresses this. BW 3.282.4-31.
[2] BH AA.3.A.6-9.
[3] BH CC.1.B.2-16. Compare Reu 1.I.77.26-8 and BW 7.306.33-8.
[4] See especially BW 1.249.22-250.7 and 3.439.20-5.

you. This is my blood of the New Testament, the covenant of grace, that is, the forgiveness of sins.' Only then comes 'Do this in remembrance of me'.[1]

The thirties present a period in which Bucer's eucharistic doctrine develops, perhaps more than any other doctrine. This does not mean a fundamental change in his doctrine, but it does betoken a profound filling out of what was expressed before, sometimes one-sidedly, sometimes with no more than a hint. What follows up to the end of his life is not so much a further development as an orientation of the debate towards his catholic and radical opponents and away from his fellow reformers.

1540–1551

In *Judges* Bucer attacks and defends the axiom that symbols confer grace. They do not, he says, do this as the papists use them, for they use them for those who are not penitent and who do not understand or eat with true faith. But, as instituted by God, they are efficacious and confer grace on those eating. Bucer can even say that God has bound his grace to them when they are properly administered, but 'not because he cannot confer it otherwise, but because he will not'.[2] This does not mean that the power is in the sacraments themselves, any more than it was in Samson's hair, 'but God, as it were, added the power'.[3]

The question of Christ's presence in the sacrament is one that the reformation in Cologne raises. In considering it Bucer once more attacks the doctrine of transubstantiation as unscriptural.[4] Using, as often before, the analogy of the gift of the Spirit in John 20, he is prepared to use the prepositions with and under, but he does not mention 'in'. 'No Christian denies that the Lord gave his disciples here as well two things—one, the sign of his breath, the other, the Holy Spirit which the Lord gave under and

---

[1] BH CC.1.B.20–2.A.6.

[2] J 513.12–30. This is not essentially a new position, but nowhere else does Bucer express with such definiteness God's unequivocal acting in the sacraments.

[3] J 512.48–9.   [4] BV 110.B.6–15.

with the sign of the breath.' Likewise, 'the body and blood of Christ are given under or with the bread and wine, not...under or with the accidents of bread and wine'.[1] He expresses this more dramatically when he writes 'we do not sing *Huc corda*, but *Sursum corda*', and insists that the heart and mind are to be raised above all sensible things and that through faith the Lord is to be grasped and enjoyed in his heavenly glory.[2]

The presence of Christ is related to Christ's work and our faith:

For indeed all grace and consolation in the holy sacraments come in no way *opere operantis Ministri*, that is, from the work of the officiating minister, but *opere operato*, that is, from the accomplished work of Christ, which is presented to us there according to his word and command. But there must also be the *opus operantis sumentis et Sacris Christi utentis*, the work of the one who receives, who makes use of the sacrament of Christ, namely true faith in Christ and his promise, which grasps and enjoys the work of Christ. Not that even the faith, through itself, merits something for us, or brings or adds something to the work and merit of Christ, but that it receives the work and merit of Christ.[3]

It is the question of the presence of Christ that marks Bucer's last writings.[4] His position remains that of the middle way. He rejects the idea of transubstantiation as he rejects that of the memorial of an absent Christ, a Christ who is in heaven and hence absent from the holy communion.[5] In relating the presence to receiving the sacrament in faith, he uses a new formula, saying that 'the body and blood of the Lord were given by him not to the bread and wine, but to the disciples', and that not for any use, but 'to be eaten and drunk'. The bread and wine are the body and blood of Christ, but only as eaten by the disciples, and as Christ

---

[1] BV iii.A.34–8, B.20–4.
[2] BV 125.B.2–8.
[3] BV 193.A.20–31. The importance of administering and receiving the sacrament according to Christ's institution can be seen in BV 93.A.26–B.10. Compare TA 248.5–12, 45–9.
[4] This is not the place for a detailed analysis of Bucer's sacramental writings in England and the variations that they present. See Hopf, *op. cit.* p. 50.
[5] TA 598.37–48, 601.14–16, 602.1–4, 605.47–8, 606.1–15. Hopf refers to the analogy that Bucer makes with the sun in this context (*op. cit.* p. 48).

commanded.[1] Here again the role of the Holy Spirit, which is less evident in the discussion of the forties, is shown, though in a somewhat ambiguous formula. The true reception of the bread and wine is said not to be by the senses or by natural reason 'but through faith and by the energy of the Holy Spirit'.[2]

God uses the sacraments[3] and intends them to be used. The fact that God can dispense with his sacraments, and is not, in that sense, bound to them, does not make us free to use them at will. 'He is able to present his benefits to whom he wills, without any signs. While, however, he offers them to us in sure signs, if we neglect these signs we repudiate also his benefits. For not we ourselves, but he himself is to prescribe to us in what way we receive his gifts.'[4]

It is in the total context of his eucharistic theology, as we have traced it, that we see both the main lines of Bucer's thought and his understanding of the role of the Holy Spirit within it. The Holy Spirit makes faith possible in the recipient, without which he would be unable to perceive or receive the things of the Spirit. He persuades the believer of that which is represented and offered to him in the sacrament. He makes present to him the divine love manifested in Christ, which is now present not bodily, but only through the Spirit. That the role of the Holy Spirit seems less dominant here than elsewhere in Bucer's theology is due in part to the nature of the sacrament itself and perhaps in part to an impoverished understanding of the work of the Spirit in the traditional Christian interpretation of holy communion. It is, however, significant that the role of the Spirit for Bucer does not lie at the circumference of his understanding of holy communion, but at its heart.

[1] TA 609.40–5; EE 156.E.1–6. [2] TA 606.4–6; EE 156.D.7–10.
[3] TA 587.5–9. [4] TA 608.45–609.4. Compare TA 248.29–41.

CONCLUSION

There is no presentation of another's theology which is not in some measure an interpretation. The choice of quotations, the way they are related to each other, the framework in which they are placed, all betray the author's own interpretation. Yet, within these limitations, this study of Bucer's theology has sought to let Bucer speak in his own accents. There has been comment, but the comment has been aimed to let Bucer's theology, rather than the author's, stand out more clearly. Now it is necessary to lay bare some of the questions that a study of Bucer's theology raises—in particular four that concern essentially the role of the Holy Spirit in his theology.[1]

I. THE HOLY SPIRIT AND SALVATION

Much of the power of Bucer's theology derives from his doctrine of predestination. Whatever difficulties a son of the Wesleys may have with Bucer's understanding of this doctrine, he can nevertheless recognise its strength and fruitfulness in the development of Bucer's thought.

It gives a wholeness to his understanding of salvation, keeping him from an over-emphasis on justification by faith on the one hand and the pursuit of a life of holiness on the other. Justly or unjustly Luther was seen to sever faith from a life of love,[2] and the

[1] See Appendix, pp. 273-4.
[2] Luther undoubtedly urged that true faith was active in love, but he was often understood as releasing people from a life of love in conformity with the will of God. This was the charge of the radicals (see, for example, G. H. Williams, *Radical Reformation*, p. xxv) as well as of the catholics.

A valuable discussion of Luther's position is to be found in Ragnar Bring, *Förhållandet mellan tro och gärningar inom luthersk teologi*. See, for example, his comment on p. 20: 'For Luther there is no religion without morality. Nor can one say that morality is subordinated to religion. The religious relationship certainly implies that God is the one who determines and effects everything. But man does not thereby become passive. Faith, in which he receives everything from God, becomes on the contrary the point of departure for a new

catholics and radicals to sever the life of love from faith. Bucer views salvation from the standpoint of predestination, so that he does not lose sight of its source or its goal, of God's part or of man's part in it. It is God's work from first to last and always dependent on his grace; yet the sovereign grace of God is not allowed to obscure man's co-operation with God. It is an act of forgiveness to man in his sin and frailty; but man's constant need of forgiveness is not allowed to obscure the vision of the sons of God conformed to the image of God's Son and sharing in his glory.

Some of the ways in which Bucer holds these tensions together do not do justice to his purpose. His description of various causes of salvation, his discussion of twofold and threefold justification, and his treatment of free will sometimes lack clarity and betray his not always exact use of terms.

His concern is to be faithful to the biblical evidence which speaks of man's part in his salvation (as well as God's part) and of man's being justified by works (as well as by faith). It is not easy to hold the biblical paradoxes together, and Bucer generally succeeds remarkably in doing so. Nevertheless he does not always use the distinctions necessary to make his purpose clear. Thus the word cause when applied to man's good works as a cause of salvation ought to be clearly distinguished from its use when applied to God's election. Similarly the use of the term will, considered as free, when one speaks of man's psychological co-operation in his salvation, should be distinguished from its use as bound or enslaved, when one speaks of man's inability to do anything for his salvation theologically.

The accent on sanctification in Bucer's theology is related not only to his doctrine of predestination, but also to his doctrine of the Holy Spirit. In theologians and movements where the doctrine of the Spirit is stressed there is almost invariably a strong emphasis

activity, in which he works as God's instrument, his tool. It is precisely through faith that he is turned away from himself and out towards his neighbour and the world. It is therefore precisely faith which is the condition for or includes in itself a new morality.'

on sanctification. This is one of the major consequences of Bucer's doctrine of the Spirit. It may well be that the traditions of piety which he inherited in Alsace led him to emphasise the new life of the Christian, but undoubtedly the biblical understanding of the Spirit as the Spirit of holiness contributed to this.

It is precisely this stress on sanctification that may have led in part to Bucer's success with the anabaptists in Hesse. It is certainly noteworthy that it is the absence of lives whose quality commends the gospel that is one of Erasmus' charges against the reformers.[1] Moreover, in Calvin, it is an aspect of Bucer's theology that found a new and lasting expression.

Besides safeguarding a more comprehensive view of salvation, predestination also shaped Bucer's attitude to the word and sacraments. The doctrine of predestination is first developed in a reference to baptism in his debate with Treger, where he distinguishes baptism with water from baptism with the Spirit. In this way he was able to reject an automatic view of the sacraments. It is the same doctrine, however, that enables him later to accept a view that speaks of the sacraments as a means of grace. The difference between the two periods in his theology is essentially one of accent, but it is nonetheless a difference.[2]

The doctrine of predestination, however, raised some problems that Bucer did not resolve so satisfactorily, chief among them being the way in which the elect share in the Holy Spirit.

[1] See his letter to Bucer of 11 November 1527 (a translation is given in Johan Huizinga, *Erasmus of Rotterdam*, pp. 243–6). The claim of his conscience and the discord of the leaders of the reformation are given by Erasmus as reasons for not joining the church of the reformers. A further reason is the life of those who embrace the reformed faith.

'If the husband had found his wife more amenable, the teacher his pupil more obedient, the magistrate the citizen more tractable, the employer his workman more trustworthy, the buyer the seller less deceitful, it would have been great recommendation for the Gospels' (p. 245). Compare a similar comment referred to by Huizinga on p. 177.

[2] This is discussed further in § 3.

The doctrine of election was also a weapon against the anabaptist rejection of infant baptism.

Conclusion

Bucer makes a consistent distinction between the way the elect and reprobate participate in the Holy Spirit. Thus the reprobate could have the gifts of the Spirit, but not the fruit of the Spirit. They could be convinced of the truth, which is the work of the Holy Spirit, but not persuaded of it, so that they embrace it. The two ways in which the reprobate participate in the Spirit are in a sense parallel to the way in which the elect participate in him. The one (the gifts of the Spirit) is independent of the proclamation of the gospel, the other (what amounts to the sin against the Holy Spirit) is normally dependent on it.[1] The second of these corresponds broadly to the vocation and justification of the elect, an action of the Spirit normally linked to a proclamation of the gospel. The first corresponds to some uses of the phrase the seed of God, together with the idea of the elect as having the Spirit before they hear and respond to the word.

There is no point at which Bucer makes clear what it means for the elect to have the Spirit before they hear the word. It is presumably not to be understood in a full sense of the Spirit of sonship, because he speaks of God's saving the elect without preaching as, in effect, an exception, the implication being that God uses the outward word and sacraments to effect their salvation. Yet he uses the particular example of John the Baptist who had the Holy Spirit from his mother's womb.[2] This would imply more than an action of the Holy Spirit in the lives of the elect, making them ready to respond to the gospel when it is proclaimed. Bucer does not appear sensitive to this difficulty, perhaps because he uses the reference to John the Baptist primarily in a context in which he is concerned to prove that the word and sacraments are not automatic bearers of the Spirit and the gifts of God, but require the presence of the Holy Spirit if they are to be received for salvation.

[1] The gifts of the Spirit are discussed in ch. 9, the sin against the Holy Spirit in ch. 1.
[2] The problem is not unlike that posed by the gift of the Holy Spirit to an infant in baptism, before he is able to make any personal response to the gospel (through its proclamation in preaching or in the life of the church). It is different, however, in that it is independent of outward means.

2. THE HOLY SPIRIT AND CHRIST

A weakness in Bucer's theology that many have argued is in his understanding of the person and work of Christ. Much that has been said in this debate has given a distorted picture of what Bucer actually thought; but there is a measure of truth in the criticism.

Bucer preserves a sense of the unity of scripture, which is the tradition of the New Testament and of the fathers. Yet, in doing so, he does not sufficiently stress the distinctness of the New Testament. He does not by-pass the life and work of the incarnate Christ, nor does he put the people of the Old Testament on a level with the people of the New Testament. But he does not seem sensitive to the difference that there is (at least from the human side) between having faith in the Christ who is to come and having faith in the Christ who has come and who is present through the Holy Spirit in his church.

The reason is perhaps to be found in a theology which is inclined to view salvation from the godward side and which presents God as not confined within the processes of human history (so that for God the death of Christ is present, as all things are present to him). It is here, rather than in the universalism of the Friends of God of the Upper Rhine[1] or in a pervading humanism, that the chief clue may well lie. Whatever the origin of this weakness, it is a point where Bucer does not sufficiently do justice to that element in the New Testament which stresses the newness of the situation created by the life, death, and resurrection of Christ, and the gift of the Holy Spirit.

3. THE HOLY SPIRIT AND THE WORD

The charge of spiritualism that has been levelled against Bucer concerns the relation of the Holy Spirit and the word in all senses in which we have used the latter term, except for the magistrate

---

[1] Compare G. H. Williams, *Radical Reformation*, pp. 836–8.

seen as servant of the word. Here, however, we shall consider it as it applies to God's use of outward means in general, and to the Bible and preaching in particular.

The spiritualists were as varied among themselves as the reformers, and to ascribe to them an identical theology remains a distortion of the facts, however convenient it may be for the theologian. Yet, for brevity and simplicity, we may describe spiritualism as separating the Spirit from what is outward, either as being essentially opposed to what is outward or as being superior to it.

Franck represents this point of view when he writes:

Therefore, I believe that the outward church of Christ, including all its gifts and sacraments, because of the breaking in and laying waste by Antichrist right after the death of the apostles, went up into heaven and lies concealed in the Spirit and in truth. I am thus quite certain that for fourteen hundred years now there has existed no gathered church nor any sacrament.[1]

Along with this, I ask: what is the need or why should God wish to restore the outworn sacraments and take them back from Antichrist, yea, contrary to his own nature (which is Spirit and inward) yield to weak material elements? For he has been for fourteen hundred years now himself the teacher and baptizer and governor of the Feast, that is, in the Spirit and in truth without any outward means...[2]

God permitted, indeed gave, the outward signs to the church in its infancy, just like a doll to a child, not that they were necessary for the Kingdom of God, nor that God would require them of our hands.[3]

Therefore even as the Spirit of God is alone the teacher of the New Covenant, so also he alone baptizes and alone avails himself of all things, namely, in the Spirit and in truth. And just as the church today is a purely spiritual thing, so also is all law, promise, reward, spirit, bread, wine, sword, Kingdom, life—all in the Spirit and no longer outward, etc.[4]

[1] L.C.C. xxv, p. 149.   [2] L.C.C. xxv, p. 154.
[3] L.C.C. xxv, p. 155.   [4] L.C.C. xxv, p. 150.

Conclusion

The opposition to what is outward includes the Bible, which is subordinate to the inward word and, at best, a testimony to it:

I should wish, however, that thou wert not so addicted to the letter of Scripture, thus withdrawing thy heart from the teaching of the Spirit, and that thou wouldst not drive out the Spirit of God as though it were Satan, crowding him against his will into the script and making Scripture thy god (which has often happened and still happens). Thou shouldst much rather interpret the Scripture as a confirmation of thy conscience, so that it testifies to the heart and not against it. Again, thou shouldst not believe and accept something (merely) reported by Scripture—and feel that God in thy heart must yield to Scripture. It were better that Scripture should remain Antichrist's! St Paul speaks not in vain that the letter killeth. And yet it is (precisely visible letters) which almost all and especially the learned divines consider to be the sole pre-eminent word of God—supposing God's word really could be written—and the sole teacher.[1]

Bucer's position stands in contrast to this view with its opposition to the outward and its subordination of the Bible to the inward word. His opposition of inward and outward, especially apparent in his earliest writings, where he is often supposed to be spiritualist, is related to his doctrine of election and his insistence on inward reality. In the first of these he is clearly arguing in a different way from the spiritualists, for he allows the effectiveness of the word and sacraments in the case of the elect or those who have faith, though only in their case.[2]

In the second he seems closer to them as he regards the new covenant as concerned with the Spirit and not with outward ceremonies. (However, he does not regard the outward ceremonies of preaching, baptism, and holy communion as superseded in the new covenant, but rather as given in it.) Yet he seeks to affirm the inward (for example, the baptism of the Holy Spirit, or the true feeding on the true body of Christ) not against the outward, nor in separation from it, but in distinction from it. In

[1] L.C.C. xxv, pp. 159–60.
[2] The detailed arguments can be found in the chapters on Preaching, the Sacraments, Baptism, and Holy Communion.

other words, he is arguing that the outward is not the automatic bearer of the inward. Without the work of the Spirit who makes alive, the outward is dead, mere flesh.[1]

Furthermore, Bucer totally rejects the spiritualists' subordination of the Bible to the inward word. For him the Bible is the certain word of the Holy Spirit, and by it every inward word must be tested. It authenticates the inward word, not the reverse. Bucer's own use of the term inward word means the inward teaching of the Holy Spirit—a teaching that is never contrary to scripture, and that is distinguished, but not necessarily or usually separated from the outward word of preaching.

There is, nevertheless, one point at which Bucer's understanding of the relation of word and Spirit, especially in the sense of the spoken word of preaching, is less coherent. He holds that the Holy Spirit is needed to understand and respond to the word. The gift of the Holy Spirit to enable this, however, is sometimes seen as preceding, sometimes as following, though perhaps more often as simultaneous with the word. This variety does in some ways represent a certain ambiguity in the biblical examples with which Bucer seeks to come to terms, and may be thought to preserve the liberty of the Spirit to act as and when he wills. Bucer's failure, however, to present a coherent picture of the action of the Spirit here, is due largely to the fact that this whole

---

[1] Bucer's concern is different from Luther's. Luther attacks the spiritualists for opposing the Spirit to what is outward and for rejecting the very means by which God offers his Spirit. Bucer opposes them for ignoring the testimony of scripture to the use of outward means. Luther's position is given in Gordon Rupp's article, 'Word and Spirit in the First Years of the Reformation': 'We say that all is Spirit, spiritual and a spiritual thing which comes from the Holy Spirit, be it as bodily and outward and visible as it likes. Contrariwise, that which is apart from the Spirit is flesh, and comes from the natural power of the flesh, be it never so inward and invisible.' W.A. 23.203.7. 'With the very words "Spirit, Spirit, Spirit", he kicks away the very bridge by which the Holy Spirit can come to you, namely the outward ordinances of God like the bodily sign of baptism and the preached Word of God and teaches not how the Spirit comes to you, but how you come to the Spirit, so that you may sail up into the sky, ever so high, and ride upon the wind, only he can't tell you how or when or what it is, but only that you shall have the same experience that he has.' W.A. 18.137.5.

discussion is part of the controversy with Luther, in which he is rejecting the view that the word itself automatically brings the Spirit.

His doctrine of election which in part enables him to resolve this problem, at the same time leaves it unresolved. It enables him to accept the word as a means of grace with the elect. Yet it could be that to bind the Spirit to the word, even in the case of the elect, would imply, among other things, that God wills to call the elect on the first occasion that the gospel is preached to them. It is not certain that Bucer would want to say this. Bucer's view would appear to require a parallelism in God's action outwardly in the word and inwardly in the Spirit, so expressed that God's action is not limited to his action in the elect enabling them to receive, but takes place also through the word and sacraments which he is using. But even such a formulation might have to be modified by some reference to his understanding of the presence of the Holy Spirit in the elect before they hear the outward word.

4. THE HOLY SPIRIT AS PERSONAL

Bucer's references to the Holy Spirit as the force or energy of God have misled some scholars into judging that his view of the Holy Spirit is impersonal. Lang refers to the Spirit as conceived, at least sometimes, in physical terms, although he gives only a hesitant example to prove his point.[1] Temmel speaks of the Spirit

[1] '...der Christ soll ganz frei werden von allen Mitteldingen und relativen Grossen; bis ins Kleinste soll er sich von dem Höchsten allein bestimmt wissen. So viele Vorzüge dieser Auffassung zur Sicherung der Freiheit und Innerlichkeit des Christenlebens beiwohnen, so liegt andererseits, die Gefahr der Schwärmerei, d. h. des Übersehens der geordneten Wege, Gott zu erkennen und zu folgen, wie wir schon oben bemerkten, sehr nahe. In jedem Falle aber, wo es wirklich geschieht, ist der Geist nicht mehr ein rein religiöser Begriff, sondern nach Art einer physischen Kategorie gedacht. Anschaulich wird dies z. B. in einer Äusserung wie der folgenden: "Spiritus *sphragis* illa est, qua electi obsignantur, ut ipsi se filios Dei esse sciant, et *agnoscantur tales quoque ab aliis*". Sofern diese äussere Erkennbarkeit nicht einzig auf die Früchte geht, von den weiterhin die Rede ist, hat der Geistesbesitz offenbar etwas Naturhaftes.' Lang, *op. cit.* pp. 126–7.

Conclusion

in Bucer as a *Lebensprinzip*,[1] though without any compelling evidence to support his view.

It is not easy to consider these positions, as it is by no means clear what precisely is meant by regarding the Holy Spirit as something physical or as a *Lebensprinzip*. What can be said is that Bucer distinguishes the work and activities of the Spirit from his person.[2] For him the Spirit is not just a force; he is the living God himself to whom we may pray as we may pray to the Father and the Son,[3] and who prays for us.[4] This experience of the Holy Spirit in prayer, quite apart from the total picture of his work that has been presented in this study, gives the lie to a view that sees the Holy Spirit in Bucer as some impersonal, supernatural force.[5]

Most often the source to which Bucer's doctrine of the Holy Spirit is ascribed colours the understanding of his doctrine, as the ascrip-

---

[1] 'Geist ist für Bucer Lebensprinzip, von dem das Herz beherrscht wird.' Leopold Temmel, 'Glaube und Gewissheit in der Theologie Martin Bucers vornehmlich nach seinem Römerbriefkommentar', p. 65.

[2] 'Lastly, this also is to be noted, that all these names by which scripture proclaims this one of whom we speak the Breath of God, the Holy Spirit, indeed express to some extent what he effects in us, but not what he is in himself. For he is himself God, just as the Word is. For neither the Word nor the Spirit of God is other than God himself, in whom there are no accidents, [but] in whom everything is substance.' 80.A.17; 26.C.28–D.1; 63.B.22–64.C.1.

[3] Against Hofmann, Bucer, citing Acts 7:59, affirms the rightness of prayer to Christ and the Holy Spirit. KR 2.83.24–7.

[4] R 396.E.18–401.B.15.

[5] Nevertheless, some of the ways in which Bucer speaks of the Holy Spirit are strange to our ears. He can speak of Christians as being more adult in the Spirit than those who lived before Christ, and also of the Spirit given to Christians as a more adult Spirit. His view is that men shared in the Spirit before Christ, but that they shared less fully. (He interprets John 7:39 to mean that the Spirit was not given fully before Christ was glorified.) The Spirit was not different in the Old Testament, but he was differently apprehended. Indeed before Christ men experienced the Spirit as the Spirit of fear, rather than as the Spirit of liberty. 'Dominus unus mediator Dei et hominum, qui semper in medio suorum est, semper spiritu suo agit in sanctis administrationibus verbi sui et symbolorum: semper item cum addictione favoris paterni, spiritum suum per sacramenta impertiit: sed pro certa mensura, quam pro tempore variavit. Spiritum enim quo adflavit populum veterem, collatum spiritui quem a sua glorificatione in credentes sibi effudit, Paulus vocat spiritum servitutis et timoris: cum hunc appellet spiritum libertatis et adoptionis filiorum.' R 324.E.8–15.

tion of it to Erasmus and mysticism colours Köhler's position.[1] Since this study has revealed no certain source for Bucer's doctrine, it has been easier to present Bucer's theology of the Spirit simply as it appears in his writings, though with the recognition that there are many influences at work on his thought, beside the primary one, the Bible.

There are many clues to the understanding of Bucer's theology;[2] of these his doctrine of the Spirit is one, but not the only one. Indeed, isolated from the doctrines of predestination and the word, it would be misleading. But there is no clue more important than his endeavour to be, in Wesley's words, 'a man of one book'. Much of the balance and comprehensiveness of this theology derives from his attempt to be faithful to the scriptures.[3]

He lacked the fresh creative insights of Luther and the systematic genius of Calvin. Part of his role in the reformation may have been to take hold of Luther's astonishing rediscovery of the gospel and to mediate it to Calvin in a context at once more corporate and more complete.[4] The corporate note sounded in Bucer's

[1] Köhler, *Dogmengeschichte*, p. 418. Compare Lang's reference to mysticism (*op. cit.* pp. 139–41).

[2] Müller mentions Bucer's doctrine of original sin (*op. cit.* p. 237) and the contrast of *Deus verax* and *homo mendax* (*op. cit.* p. 248).

[3] Torrance's comment may be noted: 'If Luther's theology is to be interpreted over against the development of Western thought, particularly in its mediaeval form, that of Butzer is to be understood in terms of the Catholic Church and patristic theology of the first six centuries, for here we have a great attempt to get behind mediaevalism and, as Calvin put it, writing from Strasbourg, to restore the face of the ancient Catholic Church. In further contrast to the Lutheran position, Butzer's theology is more broadly based on the teaching of Scripture. Ephesians, Galatians, the Johannine writings, for example, are interpreted together, and so the Biblical ideas of election and adoption into the Body of Christ are placed alongside the doctrines of rebirth and justification by faith, and they are thought into each other, while the ministry of the Gospel, as well as the Gospel itself, becomes a *de fide* matter. It was in line with this that, while Luther laid all the stress upon the Word of God, Butzer (to be followed by Calvin) came to lay stress upon the Word and Spirit in their inseparable conjunction.' *Kingdom and Church*, pp. 73–4.

[4] This is not meant to detract from an appreciation of Bucer as a reformer and theologian in his own right. Nevertheless, the parallels between his thought and that of Calvin are striking. The influence of Bucer on Calvin can therefore scarcely be doubted, though it should not be assumed that there was no influence

understanding of the church and the varied ministry of teaching, preaching, service, and pastoral care, and the more complete grasp of salvation expressed in the place given to sanctification and pastoral discipline, derive from Bucer's less one-sided interpretation and presentation of scripture.[1]

Other aspects of Bucer's thought may commend themselves to the twentieth-century reader before his doctrine of the Holy Spirit. The comprehensiveness of his theology, his openness to learn from those not in the historic Christian tradition, his search for unity with his fellow Christians on the right hand and on the left, his strong emphasis on the primacy of love in the Christian life, his sense of man's life as corporate and finding its fulfilment in a new community of faith and love, his vision of the kingly rule of Christ embracing the total life of man, political, social, and cultural—all these find a more immediate echo in the thought of contemporary Christians. But cut off from the source of his doctrine they become distortions of what he had to say, an ideology rather than a theology.

They need to spring out of an encounter with the living God. It is the doctrine of the Holy Spirit that expresses and safeguards this.[2] It bridges the gap between us and the historical revelation

the other way. Instances of the influence of Bucer on Calvin are to be found, for example, in Lang, *Der Evangelienkommentar* and Wendel, *Calvin: The Origins and Development of his Religious Thought*, especially pp. 137–44.

[1] On Luther and Zwingli, Pollet comments: 'Si cependant on cherchait un parallélisme avec l'attitude de Luther, on trouverait dans Rom., IX, 20 sq. (la prédestination, effet de la toute-puissance absolue de Dieu) le verset qui a fourni à Zwingli le leitmotiv de sa théologie, correspondant à ce qu'a pu être Rom., I, 17 (la justification par la foi) pour Luther.' *Dictionnaire de Théologie Catholique* 15, II, 3752. It might not be too fanciful to suggest that Rom. 8:28–30 would represent Bucer's position, a text embracing in some measure those offered for Luther and Zwingli.

[2] In the twentieth century the Pentecostal and Holiness churches offer a challenge to the main Christian tradition similar to that offered by the radicals of the sixteenth century, and in many ways more consciously biblical. It remains to be seen how far their contribution to an understanding of the doctrine of the Holy Spirit will be accepted by the evangelical and catholic traditions and to that extent bring them new life. See Lesslie Newbigin, *The Household of God*.

of God in Christ, which becomes otherwise a distant and pious memory. For it is the Holy Spirit who makes Christ present, evoking our faith in him, uniting us to him and his people, and conforming us at last to his image in the glorious liberty of the children of God.[1] It is fitting, therefore, that the commission of Bucer that sends men out from the worship of God in church to a worship continued in the world and consummated in heaven is 'Go forth; and the Spirit of the Lord lead you to eternal life. Amen.'[2]

[1] The *Catechism* summarises the role of the Holy Spirit in these words:

Teacher: What is the chief work of the Holy Spirit in you?

Child: That he assures me absolutely of the promises of a gracious God, so that from the heart and with a truly childlike confidence I can recognise and call on God as my Father through our Lord Jesus Christ and can say 'Abba, dear Father'. Therefore Saint Paul calls him the seal of the elect, with whom God seals them and marks them for eternal life (Rom. 8 and Gal. 3).

Teacher: ...Thus as there are therefore three persons, Father, Son, and Holy Spirit, and yet in being only one sole God, so there is also only faith in God, Father, Son, and Holy Spirit, although it has something different in view with the Father, the Son, and the Holy Spirit. With the Father that he is the source and goal of all things and that he wills to be our Father. With the Son that as everything is made through him, so also everything is to be restored and completed through him. Therefore he became man, to pay for our sins in our nature and to be our Head and Saviour. With the Holy Spirit that through the Power of God we are renewed and made blessed in soul and body, in reason, will, and action. In this present, to a holy life, pleasing to God; in the future, to the blessed rest which is in Christ; and at the last day, to an eternally blessed immortality. GC C.1.A–2.A.4.

[2] BW 7.309.32–3.

APPENDIX

Three issues that have not been referred to can be mentioned here. They concern the relation of the Holy Spirit to the Trinity, his relation to creation, and the use of the term Holy Spirit as equivalent to such terms as the Spirit of God, the Spirit of the Father, or the Spirit of Christ.

A. There is little discussion by Bucer of the person of the Holy Spirit. He accepts the traditional formulations and is content to reiterate them. He asserts that there is no difference of substance between the Father, the Son, and the Holy Spirit (37.A.12–17; 12.C.12–16; 591.B.9–13), who may be described as 'one in being, power, and action' (GC A.5.B.7–11).

Their unity does not, however, contradict their trinity. Against Jewish commentators he affirms in the *Psalms* that scripture speaks of them distinctly as three persons (P 17.A.4–16, 134.B.24–C.10). Writing against Servetus he rejects the view that the Trinity means only a trinity of action and not a trinity of persons, so that one could speak of the Holy Spirit or Christ as beginning or ending.

'Trinitatem quam adversarius ponit, quamvis ubique eam inculcet, plenius tamen legis in eius libro L.5. Ea est huiusmodi: deus apparuit aliter in Christo homine, aliter in flatu, quo spiritus sanctus advenit; igitur est trinitas. Deus per se invisibilis, in Christo visibilis, aliter tamen quam in flatu; tria ergo sunt, deus, Christus, flatus. Personam Christi et flatus intelligit representationem horum, qua deus olim Christo et huic flatui variis apparitionibus praelusit. Pernegat autem vel verbum vel spiritum sanctum naturae vocabula sed actionum dumtaxat, quae et caeperint et desierint...[by contrast the Christian] abhorreatque dicere, verbum dei, quo sunt omnia condita et portantur, aut spiritum sanctum dei, quo omnia perfecta sunt et perficiuntur, vel caepisse vel desiisse, aut illud nihil quam carnem Christi, hunc nihil aliud esse quam flatum, qui advenit discipulis in die pentecostes, quae sunt Hispani istius blasphemiae.' KR 1.595.22–596.13.

Already in 1530 he added a comment to *St Matthew* to point out the distinction between the person and work of the Holy Spirit, 80.A.17; 26.C.28–D.1; 63.B.22–64.C.1. See p. 269, n. 2.

B. There are few references to the work of the Holy Spirit in creation. Bucer refers to it in expounding Ps. 104:30 (P 269.C.1–5). Compare the reference in the 1529 edition of *Psalms* (276.A.18–20), which was not included in the 1532 edition (P 222.C.23). See also the *Gospels* (1530 and 1536) (14.B.13; 5.C.27–D.6; 574.C.16–25). This doctrine, however, plays no significant part in this thought.

C. Bucer appears to use terms like the Spirit of God, the Spirit of the Father, and the Spirit of Christ as equivalent to the Holy Spirit. There are a number of examples where the terms are used indiscriminately or interchangeably in the same context, sometimes as a result of the various biblical texts to which he alludes. BW 2.137.1–6 and 141.23. Compare 209.A.10–21, 218.B.6–9; 76.D.18–25, 80.A.19–20; 742.D.8–15, 750.D.21–2. See also R 380.E.10–19.

SELECT BIBLIOGRAPHY

Bucer's writings are given in the order in which they appear in the bibliography by Robert Stupperich (see *Bibliographia Bucerana* by Robert Stupperich, published as the second part of Heinrich Bornkamm, *Martin Bucers Bedeutung für die europäische Reformationsgeschichte*, Gütersloh, 1952). The full titles may be found by reference to the bibliography. Here an abbreviated or translated title, which corresponds to the title used in the text of the book, is given. It is preceded by the abbreviation used in the footnotes and the number in the bibliography. It is followed by a reference to the date, (and where this is different) to the edition used, and in the case of *Martin Bucers Deutsche Schriften* by the page references. Writings that are not included in Stupperich's bibliography are given separately after the main list.

In the footnotes the commentaries on the gospels have been referred to without a preliminary letter, but are clearly recognisable from the fact that the references are given in groups of three, separated by semicolons. The first reference is to *St Matthew* or *St John*, the second to *Gospels* (1530), the third to *Gospels* (1536). The first volume of *St Matthew*, covering chapters 1–7, corresponds in *Gospels* (1536) to pages 1–206, the second volume to pages 206–524, the sections on St Mark and St Luke to pages 525–60. *St John* corresponds to pages 561–798. Where a quotation is missing from one edition, the line reference given indicates the point at which the omission or addition occurs. The context of the discussion makes it clear in which edition the change occurs. Important differences from one edition to another are generally noted in the text or in the footnotes.

References are given to the page, the side of the page, the section on a page, and the line. For simplicity a uniform method has been followed.

A. The page is given according to the edition quoted. Where the original number is inaccurate, usually through a misprint, the correct number is given in its place. This is preceded by a letter, when it was used in the original edition. The letter is invariably capitalised. In editions where the letters of the alphabet are used a second time, a double capital is used to represent the letter used the second time.

Select Bibliography

B. The side of the page (recto and verso) is indicated by the letters A and B, after the number of the page, where the sides are not separately numbered, or where sections on the page are not given.

C. The sections of a page are given as in the original editions, with the relevant letter (A–F) following the page number.

D. The lines have been numbered as accurately as is possible according to the side or section quoted. Often the reference given covers the passage in which a quotation is found and not just the quotation itself.

Besides the original editions of Bucer's works, of which details are to be found in *Bibliographia Bucerana*, the following editions of his works have been used:

Martini Buceri Opera Latina. Vol. 15: *De Regno Christi.* Paris and Gütersloh, 1955.

Martin Bucers Deutsche Schriften. Vols. 1–3, 7. Paris and Gütersloh, 1960 ff.

D. Martin Luthers Werke. Kritische Gesamtausgabe. Weimar 1883 ff.

von Schubert, Hans. *Zwei Predigten Martin Bucers. Beiträge zur Reformationsgeschichte, Prof. D. Köstlin gewidmet.* Gotha, 1896.

Reu, Johann Michel. *Quellen zur Geschichte des kirchlichen Unterrichts in der evangelischen Kirche Deutschlands zwischen 1530 und 1600.* Vol. 1.I: *Quellen zur Geschichte des Katechismus-Unterrichts: Süddeutsche Katechismen.* Gütersloh, 1904.

'Von der Kirchen mengel und fähl und wie dieselben zu verbessern.' A.R.G. Ergänzungsband 5, *Festschrift für Hans von Schubert.*

Friedensburg, Walther. 'Von der Wiedervereinigung der Kirchen.' A.R.G. 31. 1934.

Pollet, J. V. *Martin Bucer: Etudes sur la Correspondance.* Vol. I, Paris, 1958. Vol. II, Paris, 1962.

Krebs, Manfred and Rott, Hans Georg. *Quellen zur Geschichte der Täufer.* Vol. VII. *Elsass, I, Stadt Strassburg 1522–1532.* Gütersloh, 1959. Vol. VIII. *Elsass, II, Stadt Strassburg 1533–1535.* Gütersloh, 1960.

Select Bibliography

I. BUCER'S WORKS

	1.	Das ym selbs	(1523)	BW 1.44–67
	2.	Summary	(1523)	BW 1.79–147
	3.	Verantwortung	(1523)	BW 1.156–84
	7.	Against Treger	(1524)	BW 2.37–173
	8.	Grund und Ursach	(1524)	BW 1.194–278
	12.	Psalter	(1526)	BW 2.187–223
AP	13.	Apologia	(1526)	
	14.	St Matthew	(1527)	
PR	15.	Preface	(1527)	
	16.	Getrewe Warnung	(1527)	BW 2.234–58
E	17.	Ephesians	(1527)	
	19.	Berner Predigt	(1528)	BW 2.281–94
	20.	St John	(1528)	
	21.	Vergleichung	(1528)	
Z	22.	Zephaniah	(1528)	
	24.	Gutachten	(1529)	BW 3.443–71
P	25.	Psalms	(1529)	1532 edition
				(= 25 b)
	27.	Ursach	(1530)	BW 3.322–38
	28.	Gospels (1530) also (Preface 1530)	(1530)	
	28 a	Gospels (1536) also (Preface 1536)	(1536)	
Q	33.	Quomodo	(1531)	R.H.P.R. 26, 1946
	35.	Tetrapolitana	(1531)	BW 3.36–185
		Apology	(1531)	BW 3.194–318
	37.	Confutatio	(1531)	KR 1.592–8
H	40.	Handlung	(1533)	
QD	42.	Quid de baptismate	(1533)	
BH	43.	Bericht	(1534)	
GC	48.	Catechism	(1534)	
D	50.	Dialogi	(1535)	
R	55.	Romans	(1536)	1562 edition
				(= 55 a)
SC	56 a	Shorter Catechism	(1537)	Reu 1.I
			(1539)	Reu 1.I
			(1543)	Reu 1.I
			(1544)	1544 edition
	58.	Benfelder Predigten	(1538)	BW 7.18–65

Select Bibliography

	59. Von der waren Seelsorge	(1538)	BW 7.90–241
	60. Ziegenhainer Zuchtordnung	(1539)	BW 7.260–77
	61. Kasseler Kirchenordnung	(1539)	BW 7.279–318
	68. Abusuum ecclesiasticorum	(1541)	
AC	69. Acta colloquii	(1541)	
DV	73. De vera ecclesiarum	(1542)	A.R.G. 31, 1934 (= 73 a)
BV	86. Bestendige Verantwortung	(1545)	
VD	95. Von der Kirchen mengel und fähl	(1546)	A.R.G. Erg. 5, 1929
V	96. Ein Summarischer vergriff	(1548)	
J	101. Judges	(1544?)	1554 edition
	103. De Regno Christi	(1550)	OB 15
	110. De vi et usu	(1550–1)	TA
EE	112. Ephesians (1550)	(1550)	1562 edition
TA	115. Tomus Anglicanus	(1577)	
	120. De ordinatione	(1549?)	TA
ZP	151a Zwei Predigten	(1531 and 1540 (?))	von Schubert

Additional Works

BW 1.281–4	Bucer's Book List (1518)
BW 1.310–44	Dass D. Luthers Lehr (1523)
BW 3.404–8	Propositiones ministrorum Ecclesiae Argentinensis (1524) (abbreviated as Strasbourg Propositions)
BW 3.432–41	An Johann Ritter Landschad von Steinach (1525)
Pollet 1.12–18	Letter to Martin (1526)
1.23	Strasbourg Confession (1529)
1.58–61	Zürich Interpretation (1530) (also BW 3.395–7)
1.68–79	Schweinfurt Confession (1532)
1.91–122	Reply to Wolfhart (1532)
1.126–41	Augsburg Summary (1533)
1.165	Exhortation (1536)
1.166	Explanation (1536)
1.167–70	Speech to the Council (1536)
1.171–3	Address (1536)
KR 2.25–32	Articles (1533)
2.193–8	Contra Bernard Wacker (1533)
2.198–200	Bericht uber dem eusserlichen und innerlichen Wort (1533)

Select Bibliography

2. TABLE OF ABBREVIATIONS

(a) Bucer's Works (where relevant the number in Bibliographia Bucerana is given)

AC	Acta colloquii	(69)
AP	Apologia	(13)
BH	Bericht	(43)
BV	Bestendige Verantwortung	(86)
BW	Martin Bucers Deutsche Schriften	
D	Dialogi	(50)
DV	De vera ecclesiarum	(73a)
E	Ephesians	(17)
EE	Ephesians (1550)	(112)
GC	Catechism	(48)
H	Handlung	(40)
J	Judges	(101)
KR	Krebs and Rott: Quellen zur Geschichte der Täufer	
OB	Martini Buceri Opera Latina	
P	Psalms	(25b)
PR	Preface	(15)
Q	Quomodo	(33)
QD	Quid de baptismate	(42)
R	Romans	(55a)
SC	Shorter Catechism	(56a)
TA	Tomus Anglicanus	(115)
V	Ein Summarischer vergriff	(96)
VD	Von der Kirchen mengel und fähl	(95)
Z	Zephaniah	(22)
ZP	Zwei Predigten	(151a)

(b) Other Works

A.R.G.	Archiv für Reformationsgeschichte. Gütersloh.
A.R.G. Erg.	Archiv für Reformationsgeschichte, Ergänzungsband.
L.C.C.	Library of Christian Classics. (See bibliography under Matthew Spinka and George Huntston Williams.)
P.T.R.	Princeton Theological Review.
R.H.P.R.	Revue d'Histoire et de Philosophie religieuses. Strasbourg.

Select Bibliography

W.A.	Weimar Ausgabe. (See Luther, Martin.)
W.A.Br.	Weimar Ausgabe. Briefwechsel. (See Luther, Martin.)

3. LITERATURE

Anrich, Gustav. *Martin Bucer*. Strasbourg, 1914.

Baum, Johann Wilhelm. *Capito und Butzer: Strassburgs Reformatoren*. Elberfeld, 1860.

Bellardi, Werner. *Geschichte der 'Christlichen Gemeinschaften' in Strassburg (1546–1550)*. Leipzig, 1934.

Bornkamm, Heinrich. *Martin Bucers Bedeutung für die europäische Reformationsgeschichte*. Gütersloh, 1952.

Brecht, Martin. *Die frühe Theologie des Johannes Brenz*. Tübingen, 1966.

Bring, Ragnar. *Förhållandet mellan tro och gärningar inom luthersk teologi*. Helsinki, 1934.

Burckhardt, A. E. *Das Geistproblem bei Huldrych Zwingli*. Leipzig, 1932.

Clark, James M. *The Great German Mystics*. Oxford, 1949.

Courvoisier, Jaques. *La notion d'Eglise chez Bucer dans son développement historique*. Paris, 1933.

Eells, Hastings. 'Martin Bucer and the Conversion of John Calvin.' P.T.R. XXII, 3. 1924.

'Sacramental Negotiations at the Diet of Augsburg, 1530.' P.T.R. XXIII, 2. 1925.

'The Genesis of Martin Bucer's Doctrine of the Lord's Supper.' P.T.R. XXIV, 2. 1926.

Martin Bucer. New Haven, 1931.

'The Failure of Church Unification Efforts during the German Reformation.' A.R.G. 42. 1951.

Ellwein, Eduard. *Vom neuen Leben*. *De novitate vitae*. Munich, 1932.

Grützmacher, Richard H. *Wort und Geist*. Leipzig, 1902.

Heitz, Jean-Jacques. 'Etude sur la formation de la pensée ecclésiologique de Bucer d'après les traités polémiques et doctrinaux des années 1523–1538.' Thèse Strasbourg, 1947.

Hendry, George S. *The Holy Spirit in Christian Theology*. London, 1957.

Hopf, Constantin. *Martin Bucer and the English Reformation*. Oxford, 1946.

Huizinga, Johan. *Erasmus of Rotterdam*. London, 1952.

Itti, Gérard. 'Dans quelle mesure Bucer est-il piétiste?' Thèse Strasbourg, 1936.

Select Bibliography

Koch, Karl. *Studium Pietatis. Martin Bucer als Ethiker.* Neukirchen, 1962.

Köhler, Walther. *Zwingli und Luther, Ihr Streit über das Abendmahl nach seinen politischen und religiösen Beziehungen.* Band 1, Leipzig, 1924. Band 11, Gütersloh, 1953.

Dogmengeschichte als Geschichte des christlichen Selbstbewusstseins. Band 11: *Das Zeitalter der Reformation.* Zürich, 1951.

Kohls, Ernst-Wilhelm. *Die Theologie des Erasmus.* Basel, 1966.

Krusche, Werner. *Das Wirken des Heiligen Geistes nach Calvin.* Berlin, 1957.

Lang, August. *Der Evangelienkommentar Martin Butzers und die Grundzüge seiner Theologie.* Leipzig, 1900.

Lortz, Joseph. *The Reformation in Germany.* Vols. 1 and 2. London, 1968.

Luther, Martin. *D. Martin Luthers Werke. Kritische Gesamtausgabe.* Weimar, 1883 ff.

Lutz, Pierre. 'Le commentaire de Martin Bucer sur le livre des Juges.' Thèse Strasbourg, 1953.

Lyonnet, Stanislas (and Imbart de la Potterie). *La Vie selon l'Esprit.* Paris, 1965.

Morii, Makoto. 'La notion du Saint-Esprit chez Calvin dans son développement historique.' Thèse Strasbourg, 1961.

Müller, Johannes. *Martin Bucers Hermeneutik.* Gütersloh, 1965.

Newbigin, Lesslie. *The Household of God.* London, 1953.

Noesgen, K. F. *Geschichte der Lehre vom Heiligen Geiste.* Gütersloh, 1899.

Oberman, Heiko. *The Harvest of Medieval Theology.* Cambridge, Massachusetts, 1963.

Forerunners of the Reformation. London, 1967.

Packer, J. I. (and O. R. Johnston). *Martin Luther on the Bondage of the Will.* London, 1957.

Peter, Rodolphe. 'Le Maraîcher Clément Ziegler, l'homme et son œuvre.' R.H.P.R. 34. 1954.

Pollet, J. V. 'Zwinglianisme.' *Dictionnaire de Théologie Catholique.* Vol. 15.11. Paris, 1950.

Prenter, Regin. *Spiritus Creator: Studien zu Luthers Theologie.* Munich, 1954.

Ritschl, Otto: *Dogmengeschichte des Protestantismus.* Band 3: *Reformierte Theologie des 16. und 17. Jahrhunderts.* Göttingen, 1926.

Robinson, Hastings. *Original Letters Relative to the English Reformation 1537–1558.* Vol. 2. Cambridge, 1847.

Rott, Jean. 'Bucer et les débuts de la querelle sacramentaire.' R.H.P.R. 34. 1954.

Select Bibliography

Rupp, E. Gordon. *The Righteousness of God.* London, 1953.

'Word and Spirit in the First Years of the Reformation.' A.R.G. 49. 1958.

Scherding, Pierre (and François Wendel). 'Un Traité d'exégèse pratique de Bucer.' R.H.P.R. 26. 1946.

Seeberg, Reinhold. *Lehrbuch der Dogmengeschichte.* Band IV.2: *Die Fortbildung der reformatorischen Lehre und die gegenreformatorische Lehre.* Stuttgart, 1960.

Spinka, Matthew. *Advocates of Reform: From Wyclif to Erasmus.* Library of Christian Classics: Vol. XIV. London, 1953.

Spitz, Lewis. *The Religious Renaissance of the German Humanists.* Cambridge, Massachusetts, 1963.

Strasser, Otto Erich. *La pensée théologique de Wolfgang Capiton dans les dernières années de sa vie.* Neuchâtel, 1938.

Strohl, Henri. 'La théorie et la pratique des quatre ministères à Strasbourg avant l'arrivée de Calvin.' Bulletin de la Société de l'Histoire du Protestantisme français, 84. Paris, 1935.

'La notion d'Eglise chez les Réformateurs.' Recherches théologiques, 1. Paris, 1936.

'Un aspect de l'humanisme chrétien de Bucer.' R.H.P.R. 18. 1938.

Bucer, humaniste chrétien. Paris, 1939.

'Bucer, interprète de Luther.' R.H.P.R. 19. 1939.

Martin Bucer. Traité de l'Amour du Prochain. Paris, 1949.

La pensée de la Réforme. Neuchâtel and Paris, 1951.

Strype, John. *Memorials of Archbishop Cranmer.* Vols. 1–3. Oxford, 1848.

Stupperich, Robert. 'Die Kirche in M. Bucers theologischer Entwicklung.' A.R.G. 35. 1938.

'Strassburgs Stellung im Beginn des Sakramentsstreits.' A.R.G. 38. 1941.

'Stand und Aufgabe der Butzer-Forschung.' A.R.G. 42. 1951.

Temmel, Leopold. 'Glaube und Gewissheit in der Theologie Martin Bucers vornehmlich nach seinem Römerbriefkommentar.' Dissertation Vienna, 1950.

Törnvall, G. *Andligt och världsligt regemente hos Luther.* Stockholm, 1940.

Torrance, Thomas. *Kingdom and Church.* Edinburgh, 1956.

Usteri, Johann Martin. 'Die Stellung der Strassburger Reformatoren Bucer und Capito zur Tauffrage.' Theologische Studien und Kritiken, 57. Gotha, 1884.

Select Bibliography

van de Poll, G. J. *Martin Bucer's Liturgical Ideas*. Assen, 1954.

Watson, Philip. *Let God be God!* London, 1947.

Weber, Hans Emil. *Reformation, Orthodoxie und Rationalismus*. Band 1.1: *Von der Reformation zur Orthodoxie*. Gütersloh, 1937.

Wendel, François. *L'Eglise de Strasbourg: sa constitution et son organisation 1532–1535*. Paris, 1942.

Martin Bucer. Strasbourg, 1952.

Calvin: The Origins and Development of his Religious Thought. London, 1963.

Wesley, John. *The Works of John Wesley*. London, 1829–31.

Williams, George Huntston (and Angel M. Mergal). *Spiritual and Anabaptist Writers: Documents Illustrative of the Radical Reformation and Evangelical Catholicism*. Library of Christian Classics: Vol. xxv. London, 1957.

The Radical Reformation. Philadelphia, 1962.

INDEXES

INDEX OF REFERENCES TO BUCER'S WORKS

Index of References to Bucer's Works

INDEX OF AUTHORS

INDEX OF PROPER NAMES

INDEX OF SUBJECTS

Index of Subjects

Index of Subjects